I TABLESPOON
I TEASPOON
½ TEASPOON
¼ TEASPOON

THE ART OF MAKING SOUFFLÉS

Individual Cheese Soufflés make lunch or supper glamorous and easy.

THE ART OF MAKING SOUFFLÉS

FREDERICA L. BEINERT

DOUBLEDAY & COMPANY, INC.
GARDEN CITY, NEW YORK
1967

BOOKS BY FREDERICA L. BEINERT

The Art of Making Sauces and Gravies

The Art of Making Soufflés

PHOTOGRAPH CREDITS

Frontispiece Individual Cheese Soufflés KRAFT FOODS
Plate 1 Basic Cheese Soufflé TABASCO
Plate 2 Cheese and Bacon Soufflé GENERAL FOODS
Plate 3 Spinach Soufflé POULTRY AND EGG NATIONAL BOARD
Plate 4 Raisin Angel Puff CALIFORNIA RAISIN ADVISORY BOARD
Plate 5 Potato Puff AC'CENT INTERNATIONAL
Plate 6 Quick Mushroom Soufflé CAMPBELL SOUP COMPANY
Plate 7 Toasted Nut Soufflé DIAMOND WALNUT GROWERS, INC.
Plate 8 Easy Frozen Caramel Nut Soufflé STANDARD BRANDS, INC.
Plate 9 Cold Orange Soufflé FLORIDA CITRUS COMMISSION
Plate 10 Vanilla Pudding Soufflé Pie BEST FOODS DIVISION, CORN PRODUCTS COMPANY
Plate 11 Easy Frozen Chocolate Soufflé STANDARD BRANDS, INC.
Plate 12 Cold Mocha Soufflé GENERAL FOODS
Plate 13 Cold Pineapple Soufflé PINEAPPLE GROWERS ASSOCIATION

LIBRARY OF CONGRESS CATALOG CARD NUMBER 67-19066

PRINTED IN THE UNITED STATES OF AMERICA
FIRST EDITION

A recipe book always represents the inspiration and co-operation of many people over a long period of time. The author's deep gratitude goes to teachers who made the principles of good food preparation a lasting joy; and to home economics colleagues who always generously share product use information. For this book in particular, special thanks are given to Kathryn Freeman for untiring help in preparation of the manuscript, and to Cynthia Dignan who types, not only with perfection, but with interest and understanding.

CONTENTS

ILLUSTRATIONS

INTRODUCTION

If you've always wanted to make good soufflés but never had courage to try—or if you've tried and tried and never quite succeeded—this book is for you. It's designed, too, for those accomplished cooks who like to find, under one cover, a complete soufflé recipe book. Here are recipes for all the types and kinds of soufflés and soufflélike dishes anyone could wish to know about and make.

There's a story told about a bride who wanted her first "real" dinner party to be a gourmet's dream. She planned a fairly elaborate menu, with soufflé for dessert, and engaged a part-time helper to cook and serve the meal. All went smoothly until midway through dinner when the cook slipped a note onto the hostess' lap. As unobtrusively as possible it was unfolded—and the hostess read, with horror, "Heavenly days ma'am, what do I do now, the wind's gone out of the puddin'?"

Both hostess and cook could have used this book and kept the "wind in the puddin'." The first chapter is devoted to all the basic facts about soufflés that lead to imaginative, creative, and successful cookery. There's nothing magic about soufflés. Many are much less trouble to make and take much less time than a number of popular cakes and cookies.

There are soufflés that are hearty enough to serve as the main dish at a meal, others that make savory accompaniments to an entrée. Some, with delicate richness, are the most delectable of desserts. Many soufflés are rushed to the table piping hot, while others are chilled before serving. Recipes for all of these are presented here together with directions for making a variety of soufflé puddings, omelet soufflés and other dishes that are first cousins to a true soufflé. There are, too, small-size recipes for soufflés to serve two or three people, and timesaver soufflés for the busy homemaker who wants to produce a glamorous food in a hurry. To complete the picture there is a chapter devoted to sauces to serve with soufflés, and a glossary of terms and techniques most helpful in soufflé preparation.

THE ART OF MAKING SOUFFLÉS

1

HOW TO MAKE AND SERVE SUCCESSFUL SOUFFLÉS

Perfectly prepared and served soufflés are high on the list of foods worthy of culinary accolades. Their high and delicate appearance and their long-standing reputation for temperamental behavior have added leaves to the laurels of the superb cook. But these same characteristics have caused many a timid cook to shy away from learning, at firsthand, how simply soufflés can be made and how easy it is to handle them correctly.

A soufflé is a dramatic production, to be sure, but its basic ingredients are quite ordinary. Understanding why and how to handle the ingredients properly is the key to understanding how a soufflé is made to rise and what causes it to fall. Once the few helpful tricks for each type of soufflé are mastered, creative imagination takes over. Then the variety of soufflés that can be made and served with pride becomes almost endless.

Types of Soufflés

In simplest terms, a soufflé is an egg dish, since eggs are the basis for its delicate texture and appearance. The base into which the eggs are blended, and which often serves to stabilize the airy mixture, is used to describe the types of soufflés. Thus, there are soufflés with a white sauce base and those based on a custard. There are simple egg-white-based soufflés, which are baked, and similar ones steamed in a double boiler. Cold soufflés have a gelatine mixture as stabilizer, and many of these resemble a molded cold mousse.

Soufflélike dishes, too, fall into several categories. Soufflé omelets resemble the fluffy omelet but are sweetened, variously flavored, and easier to handle than the foamy omelets from which they are derived. Soufflé puddings are airy and light, but not so light and delicate as a true soufflé. They are less prone to collapse than soufflés, and many can be reheated, if necessary, for delayed serving. The recipes termed pseudo-soufflés closely resemble true soufflés in texture but use fewer eggs as well as using a variety of starchy foods instead of sauce as base. They are much like fondues.

All these soufflés and soufflélike dishes fall into three main groups according to use. Those with a white sauce base and hearty ingredients such as meat, poultry, fish, seafood, or cheese, can be served as the main dish at lunch, brunch, or supper. Savory soufflés containing well-seasoned vegetables, rice, mushrooms, noodles, and the like are excellent accompaniments for the entrée. And the sweet dessert soufflés, flavored with fruits, nuts, chocolate, soft cheeses, liqueurs, or wines, are a perfect finishing touch to any meal. In addition, some of the hearty soufflés and many of the savory ones can be served, baked in individual portions, as a first course.

Not truly soufflés, but a boon to the hurried or harried cook, are the light and puffy dishes that can be made with the minimum of effort, using prepared foods such as pudding mix or canned soup as the base. These might be called emergency shelf soufflés, whipped up at the drop of a hat for the unexpected guest.

Tools and Techniques for Successful Soufflés

BAKING DISH OR MOLD

The ideal soufflé dish has straight sides and a flat bottom. Plain or decorated, fluted, silvered, or gilded, this type of dish comes in graduated sizes ranging from 4 ounces to 3-quart capacity. For single portions of a hearty, savory, or sweet soufflé an 8 or 12-ounce size is best. A 1-quart dish holds 4 servings; the 1½-quart size will serve 4 or 5 adequately; and the 2-quart dish provides 6 good servings. Many good cooks prefer using two 1½-quart dishes instead of a 3-quart size for hot soufflés in the belief that baking is more perfect when the total volume in the soufflé dish is not too great. To determine the capacity of a soufflé dish, measure the amount of water that will fill it just to the indentation that forms the rim.

A deep casserole with straight, rounded, or sloping sides can be used successfully for many soufflés and soufflé puddings. The rise, however, may not be quite so high, the shape of the finished product somewhat different. Of course, the master of the art of soufflé making can and will choose, for variety and attractive serving, interestingly shaped baking or molding dishes of right capacity with perfect results because of deftness in handling the soufflé.

BEATERS

The type of beater used to whip egg whites determines, to some extent, the high rise of the soufflé. Greatest volume is obtained by using a wire whisk or flat wire whip. A rotary hand beater produces the next highest volume. But an electric beater or mixer, while producing a stable, fine-celled foam may yield less total volume of beaten egg whites. An electric blender is not suitable for producing properly beaten egg whites.

BLENDERS AND STIRRERS

For blending together the ingredients of sauces for soufflés a wooden spoon is perfect. This tool is always cool to the hand, gentle but efficient where combining of different types and textures of ingredients is concerned. It may be used, too, for folding in beaten egg whites, if desired. A rubber spatula, however, is often preferred for folding since it so easily lifts as well as cuts through the mixture.

CUTTERS AND CHOPPERS

A French chef's knife is the all-purpose tool for cutting, dicing, chopping, or mincing ingredients. Mechanical choppers or dicers can, of course, be used, but the French knife technique is quicker in most cases. Kitchen shears are fine for mincing parsley or chives. Cut up foods can be minced, too, by whirling in an electric blender for a few seconds.

SIEVES

For puréed ingredients such as fruits or vegetables, several types of tools may be used. For a moderately coarse purée the food may be pushed through a Foley blender. For very fine purée, a wooden spoon can be used to push the food through a finely meshed sieve. An electric blender will purée many foods evenly and smoothly when small batches of the food are whirled in it for 8 to 10 seconds.

DOUBLE BOILERS

The shape of a double boiler used to steam a soufflé will, of course, determine the appearance of the product. In lieu of a double boiler a tightly covered bowl set in a saucepan or skillet containing hot, not boiling, water can be used. Similarly, in cooking a custard sauce base, two saucepans, one smaller than the other, can be used to simulate a double boiler.

PREPARING A SOUFFLÉ DISH

To grease or not to grease a soufflé dish is a confusing question. The purist maintains that a soufflé clings to an unbuttered dish, thus climbing better as it bakes. Modern experience, however, indicates that an unbuttered dish does not appreciably increase the height of a soufflé.

For many soufflés, eating quality is enhanced by the preparation of the dish. The dish may be oiled, using a pastry brush to distribute a very fine film of vegetable oil on the bottom only (if preferred) or bottom and sides of the dish. Softened or creamed (not melted) butter or margarine may be spread similarly, using brush or fingers.

Coating the greased surface of the soufflé dish makes it a bit less slippery, and gives opportunity for the addition of a little flavor and texture to enhance the crust of the finished product. A properly light coating is brought about by dusting onto the greased surface fine granulated sugar, fine dry bread crumbs or macaroon crumbs, sifted flour, or finely ground nuts. The coating selected should always, of course, be compatible in flavor with the soufflé.

COLLARING A SOUFFLÉ DISH

A collar on a soufflé dish serves several purposes. When a soufflé dish is filled ⅔ to ¾ full of soufflé mixture before baking, a collar is not necessary, for the well-baked soufflé will rise above the dish without one. To extend the usefulness of the dish, however, by filling it nearly to the rim, a collar is advisable to guide the high rise. This is particularly true in making spectacular individual soufflés in small-sized soufflé dishes.

A collar is a must for an attractively molded cold soufflé so that it resembles a highly puffed baked soufflé.

To collar the dish, cut a strip of foil or waxed paper long enough to go around the dish and overlap about 2 inches. Fold foil or paper in half lengthwise, then fold in half again. Butter or oil one side of the folded foil or paper and, if the dish is also dusted with a fine dry food, dust it also. Place the foil or waxed paper, prepared side in, around the rim of the soufflé dish, extending 1 or 2 inches above the rim. Tie it on securely with string, or fasten at the overlap with tape, paper clips, or straight pins. The collar should be removed most carefully from a hot or cold soufflé so as not to break the surface. In a hot soufflé such a break can hasten collapse of the product.

So as to concentrate all effort on making the soufflé, always prepare the soufflé dish as needed before beginning to combine ingredients.

PREHEAT OVEN

The oven should always be preheated to the right baking temperature before a soufflé is put into it. A part of soufflé success is the immediate penetration of the right heat into the soufflé. This helps to deter any possible separation or drainage of liquid ingredients, thus keeping the soufflé intact.

Some authorities recommend heating the soufflé dish in a pan of hot water in the preheating oven before putting the soufflé mixture in it. This is said to hasten the heating and baking of the soufflé as well as to deter drainage of liquids.

SOUFFLÉ BASE

One of the secrets of success of hot soufflés is to see that the sauce or custard base is perfectly smooth. Lumps not only add an unpleasant touch to taste and texture, but they can interfere with uniform rising of the soufflé during baking. Careful cooking and constant stirring over low and medium heat can prevent lumps from forming. Savory ingredients such as onion are grated or finely minced when incorporated into a white sauce so as not to detract from its smoothness. And it is helpful, as a sauce is cooled to the proper temperature for blending with other ingredients, to stir it occasionally to keep a skin from forming since the skin can cause small lumps if it does form and is stirred in.

EGG YOLKS

The egg yolks in a soufflé add both lightness and thickening power. They may be added to the sauce in two ways. A portion of hot sauce may be beaten into thick, beaten egg yolks a little at a time to warm them, then the warmed mixture is stirred into the remaining sauce; or the sauce may be cooled for 10 to 15 minutes and the beaten egg yolks briskly stirred into it. Either way the egg yolks are warmed and lightly cooked in the sauce. If preferred, the egg yolk and sauce mixture can be cooked and stirred over low heat for 1 or 2 minutes after combining, then cooled to the right temperature for folding in beaten egg whites.

EGG WHITES

A very important part of successful soufflé making is the preparation and addition of the egg whites. The whites should be carefully separated from the yolks, and if a speck of yolk accidentally appears, it should be completely removed with a bit of eggshell. Though eggs are most easily separated at refrigerator temperature, the egg whites beat to greatest volume when warmed to room temperature. This is done by separating them 30 to 60 minutes before beating and letting them stand outside the refrigerator, or by warming them for a few minutes in a bowl set in a container of warm water.

Salt sprinkled on egg whites before beating tends to shorten the beating time. Cream of tartar, added when the egg whites have been beaten to the foamy stage, tends to increase volume and stability. When it is desirable to add the egg whites to the soufflé in the form of a meringue, they should be beaten first to soft peaks. Sugar is then added gradually while beating continues until stiff glossy peaks form. The sugar crystals should, at this time, be thoroughly dissolved. Meringue is said to be more stable for folding into sauce than plain beaten egg whites.

Egg whites beaten to stiff but not dry or to stiff glossy peaks will not slide out of the bowl when it is tipped. The peaks will stand high when the beater is withdrawn but will bend over a little bit. If the shiny look disappears and the peaks stand straight up, or the beaten whites slide out of the bowl, the beating has been carried too far. Overbeaten egg whites will not blend smoothly into the sauce mixture and will leave visible egg white flecks throughout the soufflé.

There is no hard and fast rule as to folding sauce into beaten egg whites or beaten egg whites into sauce. Both methods are successful.

Egg whites may be folded into sauce all at once, if desired, or a portion of the beaten egg whites may be stirred into the sauce until thoroughly blended to lighten the sauce mixture, then the remainder gently folded in.

FORMING A TOP HAT

After the soufflé mixture has been poured into the prepared soufflé dish the attractive finishing touch known as a top hat or crown may be formed before the soufflé is baked. Using a spoon or spatula, trace a circle 1 inch deep about 1 inch from the edge of the dish. This allows the soufflé to rise higher in the center, creating a top hat effect.

BAKING TEMPERATURES

The temperature at which a soufflé is baked has much to do with the character of the finished product. The French-style soufflé is baked in a hot (400° F.–425° F.) oven for quick rising and browning, with center very moist. This is the "soufflé with a bleeding heart," self-sauced by its undercooked center. The American-style soufflé, cooked for a longer time at slow or moderate temperature (325° F.–375° F.) is a bit drier since it is cooked through, doesn't rise quite so high, but doesn't collapse so easily either.

SERVING TIP

A hot dessert soufflé must be served at peak of perfection, right out of the oven. Have dessert dishes and silver in place on the table before presenting the soufflé. And to serve it quickly and easily, cut portions with a fork, then spoon them lightly onto the dessert plate. The fork does less damage to the structure of the soufflé than a spoon would do in cutting, thus slightly deterring collapse.

TIME AND TEMPER SAVERS

Always try out a soufflé at a family meal before preparing it for guests.

Make the basic sauce ahead of time and refrigerate it in a covered container. Remove it from the refrigerator 30 to 60 minutes before completing the recipe, to allow it to warm to room temperature, or stir it over hot water for a few minutes.

Some soufflés, such as individual cheese soufflés, can be completely prepared and poured into soufflé dishes, then refrigerated for an hour or more before baking. They can then be baked quickly in a very hot oven, and served with a soft center.

It is possible to freeze some types of soufflés, thaw them for an hour, and bake them as if freshly made.

Soufflés baked in hot water are said to hold up longer for serving than some of those baked in dry heat.

Tapioca-based soufflés hold up very well during table service.

Soufflés made with a cornstarch base can be reheated.

It is best to serve a soufflé the minute it is ready to come from the oven, yet, many soufflés can be made to wait for the guests—but not too long. Turn the oven to lowest possible heat after the soufflé is baked, or turn off the heat, but do not open the door. The soufflé will dry a bit but can be held for 15 to 30 minutes.

Prepare dessert soufflé components completely before serving dinner. Combine just as the main course is finished. Bake French-style in hot oven quickly, while table is cleared and dessert service placed. Serve at once, high and brown, with moist, creamy center.

The bain-marie, a water-bath cooker, is the French version

of the double boiler. It is used for poached or steamed soufflés. If a bain-marie is used for any of the double boiler soufflé recipes in this book, care must be taken to fit the recipe to the capacity of the French utensil.

As a change, select a dessert soufflé recipe that takes as long to bake as it takes to serve and eat dinner. Put it into the oven as dinner is served. It's ready for eating when dessert time comes.

If you wish, divide a full recipe of soufflé into portion-sized soufflé dishes. Bake at same temperature required for large soufflé, but shorten baking time by about one third.

Try the trick of a famous chef. He said a pinch of cornstarch sprinkled onto egg whites as they are beaten helps hold up the soufflé for serving at table. A pinch is roughly 1⁄16 of a teaspoon.

Never try to beat egg whites to good volume in a plastic bowl or in one in which there is even a trace of fat.

One extra egg white adds considerable volume to a soufflé. Keep these basic proportions in mind:

3-egg soufflé needs 1-quart dish,
yields: 2 to 3 servings
4 to 5-egg soufflé needs 1½-quart dish,
yields: 4 to 5 servings
6 to 8-egg soufflé needs 2-quart dish,
yields: 6 to 8 servings

Yes, you can peek at a soufflé, but not until 5 minutes before it is through baking. Open the oven door carefully, leave the soufflé in place (do not pull shelf forward) and touch it with your finger to see if it springs back and is done. Or, if you wish to do so, sprinkle a bit of confectioners' sugar on a dessert soufflé at this time to form a glaze during the last few minutes of baking.

The use of an alcoholic beverage for flavor in hot soufflés stimulates rising and puffing due to the effect of heat on the alcohol. Though the flavor remains, the alcohol is driven off during baking.

Remember that a soufflé rises because the heat of the oven expands the air trapped in beaten eggs. A soufflé falls when cool air striking the warm food causes the trapped air to contract.

Undercooking causes a soufflé to shrink excessively when it is taken from the oven. A properly baked soufflé will shrink somewhat as soon as it's taken away from heat, but slowly at first. Overcooking seems to toughen a soufflé and may cause some separation of ingredients, which makes it seem curdled.

An uneven top or cracks in the top of a baked souffle are perfectly normal.

Watch for these common errors in soufflé preparation:

- Lumpy sauce or custard base.
- Food solids in too large pieces.
- Egg yolks improperly added to hot sauce, resulting in hard, cooked particles.
- Egg whites too cold to beat to good volume.
- Egg whites beaten too much, breaking into flecks.
- Rough handling in blending in beaten egg whites resulting in loss of trapped air.
- Wrong type of baking dish.
- Wrong time and temperature combination resulting in underbaking or overbaking.

COLD SOUFFLÉS

These feather-light beauties depend on gelatine for stability, beaten egg whites and whipped cream for height and light texture. The gelatine mixture should be handled exactly as the recipe suggests and chilled in the refrigerator to thick egg-white consistency so that it mounds up when spooned.

The completed soufflé is ready to serve when it has chilled for 3 to 4 hours. It should be delicately firm, but a bit spongy in texture. It should dent slightly and quiver just a bit when pressed lightly with a finger.

EGG WHITE SOUFFLÉS

These are probably the simplest soufflés ever devised. They are not true soufflés in that they have no sauce or custard base, but they are recognized as soufflés nonetheless. Equally well known are these egg white soufflés baked in a slow oven until delicately firm, or steamed in a double boiler. The latter may be made in a chafing dish (over hot water), and is a boon to the hostess. If left over hot water in double boiler or chafing dish, cover of utensil securely in place, this type of soufflé can be held for over an hour with very little perceptible loss of character or texture.

SOUFFLÉ OMELETS

These soufflélike desserts are not baked in a soufflé dish or casserole. Instead they are cooked and baked in a skillet or baked on an ovenproof platter. Since they are exceedingly delicate and fragile they must literally be rushed from oven to table at the very moment at which baking is finished. Traditionally the piping hot soufflé omelet is served accompanied by thoroughly chilled fruit for pleasing contrast.

SOUFFLÉ PUDDINGS

These are neither as delicate nor as dramatic as true soufflés, but make very appealing desserts. They may be turned out to serve since they tend to hold their shape when removed from the oven. To unmold most easily, let the soufflé pudding stand for 1 or 2 minutes, loosen edges with the tip of a knife, cover with a warm plate, and turn upside down quickly but gently. Some may be reheated for delayed serving.

SOUFFLÉ SAUCES

Though a well-made soufflé is a perfect thing in itself, some tastes dictate the use of a sauce to enhance the eye appeal as well as taste appeal of the dish. Savory sauces, sparked with lemon, onion, wine, and the like complement main dish and accompaniment soufflés. Sweet sauces, of course, belong to dessert soufflés. And fruits served with soufflés as garnish are, in essence, taking the place of a sauce.

Any sauce should be served with discretion, a little going a long way, so as never to hide the delicate flavor of the soufflé.

2

MAIN DISH SOUFFLÉS

These are appropriate to serve as main dish at brunch, lunch, or supper. By keeping the proportion of sauce to other ingredients constant, the variety of kinds of soufflés is limited only by imagination. Most glamorous way to use up a cup or two of leftover foods, too.

BASIC CHEESE SOUFFLÉ I

2 tablespoons butter or margarine
2 tablespoons flour
¾ cup hot milk
½ teaspoon salt
¼ teaspoon dry mustard
3 drops hot pepper sauce
1½ cups shredded sharp American or Cheddar cheese
4 egg yolks, well beaten
4 egg whites, beaten stiff but not dry

HAVE READY: 1½-quart soufflé dish or deep casserole, ungreased.

Melt butter or margarine in saucepan over low heat. Blend in flour and cook for 1 minute. Remove from heat and gradually stir in hot milk to make a smooth mixture. Cook and stir over medium heat until sauce thickens. Add seasonings and shredded cheese and stir until cheese melts and blends in. Remove from heat and cool 10 minutes. Add beaten egg yolks gradually, stirring briskly. Fold into beaten egg whites gently but thoroughly. Pour into 1½-quart soufflé dish or deep casserole. Bake in 300° F. (slow) oven for 50 minutes. If crusty soufflé with very soft center is desired, bake in 425° F. (hot) oven for 25 minutes.

YIELD: 4 servings.

BASIC CHEESE SOUFFLÉ II

¼ cup butter or margarine
¼ cup flour
1½ cups hot milk
1 teaspoon salt
½ teaspoon dry mustard
4 drops hot pepper sauce
2 cups shredded sharp American or Cheddar cheese
6 egg yolks, well beaten
6 egg whites, beaten stiff but not dry

HAVE READY: 2-quart soufflé dish or deep casserole, ungreased.

Melt butter or margarine in saucepan over low heat. Blend in flour and cook 3 minutes, stirring occasionally. Remove from heat and gradually stir in hot milk to make a smooth mixture. Cook and stir over medium heat until sauce thickens. Add seasonings and shredded cheese and stir until cheese melts and blends in. Remove from heat and cool 10 minutes. Add beaten egg yolks gradually, stirring briskly. Fold into beaten egg whites gently but thoroughly. Pour into 2-quart soufflé dish or deep casserole. Bake in 300° F. (slow) oven for 1¼ hours. If crusty soufflé with very soft center is desired, bake in 400° F. (hot) oven for 40 minutes.

YIELD: 6 servings.

BEEF MUSHROOM SOUFFLÉ

3 tablespoons butter or margarine
2 tablespoons minced onion
3 tablespoons flour
1½ cups hot diluted evaporated milk
1 teaspoon salt
2 slices fresh bread, coarsely crumbled
½ teaspoon pepper
few grains cayenne pepper
1 teaspoon Worcestershire sauce
½ pound ground raw lean beef
1 can (3 or 4 ounces) chopped mushrooms, drained
2 tablespoons minced parsley
4 egg yolks, well beaten
5 egg whites, beaten stiff but not dry

HAVE READY: 1½-quart soufflé dish, buttered.

Melt butter or margarine in saucepan over low heat. Add grated onion and sauté until light yellow. Sprinkle on flour, blend until smooth, and cook, stirring, for 1 minute. Remove from heat. Gradually add hot milk and salt, stirring to smooth mixture. Cook and stir over medium heat until sauce boils and thickens. Stir in fresh bread crumbs, peppers, Worcestershire sauce, and ground beef. Cook and stir until well heated, but do not boil. Remove from heat, add chopped mushrooms and parsley, and let cool 10 to 15 minutes. Slowly add beaten egg yolks, stirring briskly. Fold in beaten egg whites gently but thoroughly. Pour into prepared 1½-quart soufflé dish. Bake in 375° F. (moderate) oven for 50 to 60 minutes.

YIELD: 4 to 5 servings.

CHEESE AND BACON SOUFFLÉ

¼ cup quick-cooking tapioca
1⅓ cups milk
3 drops hot pepper sauce
1 cup grated Cheddar cheese, lightly packed
4 egg yolks, well beaten
3 slices crisp cooked bacon, drained and crumbled
5 egg whites, beaten stiff but not dry

HAVE READY: 2-quart soufflé dish or deep casserole, ungreased.

Combine first 3 ingredients in saucepan and let stand 5 minutes. Cook and stir over medium heat until mixture comes to a full boil. Remove from heat, add grated cheese, and stir until cheese melts. Cool 10 to 15 minutes. Add tapioca mixture gradually to beaten egg yolks, blending well. Gently stir in crumbled bacon. Fold into beaten egg whites gently but thoroughly. Pour into 2-quart soufflé dish or deep casserole set in shallow pan containing 1 inch hot water. Bake in 350° F. (moderate) oven for 50 to 55 minutes.

YIELD: 5 to 6 servings.

CHEESE AND WINE SOUFFLÉ

3 tablespoons butter or margarine
3 tablespoons flour
1 teaspoon salt
¾ cup hot milk
¾ cup dry white wine
⅛ teaspoon ground nutmeg
3 drops hot pepper sauce
1½ cups grated Swiss or American cheese
5 egg yolks, well beaten
6 egg whites, beaten stiff but not dry

HAVE READY: 2-quart soufflé dish, lightly buttered, and dusted with flour.

Melt butter or margarine in saucepan over low heat. Blend in flour and cook for 1 minute. Remove from heat. Add salt, then gradually stir in hot milk and dry white wine. Cook and stir over medium heat until sauce is thickened and smooth. Remove from heat. Add ground nutmeg, hot pepper sauce, and grated cheese, stirring until cheese melts and blends in. Let cool 5 minutes. Slowly add beaten egg yolks, stirring briskly. Fold in beaten egg whites gently but thoroughly. Pour into prepared 2-quart soufflé dish. Bake in 350° F. (moderate) oven for 45 to 55 minutes.

YIELD: 6 servings.

CURRIED CHICKEN SOUFFLÉ

¼ cup butter or margarine
2 tablespoons minced onion
1 to 1½ teaspoons curry powder
¼ cup flour
1½ cups hot chicken broth
½ teaspoon salt
¼ teaspoon pepper
¼ cup minced green pepper
2 tablespoons minced chives
4 egg yolks, well beaten
1½ cups chopped cooked chicken
5 egg whites, beaten stiff but not dry

HAVE READY: 2-quart soufflé dish, lightly buttered and dusted with fine dry bread crumbs.

Melt butter or margarine in saucepan over low heat. Add minced onion and cook for 2 minutes. Blend in curry powder, then flour, and cook for 3 minutes more, stirring constantly. Remove from heat. Gradually add hot chicken broth, stirring to smooth mixture. Add salt and pepper. Cook and stir over medium heat until sauce boils and thickens. Remove from heat, mix in minced green pepper and chives, and let cool 10 to 15 minutes. Slowly add beaten egg yolks, stirring briskly. Blend in chopped cooked chicken. Fold in beaten egg whites gently but thoroughly. Pour into prepared 2-quart soufflé dish. Bake in 375° F. (moderate) oven for 45 to 55 minutes.

YIELD: 6 servings.

CHICKEN SOUFFLÉ MADEIRA

2 tablespoons butter or margarine
2 tablespoons flour
1 cup hot light cream
1 teaspoon salt
¼ teaspoon pepper
few grains cayenne pepper
1 tablespoon Madeira wine
4 egg yolks, well beaten
1 cup minced cooked chicken
5 egg whites, beaten stiff but not dry

HAVE READY: 1½-quart soufflé dish, ungreased.

Melt butter or margarine in saucepan over low heat. Blend in flour and cook for 1 minute. Remove from heat, gradually add hot cream, then seasonings, and stir to make a smooth mixture. Cook and stir over medium heat until sauce has thickened. Remove from heat, add wine, and cool for 10 minutes. Slowly add beaten egg yolks, stirring briskly, then stir in minced chicken. Fold in beaten egg whites gently but thoroughly. Pour into 1½-quart soufflé dish. Bake in 350° F. (moderate) oven for 40 to 50 minutes.

YIELD: 4 to 5 servings.

CHICKEN LIVER AND MUSHROOM SOUFFLÉ

3 tablespoons butter or margarine
1 tablespoon minced onion
few grains garlic powder
3 tablespoons flour
½ teaspoon salt
¼ teaspoon pepper
1 cup hot light cream or milk
1 tablespoon minced parsley
4 egg yolks, well beaten
1½ cups finely chopped cooked chicken livers
1 small can (3 or 4 ounces) chopped mushrooms or ½ pound sautéed fresh mushrooms, chopped
5 egg whites, beaten stiff but not dry

HAVE READY: 1½-quart soufflé dish, well buttered.

Melt butter or margarine in saucepan over low heat. Add minced onion and garlic powder and cook for 1 minute. Blend in flour, salt, and pepper, and cook 1 to 2 minutes more. Remove from heat. Gradually add hot light cream or milk, stirring to smooth mixture. Cook and stir over medium heat until sauce boils and thickens. Remove from heat, add minced parsley, and cool for 10 mniutes. Slowly add beaten egg yolks, stirring briskly. Mix in chopped cooked chicken livers and chopped mushrooms. Fold in beaten egg whites gently but thoroughly. Pour into prepared 1½-quart soufflé dish. Bake in 400° F. (hot) oven for 30 to 35 minutes.

YIELD: 4 or 5 servings.

SWISS CHICKEN SOUFFLÉ

¼ cup butter or margarine
¼ cup flour
1 teaspoon salt
¼ teaspoon pepper
1½ cups hot milk
4 egg yolks, well beaten
1 cup finely shredded Swiss cheese
2 cups minced cooked chicken
4 egg whites, beaten stiff but not dry

HAVE READY: 1½-quart soufflé dish, ungreased.

Melt butter or margarine in saucepan over low heat. Blend in flour and cook for 3 minutes, stirring occasionally. Remove from heat. Add seasonings, then gradually stir in hot milk to make a smooth mixture. Cook and stir, over medium heat, until sauce is thick. Remove from heat and cool 10 minutes. Gradually add beaten egg yolks, stirring vigorously. Stir in finely shredded cheese and minced chicken, blending thoroughly. Fold into beaten egg whites gently but thoroughly. Pour into 1½-quart soufflé dish. Bake in 325° F. (slow) oven for 50 to 60 minutes.

YIELD: 5 to 6 servings.

CHICKEN TETRAZZINI SOUFFLÉ

¼ cup butter or margarine
1 can (3 ounces) chopped mushrooms, drained
¼ cup flour
1 cup hot medium cream
1 cup hot chicken broth
½ teaspoon salt
¼ teaspoon pepper
1 to 2 tablespoons sherry
½ cup grated Swiss cheese
4 egg yolks, well beaten
1 cup cooked, drained spaghettini
1 cup minced cooked chicken
5 egg whites, beaten stiff but not dry

HAVE READY: 2-quart soufflé dish, buttered, and dusted with grated Parmesan cheese.

Melt butter or margarine in saucepan; add chopped mushrooms and sauté for 2 or 3 minutes. Blend in flour, and cook, stirring frequently, for 3 more minutes. Remove from heat. Gradually stir in hot cream and chicken broth to make a smooth mixture; add salt and pepper. Cook and stir over medium heat until sauce has thickened. Remove from heat. Add sherry and grated Swiss cheese, stirring until cheese melts and is blended in. Cool 10 minutes. Gradually add beaten egg yolks, stirring briskly. Thoroughly mix in cooked spaghettini and minced chicken. Fold in beaten egg whites gently but completely. Pour into prepared 2-quart soufflé dish. Bake in 350° F. (moderate) oven for 50 to 60 minutes.

YIELD: 6 servings.

HEARTY CORN SOUFFLÉ

2 tablespoons butter or margarine
¼ cup flour
2 cups hot milk
½ teaspoon salt
¼ teaspoon pepper
1 teaspoon dry mustard
1 cup shredded sharp Cheddar cheese
1 cup canned cream-style corn
3 egg yolks, well beaten
4 egg whites, beaten stiff but not dry

HAVE READY: 1½-quart soufflé dish, well buttered, and dusted with flour.

Melt butter or margarine in saucepan over low heat; blend in flour. Cook for 2 minutes. Remove from heat. Slowly add hot milk, stirring constantly until smooth. Cook and stir, over medium heat, until sauce thickens. Add seasonings and cheese, and stir until cheese is softened and blended. Remove from heat, add corn, and let cool for 10 minutes. Add beaten egg yolks gradually, stirring vigorously. Fold in beaten egg whites. Pour into prepared 1½-quart soufflé dish. Set in shallow pan containing 1 inch of hot water. Bake in 375° F. (moderate) oven for 45 to 50 minutes.

YIELD: 4 to 5 servings.

CORN MEAL AND CHEESE SOUFFLÉ

⅓ cup corn meal
⅓ cup cold milk
1⅔ cups scalded milk
1 tablespoon butter or margarine
1 teaspoon salt
¼ teaspoon white pepper
¼ cup shredded Cheddar cheese
3 egg yolks, well beaten
4 egg whites, beaten stiff but not dry

HAVE READY: 1½-quart soufflé dish or deep casserole, ungreased.

Measure corn meal into saucepan, then moisten thoroughly with ⅓ cup cold milk. Slowly add scalded milk, stirring briskly to keep mixture smooth. Add butter or margarine. Cook and stir over medium heat until mixture is thick like mush. Remove from heat, add seasonings and shredded cheese, and stir until cheese melts and blends in. Cool for 10 minutes. Slowly add beaten egg yolks, stirring vigorously. Cool about 10 minutes. Fold in beaten egg whites. Pour into 1½-quart soufflé dish or deep casserole. Bake in 350° F. (moderate) oven for 30 to 35 minutes.

YIELD: 4 to 5 servings.

SAVORY CORNED BEEF SOUFFLÉ

3 tablespoons butter or margarine
1 clove garlic, crushed
3 tablespoons minced onion
3 tablespoons flour
½ teaspoon salt
¼ teaspoon pepper
few grains cayenne pepper
1 cup hot milk
2 tablespoons chopped parsley
4 egg yolks, well beaten
1½ cups finely shredded cooked or canned lean corned beef
5 egg whites, beaten stiff but not dry

HAVE READY: 1½-quart soufflé dish, buttered, and dusted with fine dry bread crumbs.

Melt butter or margarine in small saucepan over low heat. Add crushed garlic and minced onion and sauté for 1 or 2 minutes. Blend in flour, salt, and peppers, and cook, stirring, for 2 minutes. Remove from heat. Gradually add hot milk, then chopped parsley, stirring to smooth mixture. Cook and stir over medium heat until sauce boils and thickens. Remove from heat and let cool 10 minutes. Add beaten egg yolks, stirring briskly. Mix in shredded cooked or canned corned beef. Fold in beaten egg whites gently but thoroughly. Pour into prepared 1½-quart soufflé dish. Bake in 375° F. (moderate) oven for 35 to 45 minutes.

YIELD: 4 to 5 servings.

CRAB MEAT SOUFFLÉ

2 tablespoons butter or margarine
2 tablespoons flour
1 cup hot milk or light cream
1 teaspoon salt
½ teaspoon pepper
few grains cayenne pepper
1 tablespoon sherry or Madeira wine
1 tablespoon lemon juice
1 cup finely shredded cooked or canned crab meat
4 egg yolks, well beaten
5 egg whites, beaten stiff but not dry

HAVE READY: 1½-quart soufflé dish, ungreased.

Melt butter or margarine in saucepan over low heat. Blend in flour and cook 1 minute. Remove from heat. Gradually add hot milk or cream, stirring to smooth mixture. Cook and stir over medium heat until sauce is thickened and smooth. Remove from heat. Add seasonings, sherry or Madeira wine, lemon juice, and crab meat, mixing thoroughly to blend. Let sauce cool 15 minutes. Gradually add beaten egg yolks, stirring briskly. Fold in beaten egg whites gently but thoroughly. Pour into 1½-quart soufflé dish. Bake in 350° F. (moderate) oven for 35 to 40 minutes.

YIELD: 4 to 5 servings.

CURRIED CRAB SOUFFLÉ

¼ cup butter or margarine
¼ cup flour
1 cup hot milk
½ teaspoon salt
½ teaspoon curry powder
1 cup shredded Cheddar or Swiss cheese
4 egg yolks, well beaten
5 egg whites, beaten stiff but not dry
1½ cups (½ pound) flaked cooked King crab, lump crab meat, or canned crab meat

HAVE READY: 2-quart soufflé dish, ungreased.

Melt butter or margarine in saucepan over low heat; blend in flour. Let cook, stirring occasionally, for 3 minutes. Remove from heat. Gradually add hot milk, then seasonings, stirring until smooth. Cook and stir over medium heat until sauce is thick. Stir in cheese until melted and blended. Remove from heat and cool 10 minutes. Gradually add beaten egg yolks, stirring vigorously. Fold into beaten egg whites gently but thoroughly. Pour 2 cups soufflé mixture into 2-quart soufflé dish. Top with crab meat arranged as a layer. Pour on remaining soufflé mixture. Bake in 300° F. (slow) oven for 1 hour.

YIELD: 6 servings.

SELF-SAUCED CRAB MEAT SOUFFLÉ

¼ cup butter or margarine
3 tablespoons flour
¾ cup hot milk
½ teaspoon salt
⅛ teaspoon pepper
few grains cayenne pepper
1 teaspoon lemon juice
1 cup finely shredded lump crab meat
3 tablespoons brandy
¼ cup heavy cream
½ cup whole pieces lump crab meat
4 egg yolks, well beaten
5 egg whites, beaten stiff but not dry

HAVE READY: 2-quart soufflé dish, well buttered.

Melt butter or margarine in saucepan over low heat. Blend in flour and cook, stirring, for 1 or 2 minutes. Remove from heat. Gradually add hot milk, salt, and peppers, stirring to smooth mixture. Cook and stir over medium heat until sauce boils and thickens. Remove from heat and add lemon juice. Sprinkle shredded crab meat with brandy and stir into sauce. Blend ⅓ cup of sauce mixture with heavy cream and pour into prepared 2-quart soufflé dish. Top with whole pieces of crab meat. Gradually add beaten egg yolks to remaining sauce mixture, stirring briskly. Fold in beaten egg whites gently but thoroughly. Pour onto crab meat in bottom of soufflé dish. Bake in 375° F. (moderate) oven for 40 to 50 minutes. Spoon sauce from bottom of dish as soufflé is served.

YIELD: 6 servings.

HEARTY EGG SOUFFLÉ

¼ cup butter or margarine
¼ cup flour
1 teaspoon salt
1 cup hot milk or tomato juice
⅛ teaspoon hot pepper sauce
¼ teaspoon dry mustard (optional)
4 egg yolks, well beaten
4 egg whites, beaten stiff but not dry
2 hard-cooked eggs, sliced

HAVE READY: 1½-quart soufflé dish, lightly buttered, and dusted with fine dry bread crumbs.

Melt butter or margarine in saucepan over low heat. Blend in flour and salt and cook for 3 minutes, stirring occasionally. Remove from heat. Gradually add hot milk or tomato juice, stirring to smooth mixture. Cook and stir over medium heat until sauce thickens. Remove from heat. Add hot pepper sauce and dry mustard, if desired. Let sauce cool 10 minutes. Slowly add beaten egg yolks, stirring briskly. Fold in beaten egg whites gently but thoroughly. Pour half of soufflé mixture into prepared 1½-quart soufflé dish. Top with a layer of sliced hard-cooked eggs. Pour on remaining soufflé mixture. Bake in 350° F. (moderate) oven for 30 to 40 minutes.

YIELD: 4 to 5 servings.

DAINTY FISH SOUFFLÉ

1 tablespoon butter or margarine
2 teaspoons minced shallots or onions
½ cup dry white wine
½ cup water
¼ teaspoon salt
⅛ teaspoon pepper
½ pound sole, halibut, or whitefish
3 tablespoons butter or margarine
2 tablespoons flour
½ teaspoon salt
⅛ teaspoon pepper
1¼ cups hot milk
3 egg yolks, well beaten
4 egg whites, beaten stiff but not dry

HAVE READY: 1½-quart soufflé dish, buttered.

Combine first 6 ingredients in skillet; bring to a boil and let cook for 2 minutes. Reduce heat, add fish; simmer until fish is very tender, about 12 to 15 minutes. Remove fish with slotted turner and purée in electric blender or through a food mill. Reserve stock for Fish Soufflé Sauce (see Index).

Melt butter or margarine in saucepan over low heat, gradually stir in flour until smooth, add seasonings and cook for 1 minute. Remove from heat. Slowly stir in hot milk, blending until smooth. Cook and stir over medium heat until sauce thickens. Remove from heat, add puréed fish, and let mixture cool for 8 to 10 minutes. Slowly add beaten egg yolks while beating fish mixture briskly with a wire whisk. Stir in ⅓ of beaten egg whites, then gently fold in remaining egg whites until just blended.

Pour into prepared 1½-quart soufflé dish. Bake in preheated 350° F. (moderate) oven for 35 to 40 minutes. Serve at once.

YIELD: 4 to 5 servings.

EASY FISH SOUFFLÉ

2 teaspoons melted butter or margarine
2 tablespoons dry bread crumbs
⅓ cup butter or margarine
½ cup sifted flour
1 teaspoon salt
⅛ teaspoon pepper
2 cups cold milk
2 cups (1 pound) cooked white-meat fish, boned and flaked
4 egg yolks, well beaten
4 egg whites, beaten stiff but not dry

HAVE READY: 2-quart soufflé dish, well buttered, and generously dusted with fine dry bread crumbs.

Combine 2 teaspoons melted butter or margarine with 2 tablespoons dry bread crumbs, blending well. Set aside. Melt ⅓ cup butter or margarine in top of double boiler over boiling water. Sift together flour and seasonings and blend into melted butter or margarine. Gradually add milk, stirring to smooth mixture. Cook, stirring occasionally, until sauce is thick. Stir in flaked cooked fish. Slowly add about 1 cup hot sauce mixture to beaten egg yolks, then stir into remaining hot sauce. Remove from heat and let cool 10 minutes. Fold beaten egg whites into warm sauce gently but thoroughly. Pour into prepared 2-quart soufflé dish. Top with the buttered crumbs. Bake in 350° F. (moderate) oven for 50 to 60 minutes.

YIELD: 5 to 6 servings.

ELEGANT CHEESE SOUFFLÉ

6 tablespoons butter or margarine
6 tablespoons flour
½ teaspoon salt
1¼ cups hot milk
few grains cayenne pepper
½ cup sieved Brie cheese
¼ cup mashed Roquefort or blue cheese
¼ cup softened cream cheese
6 egg yolks, well beaten
6 egg whites, beaten stiff but not dry

HAVE READY: 2-quart soufflé dish, buttered, and lightly dusted with dry bread crumbs.

Melt butter or margarine in saucepan over low heat. Blend in flour and salt. Cook, stirring frequently, for 3 minutes, but do not brown. Slowly add hot milk, then pepper, stirring until smooth. Cook and stir, over medium heat, until sauce is thick. Add cheeses and stir until blended thoroughly. Remove from heat and cool 10 minutes. Add beaten egg yolks, stirring vigorously. Gently stir ⅓ of beaten egg whites into cheese mixture, then fold in remaining whites just until blended. Pour into prepared 2-quart soufflé dish. Bake in 350° F. (moderate) oven for 40 to 45 minutes.

YIELD: 6 servings.

FISH FILLET SOUFFLÉ

2 shallot cloves, minced
½ cup dry white wine
¾ cup water
⅛ teaspoon salt
pinch of white pepper
6 small sole fillets
3 tablespoons butter or margarine
3 tablespoons flour
1 cup hot milk
½ teaspoon salt
4 egg yolks
5 egg whites, beaten stiff but not dry
½ cup grated Swiss cheese

HAVE READY: 2-quart soufflé dish, lightly buttered.

Combine first 5 ingredients in skillet; bring to a boil and let cook for 2 minutes. Reduce heat, add sole fillets, and simmer until fish is fork tender, about 6 to 8 minutes. Carefully remove cooked fillets and arrange in prepared 2-quart soufflé dish. Reserve stock for Fish Soufflé Sauce (see Index).

Melt butter or margarine in saucepan over low heat. Gradually add flour and cook for 1 minute. Remove from heat. Slowly stir in hot milk and salt, blending until smooth. Cook and stir over medium heat until sauce thickens. Remove from heat and let cool 5 minutes. Beat in egg yolks one at a time, using wire whisk. Stir in ¼ of beaten egg whites and ¼ cup of the grated cheese. Fold in remaining beaten egg whites.

Pour over fish fillets. Sprinkle remaining ¼ cup grated cheese on top.

Bake in preheated 400° F. (hot) oven for 6 minutes. Reduce setting for heat to 375° F. (moderate) and continue baking for 20 to 25 minutes more. Serve at once. YIELD: 6 servings.

FRENCH-STYLE CHEESE SOUFFLÉ

½ cup butter or margarine
¼ cup flour
1¾ cups hot milk
½ teaspoon salt
¼ teaspoon white pepper
few grains cayenne pepper
few grains ground nutmeg
5 egg yolks, well beaten
¾ cup grated Gruyère cheese
6 egg whites, beaten stiff but not dry

HAVE READY: 1½-quart soufflé dish, buttered.

Melt butter or margarine in saucepan over low heat. Blend in flour and cook 3 to 4 minutes. Remove from heat. Slowly stir in hot milk to make smooth mixture. Cook and stir over medium heat until sauce thickens. Add seasonings; remove from heat and cool 15 minutes. Combine beaten egg yolks and grated cheese. Gradually add to sauce, stirring briskly. Fold in beaten egg whites gently but thoroughly. Pour into prepared 1½-quart soufflé dish. Bake in 425° F. (hot) oven for 25 to 30 minutes. YIELD: 4 to 5 servings.

HAM SOUFFLÉ

¼ cup butter or margarine
¼ cup flour
¼ teaspoon pepper
1 cup hot milk
4 egg yolks, well beaten
1 cup ground cooked ham
1 teaspoon dry mustard
5 egg whites, beaten stiff but not dry

HAVE READY: 1½-quart soufflé dish, buttered.

Melt butter or margarine in saucepan, over low heat; blend

in flour and pepper, and let cook, stirring, for 3 minutes. Remove from heat. Slowly add hot milk, stirring until smooth. Cook and stir, over medium heat, until sauce is very thick. Remove from heat and let cool 5 minutes. Gradually add beaten egg yolks, stirring vigorously, then mix ham and mustard in thoroughly. Fold beaten egg whites into ham mixture. Pour into prepared 1½-quart soufflé dish. Bake in 375° F. (moderate) oven for 35 to 40 minutes.

YIELD: 4 to 5 servings.

MACARONI AND CHEESE SOUFFLÉ

¼ cup butter or margarine
1 tablespoon minced onion
¼ cup flour
1 teaspoon salt
¼ teaspoon pepper
1¼ cups hot milk
4 drops hot pepper sauce
½ cup grated American cheese
4 egg yolks, well beaten
2 tablespoons minced pimiento (optional)
1½ cups cooked small elbow or shell macaroni
5 egg whites, beaten stiff but not dry

HAVE READY: 1½-quart soufflé dish, buttered.

Melt butter or margarine in saucepan over low heat. Add minced onion, and sauté for 1 minute, but do not brown. Blend in flour, salt, and pepper, and cook for 3 more minutes, stirring frequently. Remove from heat. Gradually add hot milk, stirring to smooth mixture. Cook and stir over medium heat until sauce thickens. Remove from heat. Add hot pepper sauce and grated cheese, stirring until cheese melts and blends in. Let cool 10 minutes. Slowly add beaten egg yolks, stirring briskly. Blend in pimiento and cooked macaroni. Fold in beaten egg whites gently but thoroughly. Pour into prepared 1½-quart soufflé dish. Bake in 350° F. (moderate) oven for 40 to 50 minutes.

YIELD: 5 to 6 servings.

HAM AND CHEESE SOUFFLÉ

¼ cup butter or margarine
¼ cup flour
1½ cups hot milk
½ teaspoon salt
1 teaspoon dry mustard
few grains cayenne pepper
¾ cup shredded American cheese
6 egg yolks, well beaten
1¼ cups ground cooked ham
6 egg whites, beaten stiff but not dry

HAVE READY: 2-quart soufflé dish, ungreased.

Melt butter or margarine in saucepan over low heat. Blend in flour and cook for 3 minutes, stirring occasionally. Remove from heat. Gradually add hot milk, stirring to smooth mixture. Cook and stir over medium heat until sauce thickens. Add salt, dry mustard, pepper, and grated cheese, stirring until cheese melts and blends in. Remove from heat and let cool 10 to 15 minutes. Slowly add beaten egg yolks, stirring briskly. Blend in ground cooked ham. Fold in beaten egg whites gently but thoroughly. Pour into 2-quart soufflé dish. Bake in 350° F. (moderate) oven for 50 to 60 minutes.

YIELD: 6 servings.

SWEDISH FISH SOUFFLÉ

⅓ cup butter or margarine
⅓ cup flour
2 cups hot milk
½ teaspoon salt
⅛ teaspoon white pepper
½ teaspoon sugar
2 cups flaked cooked white-meat fish
1 tiny sprig of dill, chopped, or ⅛ teaspoon dried dill weed
4 egg yolks, well beaten
4 egg whites, beaten stiff but not dry

HAVE READY: 1½-quart soufflé dish, buttered, and dusted with fine dry bread crumbs.

Melt butter or margarine in saucepan, add flour, and stir until smooth. Cook and stir over low heat for 2 to 3 minutes. Remove from heat. Slowly stir in hot milk, seasonings, and sugar, blending well. Cook and stir over medium heat until sauce thickens. Remove from heat and let cool 10 to 15 minutes. Add fish and dill to cooled sauce, then add beaten egg yolks gradually, beating sauce briskly with wire whisk or wooden spoon. Fold in beaten egg whites just until blended. Pour into prepared 1½-quart soufflé dish, set in shallow pan containing 1 inch of hot water. Bake in 375° F. (moderate) oven for 35 to 40 minutes.

YIELD: 6 servings.

FREEZE-AND-BAKE CHEESE SOUFFLÉ

3 tablespoons butter or margarine
¼ cup flour
½ teaspoon salt
¼ teaspoon pepper
1 cup hot milk
1 cup finely broken or mashed blue cheese
½ cup (4 ounces) cream cheese
4 egg yolks, well beaten
4 egg whites
¼ teaspoon cream of tartar

HAVE READY: 1½-quart soufflé dish, lined with two 16½-inch lengths of aluminum foil joined with a firm fold to make a center seam. Foil should extend 2 inches above edge of dish all around. Cut circle of foil to fit top of dish, and reserve until soufflé has frozen.

Melt butter or margarine in saucepan. Remove from heat. Stir in flour and seasonings until well blended. Cook for 2 minutes. Remove from heat. Add hot milk slowly, stirring constantly until mixture is smooth. Cook and stir over medium heat until sauce thickens. Reduce heat, add blue and cream cheese, and stir until cheese melts and is blended in. Cool for 10 minutes. Slowly add beaten egg yolks, stirring vigorously.

Beat egg whites until foamy. Sprinkle on cream of tartar, and continue beating until egg whites are stiff but not dry. Fold beaten egg whites gently but thoroughly into cheese sauce. Pour into foil lined 1½-quart soufflé dish. Freeze.

When soufflé has frozen, lift it from soufflé dish by grasping foil liner. Cover with circle of foil and fold down extended edges to secure it. Replace in freezer for storage up to 4 weeks.

To bake, replace foil-wrapped soufflé in baking dish; remove foil from top; fold overhanging foil at edge of dish to form a sort of collar. Place soufflé immediately in 300° F. (slow) oven. Bake for 1½ hours.

YIELD: 4 to 5 servings.

HAM AND MUSHROOM SOUFFLÉ

¼ cup butter or margarine
¼ cup flour
1 cup hot milk
¼ teaspoon pepper
4 egg yolks, well beaten
⅔ cup ground cooked ham
⅓ cup (3 ounce can) mushrooms, drained and minced
1 tablespoon finely chopped parsley
5 egg whites, beaten stiff but not dry

HAVE READY: 1½-quart soufflé dish, ungreased.

Melt butter or margarine in saucepan over low heat; blend in flour. Cook, stirring occasionally, for 3 minutes. Remove from heat. Gradually add hot milk, then pepper, stirring until smooth. Cook and stir, over medium heat, until sauce is thick. Remove from heat and cool for 10 minutes. Gradually add beaten egg yolks, stirring vigorously, then stir in ground ham, minced mushrooms, and parsley. Gently but thoroughly fold into beaten egg whites. Pour into 1½-quart soufflé dish. Bake in 350° F. (moderate) oven for 55 to 60 minutes.

YIELD: 5 to 6 servings.

CURRIED LAMB SOUFFLÉ

¼ cup butter or margarine
2 tablespoons minced onion
2 tablespoons minced celery
1 to 2 teaspoons curry powder
½ teaspoon salt
¼ cup flour
1½ cups hot lamb or chicken broth
1 tablespoon minced green pepper (optional)
2 cups minced cooked lamb
4 egg yolks, well beaten
5 egg whites, beaten stiff but not dry

HAVE READY: 1½-quart soufflé dish, buttered.

Melt butter or margarine in saucepan over low heat. Add minced onion and celery, and sauté for 2 minutes. Blend in curry powder and salt, then add flour, stirring until smooth. Cook, stirring, for 3 minutes. Remove from heat. Gradually add hot broth, stirring to prevent lumps. Cook and stir over medium heat until sauce boils and thickens. Remove from heat, add green pepper, if desired, and minced cooked lamb. Let cool 15 minutes. Slowly add beaten egg yolks, stirring briskly. Fold in beaten egg whites gently but thoroughly. Pour into prepared 1½-quart soufflé dish. Bake in 350° F. (moderate) oven for 45 to 55 minutes.

YIELD: 4 to 5 servings.

MUSHROOM AND CHEESE SOUFFLÉ

2 tablespoons butter or margarine
½ pound mushrooms, cleaned and trimmed, or 1 can mushrooms (4 ounces)
⅓ cup butter or margarine
⅓ cup flour
½ teaspoon salt
¼ teaspoon pepper
1 cup hot milk
½ cup grated Cheddar or Swiss cheese
6 egg yolks, well beaten
6 egg whites, beaten stiff but not dry

HAVE READY: 2-quart soufflé dish, ungreased.

Melt 2 tablespoons butter or margarine in small skillet. Chop mushrooms finely, pour into skillet, and sauté for about 10 minutes, over low heat. Melt ⅓ cup butter or margarine in saucepan, over low heat. Blend in flour and seasonings, and cook for 3 or 4 minutes, stirring occasionally. Remove from heat. Gradually add hot milk, stirring to blend smoothly. Cook and stir, over medium heat, until sauce is thick. Add cheese, and stir until melted; remove from heat and cool 10 minutes. Blend in cooked chopped mushrooms, then slowly stir sauce into beaten egg yolks until well mixed. Fold sauce into beaten egg whites gently but thoroughly. Pour into 2-quart soufflé dish set in shallow pan containing 1 inch hot water. Bake in 325° F. (slow) oven for 1 to 1¼ hours.

YIELD: 6 servings.

NORWEGIAN FISH SOUFFLÉ

2 tablespoons butter or margarine
1 tablespoon flour
1 cup hot milk
½ teaspoon salt
¼ teaspoon pepper
½ cup hot mashed potato
1 cup flaked cooked white fish
1 tablespoon minced parsley
3 egg yolks, well beaten
3 egg whites, beaten stiff but not dry

HAVE READY: 1-quart soufflé dish, well buttered.

Melt butter or margarine in saucepan over low heat. Blend in flour and cook for 1 minute. Remove from heat. Slowly stir in hot milk and seasonings. Cook and stir over medium heat until sauce thickens. Pour sauce onto hot mashed potato, and beat, with wire whisk or spoon, until mixture is light and fluffy. Add flaked fish and minced parsley, stirring to blend. Gradually add beaten egg yolks, stirring briskly. Fold in beaten egg whites. Pour into prepared 1-quart soufflé dish. Bake in 400° F. (hot) oven for 30 to 35 minutes.

YIELD: 4 servings.

CHEESY NOODLE SOUFFLÉ

¼ cup butter or margarine
¼ cup flour
1 teaspoon salt
¼ teaspoon pepper
2 cups hot milk
½ cup dairy sour cream
½ cup creamed cottage cheese
4 egg yolks, well beaten
1 cup cooked, drained, fine noodles
5 egg whites, beaten stiff but not dry

HAVE READY: 2-quart soufflé dish, buttered.

Melt butter or margarine in saucepan over low heat. Blend in flour and seasonings, and cook for 3 minutes, stirring frequently. Remove from heat. Slowly add hot milk, stirring until mixture is smooth. Cook and stir over medium heat until sauce is thickened. Remove from heat. Blend in sour cream and cottage cheese, and let cool 10 minutes. Gradually add beaten egg yolks, stirring briskly. Mix in cooked noodles thoroughly. Fold in beaten egg whites gently but completely. Pour into prepared 2-quart soufflé dish. Bake in 375° F. (moderate) oven for 35 to 45 minutes.

YIELD: 6 servings.

ONION AND CHEESE SOUFFLÉ

⅓ cup butter or margarine
¼ cup minced onion
¼ cup flour
½ teaspoon salt
⅛ teaspoon pepper
3 drops hot pepper sauce
1 cup hot milk
¾ cup grated Gruyère or Swiss cheese
5 egg yolks, well beaten
6 egg whites, beaten stiff but not dry

HAVE READY: 1½-quart soufflé dish, buttered, and dusted with fine dry bread crumbs.

Melt butter or margarine in saucepan over low heat, add onion, and sauté until tender and golden. Sprinkle on flour, stirring to prevent lumps, and cook for 2 more minutes. Remove from heat and add seasonings. Gradually stir in hot milk to a smooth mixture. Cook and stir over medium heat until sauce thickens. Add grated cheese and continue to stir until cheese melts. Remove from heat and cool 10 to 15 minutes. Gradually add egg yolks, stirring briskly. Lightly stir in about ⅓ beaten egg whites; then fold in remaining beaten egg whites gently but thoroughly. Pour into prepared 1½-quart soufflé dish. Bake in 375° F. (moderate) oven for 30 to 35 minutes.

YIELD: 5 to 6 servings.

OYSTER SOUFFLÉ

1 pint oysters
⅓ cup butter or margarine
⅓ cup minced scallions or onions
⅓ cup flour
1½ cups hot milk
1 teaspoon salt
¼ teaspoon pepper
4 drops hot pepper sauce
5 egg yolks, well beaten
1 tablespoon sherry
6 egg whites, beaten stiff but not dry

HAVE READY: 2-quart soufflé dish, buttered.

Pick over oysters to remove any bits of shell. Place in saucepan with their own liquor and cook over medium heat until their edges curl, about 4 minutes. Drain, reserving liquor, and chop. Set aside.

Melt butter or margarine in saucepan, add minced scallions or onions, and sauté for 2 or 3 minutes, but do not allow to brown. Blend in flour and cook for 3 more minutes, stirring frequently. Remove from heat. Gradually stir in hot milk and seasonings to make a smooth mixture. Cook and stir over medium heat until sauce has thickened. Remove from heat, add reserved oyster liquor and chopped oysters. Let cool 10 minutes.

Slowly add beaten egg yolks, stirring briskly. Stir in sherry. Fold in beaten egg whites gently but thoroughly. Pour into prepared 2-quart soufflé dish. Bake in 350° F. (moderate) oven for 50 to 60 minutes.

YIELD: 6 servings.

VARIATIONS: Instead of oysters use equal measure of clams or a mixture of clams and oysters.

SAVORY OYSTER SOUFFLÉ

1 dozen large oysters
2 teaspoons butter or margarine
6 tablespoons quick-cooking tapioca
½ teaspoon salt
⅛ teaspoon pepper
few grains cayenne pepper
1 teaspoon grated onion
1 tablespoon minced celery
1 teaspoon Worcestershire sauce
1¼ cups cold milk
2 tablespoons minced parsley
3 egg yolks, well beaten
4 egg whites, beaten stiff but not dry

HAVE READY: 1½-quart soufflé dish, ungreased.

Drain oysters, reserving liquid, and pick over carefully to remove any bits of shell. Melt butter or margarine in saucepan, add oysters, and sauté until edges curl, about 3 minutes. Remove from heat, cool, and cut into fine pieces. Set aside. Combine next 7 ingredients with milk and reserved oyster liquor in saucepan and let stand 5 minutes.

Cook and stir over medium heat until mixture comes to a full boil. Remove from heat, add oysters and minced parsley, and let cool about 10 minutes. Add oyster mixture gradually to beaten egg yolks, stirring to blend well. Fold into beaten egg whites gently but thoroughly. Pour into 1½-quart soufflé dish set in shallow pan containing 1 inch hot water. Bake in 350° F. (moderate) oven for 60 to 65 minutes.

YIELD: 4 to 5 servings.

PARMESAN CHEESE SOUFFLÉ

2 tablespoons butter or margarine
2 tablespoons flour
¾ cup hot milk
¼ teaspoon salt
⅛ teaspoon pepper
3 drops hot pepper sauce
½ cup grated Parmesan cheese
4 egg yolks, well beaten
5 egg whites, beaten stiff but not dry

HAVE READY: 1½-quart soufflé dish, buttered, and lightly dusted with grated Parmesan cheese or fine dry bread crumbs.

Melt butter or margarine in saucepan over low heat. Blend in flour and cook for 1 minute. Remove from heat. Gradually stir in hot milk and seasonings to make a smooth mixture. Cook and stir over medium heat until sauce thickens. Remove from heat, stir in grated Parmesan cheese, and cool for 5 minutes. Slowly add beaten egg yolks, stirring briskly. Fold in beaten egg whites. Pour into prepared 1½-quart soufflé dish. Bake in 400° F. (hot) oven for 25 to 30 minutes.

YIELD: 4 to 5 servings.

PUFFY CHEESE SOUFFLÉ

¼ cup butter or margarine
¼ cup flour
½ teaspoon salt
few grains cayenne pepper
1½ cups hot milk
2 cups grated sharp Cheddar cheese
6 egg yolks, well beaten
6 egg whites, beaten stiff but not dry

HAVE READY: 2-quart soufflé dish, ungreased.

Melt butter or margarine in saucepan, stir in flour and seasonings, and let cook over low heat for 2 or 3 minutes. Remove from heat and slowly add hot milk, stirring until smooth. Cook and stir over medium heat until sauce thickens, about 8 minutes. Reduce heat, add cheese and continue to cook and stir until cheese melts and blends into sauce. Very slowly add cheese sauce to beaten egg yolks, stirring vigorously. Cool for 8 to 10 minutes. Gently but thoroughly fold cheese sauce into beaten egg whites. Pour into ungreased 2-quart soufflé dish. Bake in 300° F. (slow) oven for 1¼ hours.

YIELD: 6 servings.

HERBED PORK SOUFFLÉ

3 tablespoons butter or margarine
3 tablespoons flour
1 teaspoon salt
¼ teaspoon pepper
1 cup hot milk
1 tablespoon grated onion
1 tablespoon minced parsley
⅛ teaspoon crushed dried thyme
⅛ teaspoon rubbed dried sage
3 egg yolks, well beaten
1½ cups finely minced or ground cooked pork
4 egg whites, beaten stiff but not dry

HAVE READY: 1½-quart soufflé dish, buttered, and dusted with fine dry bread crumbs.

Melt butter or margarine in saucepan over low heat. Blend in flour and cook for 2 minutes. Add salt and pepper. Remove from heat. Slowly stir in hot milk to make smooth mixture. Cook and stir over medium heat until sauce boils and thickens. Add onion, parsley, thyme, and sage. Remove from heat and let cool 10 minutes. Slowly add beaten egg yolks, stirring briskly. Add pork, mixing thoroughly. Fold in beaten egg whites gently but thoroughly. Pour into prepared 1½-quart soufflé dish. Bake in 375° F. (moderate) oven for 40 to 50 minutes.

YIELD: 4 to 5 servings.

SEAFOOD SOUFFLÉ

1 tablespoon sherry
1 cup shredded cooked or canned crab meat or lobster
¼ cup butter or margarine
3 tablespoons flour
1 cup hot milk
1 teaspoon salt
½ teaspoon white pepper
3 drops hot pepper sauce or few grains cayenne pepper
2 teaspoons lemon juice
4 egg yolks, well beaten
5 egg whites, beaten stiff but not dry

HAVE READY: 1½-quart soufflé dish, ungreased.

Sprinkle sherry on crab meat or lobster and let stand while sauce is made. Melt butter or margarine in saucepan over low heat, stir in flour until smooth, and cook for 2 minutes. Remove from heat. Slowly stir in hot milk and seasonings. Cook and stir over medium heat until sauce thickens. Remove from heat, add lemon juice and seafood, and let cool for 10 to 15 minutes. Gradually add beaten egg yolks, stirring briskly. Gently fold in beaten egg whites just until blended. Pour into ungreased 1½-quart soufflé dish. Bake in 350° F. (moderate) oven for 35 to 40 minutes. YIELD: 4 to 5 servings.

VARIATIONS: Use shredded cooked shrimp, or a mixture of shrimp and crab meat or lobster and crab meat.

SALMON SOUFFLÉ

¼ cup butter or margarine
2 tablespoons minced celery
1 tablespoon minced onion
¼ cup flour
1 cup hot milk
1 teaspoon grated lemon peel
1 tablespoon lemon juice
4 drops hot pepper sauce
4 egg yolks, well beaten
1 cup flaked drained canned salmon or poached fresh salmon
1 tablespoon minced parsley
5 egg whites, beaten stiff but not dry

HAVE READY: 1½-quart soufflé dish, buttered on bottom only.

Melt butter or margarine in saucepan, over low heat. Add minced celery and onion and sauté until vegetables are tender but not browned, about 2 minutes. Stir in flour until blended, and cook for 3 more minutes. Remove from heat; gradually add hot milk, stirring until smooth. Cook and stir over medium heat until sauce thickens. Remove from heat and cool for 5 to 10 minutes. Stir in lemon peel and juice and hot pepper sauce. Gradually add beaten egg yolks, stirring vigorously. Blend in flaked salmon and minced parsley. Fold into beaten egg whites gently but thoroughly. Pour into prepared 1½-quart soufflé dish, set in shallow pan containing 1 inch of hot water. Bake in 325° F. (slow) oven for 60 to 75 minutes.

YIELD: 4 to 5 servings.

VARIATION: If desired, use 1 cup flaked drained canned tuna instead of salmon.

SHRIMP SOUFFLÉ

3 tablespoons butter or margarine
2 tablespoons cornstarch
½ teaspoon salt
¼ teaspoon pepper
1 cup cold milk
1 cup finely chopped cooked shrimp
4 egg yolks, well beaten
5 egg whites, beaten stiff but not dry

HAVE READY: 2-quart soufflé dish, buttered.

Melt butter or margarine in saucepan over low heat. Remove from heat. Blend in cornstarch and seasonings; slowly stir in cold milk until mixture is smooth. Cook and stir over medium heat until sauce boils and thickens, about 5 or 6 minutes. Add chopped cooked shrimp. Remove from heat. Cool for 10 minutes. Slowly add beaten egg yolks, stirring vigorously. Cool sauce for 5 more minutes. Fold in beaten egg whites gently but thoroughly. Pour into prepared 2-quart soufflé dish set in shallow pan containing 1 inch of hot water. Bake in 350° F. (moderate) oven for 1¼ hours.

YIELD: 5 to 6 servings.

NOTE: This soufflé can be repuffed. Leave in soufflé dish; set dish in shallow pan with 1 inch hot water. Reheat in 350° F. (moderate) oven until puffed—about 25 to 30 minutes.

SHRIMP AND RICE SOUFFLÉ

2 tablespoons butter or margarine
1 tablespoon minced scallion
1½ to 2 teaspoons curry powder
1 tablespoon flour
1 cup hot milk
½ teaspoon salt
¼ teaspoon pepper
½ cup cooked rice
1 cup cooked shrimp, finely chopped
4 egg yolks, well beaten
5 egg whites, beaten stiff but not dry

HAVE READY: 1½-quart soufflé dish, lightly buttered.

Melt butter or margarine in a saucepan over low heat; add minced scallion and cook until tender but not browned, about 2 minutes. Blend in curry powder and flour until smooth, and cook for 1 minute. Remove from heat. Gradually stir in hot milk to make smooth mixture. Cook and stir over medium heat until sauce thickens. Remove from heat. Stir in salt, pepper, cooked rice, and chopped shrimp until well mixed. Gradually add beaten egg yolks, stirring briskly. Cool 10 minutes. Fold in beaten egg whites gently but thoroughly. Pour into prepared 1½-quart soufflé dish. Bake in 350° F. (moderate) oven for 45 to 50 minutes.

YIELD: 4 to 5 servings.

VARIATIONS: Instead of shrimp, use equal measure of chopped lobster, crab meat, or a mixture of lobster and shrimp, lobster and crab meat, or shrimp and crab meat.

SMOKED FISH SOUFFLÉ

1½ cups milk
½ pound smoked white fish, salmon, or finnan haddie
3 tablespoons butter or margarine
3 tablespoons flour
¼ teaspoon pepper
4 egg yolks, well beaten
5 egg whites, beaten stiff but not dry

HAVE READY: 1½-quart soufflé dish, buttered.

Scald milk in skillet, add fish, and poach until fork tender, about 10 to 12 minutes. Remove fish with slotted spoon or turner and reserve milk for sauce. Tear fish into fine flakes with fork. Melt butter or margarine in saucepan, over low heat; blend in flour. Cook for 1 minute. Remove from heat. Gradually add 1 cup reserved milk and the pepper, stirring until smooth. Cook and stir, over medium heat, until sauce is thick. Remove from heat and cool for 5 to 10 minutes. Add beaten egg yolks gradually, stirring vigorously. Add flaked fish and blend lightly. Fold in beaten egg whites. Pour into prepared 1½-quart soufflé dish. Bake in 375° F. (moderate) oven for 40 minutes.

YIELD: 4 to 5 servings.

SNAPPY CHEESE SOUFFLÉ

3 tablespoons butter or margarine
2 tablespoons cornstarch
½ teaspoon salt
¼ teaspoon pepper
¼ to ½ teaspoon dry mustard
few grains cayenne pepper
1 cup cold milk
1 cup grated sharp Cheddar cheese
4 egg yolks, well beaten
5 egg whites, beaten stiff but not dry

HAVE READY: 2-quart soufflé dish, buttered.

Melt butter or margarine in saucepan over low heat. Remove

from heat. Blend in cornstarch and seasonings; slowly stir in cold milk until mixture is smooth. Cook and stir over medium heat until sauce boils and thickens, about 5 or 6 minutes. Add grated cheese. Remove from heat, and stir until cheese melts. Slowly add beaten egg yolks, stirring vigorously. Cool sauce for 10 minutes. Fold in beaten egg whites gently but thoroughly. Pour into prepared 2-quart soufflé dish set in shallow pan containing 1 inch of hot water. Bake in 350° F. (moderate) oven for 1¼ hours.

YIELD: 5 to 6 servings.

NOTE: This soufflé can be repuffed. Leave in soufflé dish; set dish in shallow pan with 1 inch hot water. Reheat in 350° F. (moderate) oven until puffed—about 25 to 30 minutes.

SWEETBREAD SOUFFLÉ

2 pairs calf's sweetbreads
1½ quarts boiling water
1 tablespoon lemon juice
¼ teaspoon salt
¼ cup butter or margarine
¼ cup flour
1 teaspoon salt
½ teaspoon white pepper
1¼ cups hot light cream or milk
¼ cup dry white wine
4 egg yolks, well beaten
5 egg whites, beaten stiff but not dry

HAVE READY: 1½-quart soufflé dish, buttered, and dusted with very finely ground almonds.

Soak sweetbreads in cold water to cover for 1 hour. Drain. Combine boiling water, lemon juice, and ¼ teaspoon salt. Add sweetbreads and simmer gently for 15 minutes. Drain sweetbreads and plunge them into cold water for about 10 minutes. Remove from water, carefully remove tubes and membranes, then cut sweetbreads into tiny cubes and set aside.

Melt butter or margarine in saucepan over low heat. Blend in flour, 1 teaspoon salt, and white pepper. Cook for 2 or 3 minutes, stirring, but do not allow to brown. Remove from heat. Gradually add hot light cream or milk, stirring to smooth mixture. Cook and stir over medium heat until sauce boils and thickens. Add wine and remove from heat. Let sauce cool 10 to 15 minutes. Slowly add beaten egg yolks, stirring briskly. Gently stir in cubed sweetbreads. Fold in beaten egg whites gently but thoroughly. Pour into prepared 1½-quart soufflé dish. Bake in 350° F. (moderate) oven for 35 to 40 minutes.

YIELD: 4 to 5 servings.

NOTE: If desired, ⅓ cup cooked chopped mushrooms may be added when sweetbreads are stirred into sauce.

SOUFFLÉ SUISSE

2 tablespoons butter or margarine
2 tablespoons flour
1 cup hot milk
1 teaspoon salt
¼ teaspoon ground nutmeg
3 egg yolks, slightly beaten
1¼ cups finely grated Swiss Emmentaler or Gruyère cheese
½ teaspoon cornstarch
4 egg whites, beaten stiff but not dry

HAVE READY: 1½-quart soufflé dish, lightly buttered, and dusted with flour.

Melt butter or margarine in saucepan over low heat; stir in flour; cook for 1 minute. Remove from heat and gradually stir in hot milk and seasonings until mixture is smooth. Cook and stir over medium heat until sauce thickens. Remove from heat. Gradually add hot sauce to egg yolks, beating constantly. Dredge grated cheese with cornstarch, then stir into sauce until blended. Cool for 5 minutes. Gently but thoroughly fold in beaten egg whites. Pour into prepared 1½-quart soufflé dish. Bake in 350° F. (moderate) oven for 30 minutes.

YIELD: 4 to 5 servings.

TOMATO CHEESE SOUFFLÉ

3 tablespoons butter or margarine
1 teaspoon grated onion
3 tablespoons flour
½ teaspoon dry mustard
⅛ teaspoon pepper
¾ cup hot tomato juice
1 cup grated sharp cheese
4 egg yolks, well beaten
5 egg whites, beaten stiff but not dry

HAVE READY: 1½-quart soufflé dish, buttered.

Melt butter or margarine in saucepan over low heat. Add grated onion and cook for 1 minute. Blend in flour and cook 2 minutes more. Remove from heat. Blend in dry mustard and pepper; then gradually add hot tomato juice, stirring to smooth mixture. Cook and stir over medium heat until sauce just comes to a boil and thickens. Do not allow boiling to continue. Remove from heat. Add grated cheese and stir until cheese melts. Let sauce cool 5 minutes. Slowly add beaten egg yolks, stirring briskly. Fold in beaten egg whites gently but thoroughly. Pour into prepared 1½-quart soufflé dish. Bake in 375° F. (moderate) oven for 30 to 40 minutes.

YIELD: 4 to 5 servings.

TRIPLE CHEESE SOUFFLÉ

¼ cup butter or margarine
¼ cup flour
¼ teaspoon salt
⅛ teaspoon white pepper
few grains cayenne pepper
1 cup hot milk
1½ teaspoons dry mustard
⅓ cup sieved Camembert cheese with rind
⅓ cup grated Gruyère cheese
¼ cup grated Parmesan cheese
4 egg yolks, well beaten
6 egg whites, beaten stiff but not dry
2 teaspoons grated Parmesan cheese (additional)

HAVE READY: 2-quart soufflé dish, ungreased.

Melt butter or margarine in saucepan, over low heat; blend

in flour, salt, and peppers; cook, stirring, for 3 minutes. Remove from heat and gradually add hot milk, stirring until smooth. Cook and stir over medium heat until sauce has thickened. Add next 4 ingredients, and stir until cheeses are melted and blended. Remove from heat, and let cool 10 minutes. Add beaten egg yolks, stirring vigorously. Fold in beaten egg whites gently but thoroughly. Pour into 2-quart soufflé dish, and sprinkle 2 teaspoons grated Parmesan cheese on top. Bake in 375° F. (moderate) oven for 30 to 35 minutes.

YIELD: 6 servings.

VEGETABLE CHEESE SOUFFLÉ

¼ cup butter or margarine
¼ cup flour
¼ teaspoon salt
⅛ teaspoon pepper
½ teaspoon dry mustard
1 cup hot milk
1 cup shredded Swiss or Cheddar cheese
4 egg yolks, well beaten
5 egg whites, beaten stiff but not dry
1 cup chopped cooked broccoli, asparagus, spinach or green beans

HAVE READY: 1½-quart soufflé dish, buttered, and dusted with fine dry bread crumbs.

Melt butter or margarine in saucepan, over low heat; blend in flour and seasonings, and cook for 3 minutes. Remove from heat and slowly add hot milk, stirring until smooth. Cook and stir, over medium heat, until sauce is very thick. Remove from heat and stir in cheese until it melts. Slowly add beaten egg yolks stirring vigorously until well blended. Cool for 5 minutes. Gently but thoroughly fold cheese mixture into beaten egg whites. Pour ⅓ of soufflé into prepared soufflé dish. Carefully spoon chopped vegetable on as a layer. Pour on remaining soufflé mixture. Bake in 350° F. (moderate) oven for 50 to 55 minutes.

YIELD: 6 servings.

TUNA SOUFFLÉ

¼ cup butter or margarine
¼ cup flour
½ teaspoon salt
¼ teaspoon pepper
1 teaspoon finely minced shallot or onion
1 cup hot milk
¼ cup shredded Swiss or Gruyère cheese
1 can (7 ounces) tuna, drained and shredded
4 egg yolks, well beaten
5 egg whites, beaten stiff but not dry

HAVE READY: 1½-quart soufflé dish, ungreased.

Melt butter or margarine in saucepan over low heat. Blend in next 4 ingredients and cook for 3 minutes. Remove from heat. Slowly add hot milk, stirring steadily. Cook and stir over medium heat until sauce thickens. Remove from heat; add shredded cheese and tuna, blending until cheese melts. Stir briskly while slowly adding beaten egg yolks. Cool for 10 minutes. Gently but thoroughly fold tuna sauce into beaten egg whites. Pour into 1½-quart soufflé dish. Bake in 350° F. (moderate) oven for 45 to 55 minutes. YIELD: 5 to 6 servings.

TURKEY SOUFFLÉ

¼ cup butter or margarine
¼ cup flour
1 cup hot milk
1 cup hot turkey or chicken broth
1 teaspoon salt
¼ teaspoon pepper
⅛ teaspoon ground nutmeg
4 egg yolks, well beaten
¾ cup soft bread crumbs
1 teaspoon minced parsley
2 cups minced cooked turkey white meat
4 egg whites, beaten stiff but not dry

HAVE READY: 2-quart soufflé dish, well buttered, and heated in 350° F. (moderate) oven in shallow pan containing 1 inch hot water.

Melt butter or margarine in saucepan over low heat. Blend in flour and cook for 3 minutes. Remove from heat. Slowly stir in hot milk and broth to make a smooth mixture. Cook and stir over medium heat until sauce thickens. Remove from heat, add seasonings, and let cool about 10 minutes. Slowly add beaten egg yolks, stirring vigorously, then gently mix in soft bread crumbs and minced parsley. Blend in minced turkey. Fold in beaten egg whites gently but thoroughly. Pour into hot buttered 2-quart soufflé dish set in shallow pan containing 1 inch hot water. Bake in 350° F. (moderate) oven for 50 to 60 minutes. YIELD: 6 servings.

VEAL SOUFFLÉ

¼ cup butter or margarine
1 tablespoon minced onion or scallion
¼ cup flour
1¼ cups hot light cream
½ teaspoon salt
¼ teaspoon pepper
few grains cayenne pepper
⅛ teaspoon dried tarragon or thyme leaves
few grains nutmeg
2 cups finely chopped cooked veal
1 tablespoon sherry or dry white wine (optional)
3 egg yolks, well beaten
4 egg whites, beaten stiff but not dry

HAVE READY: 1½-quart soufflé dish, buttered, and dusted with fine dry bread crumbs.

Melt butter or margarine in saucepan over low heat. Add minced onion or scallion, and sauté 1 minute. Blend in flour and cook 2 to 3 minutes. Remove from heat. Gradually add hot light cream, then add salt and peppers, stirring to smooth mixture. Cook and stir over medium heat until sauce boils and thickens. Add tarragon or thyme and nutmeg. Remove from heat. Thoroughly mix in finely chopped cooked veal, and add sherry or white wine, if desired. Let cool 10 minutes. Slowly add beaten egg yolks, stirring briskly. Fold in beaten egg whites gently but thoroughly. Pour into prepared 1½-quart soufflé dish. Bake in 350° F. (moderate) oven for 45 to 50 minutes. YIELD: 4 to 5 servings.

3

ACCOMPANIMENT SOUFFLÉS

Here are savory soufflé combinations perfect for accompanying the entrée or a hearty salad. Some are hearty enough to serve as the main dish at a lunch or supper.

BROCCOLI SOUFFLÉ

3 tablespoons butter or margarine
2 teaspoons minced shallot or onion
3 tablespoons flour
½ teaspoon salt
¼ teaspoon pepper
1 cup hot milk
2 teaspoons lemon juice
4 egg yolks, well beaten
1 cup minced cooked broccoli
4 egg whites, beaten stiff but not dry

HAVE READY: 1½-quart soufflé dish, buttered, and lightly dusted with fine dry bread crumbs.

Melt butter or margarine in saucepan over low heat; add minced shallot or onion and sauté for 2 minutes. Blend in flour and seasonings and cook for 2 more minutes, stirring occasionally. Remove from heat. Slowly stir in hot milk to make a smooth mixture. Cook and stir over medium heat until sauce has thickened. Remove from heat, add lemon juice, and let cool 10 minutes. Slowly add beaten egg yolks, stirring vigorously; carefully blend in minced broccoli. Fold in beaten egg whites gently but thoroughly. Pour into prepared 1½-quart soufflé dish set in shallow pan containing 1 inch hot water. Bake in 350° F. (moderate) oven for 40 to 50 minutes.

YIELD: 6 servings.

RAW CARROT SOUFFLÉ

6 tablespoons butter or margarine
7 tablespoons flour
1½ cups hot milk
1 tablespoon flour
1½ cups grated raw carrots
4 egg yolks, well beaten
1 tablespoon grated onion
¼ teaspoon pepper
6 egg whites
1 teaspoon salt

HAVE READY: 1½-quart soufflé dish, ungreased, set in shallow pan containing 1 inch hot water in 325° F. (slow) oven to heat.

Melt butter or margarine in saucepan over low heat. Blend in 7 tablespoons flour and cook for 3 minutes, stirring frequently. Remove from heat and gradually add hot milk, stirring to smooth mixture. Cook and stir over medium heat until sauce thickens. Remove from heat and cool 5 minutes. Blend 1 tablespoon flour with grated raw carrots and stir into beaten egg yolks. Add grated onion and pepper. Slowly add egg yolk mixture to cooled sauce, stirring briskly. Beat egg whites and salt until stiff glossy peaks form. Fold carrot mixture, one fourth at a time, into beaten egg whites, gently but thoroughly. Pour into heated 1½-quart soufflé dish set in pan containing 1 inch hot water. Bake in 325° F. (slow) oven for 60 to 70 minutes.

YIELD: 5 to 6 servings.

CARROT AND RAISIN SOUFFLÉ

3 tablespoons butter or margarine
4 tablespoons flour
1 cup hot milk
1 teaspoon salt
1 teaspoon prepared horse-radish, drained
2 cups grated raw carrot
¾ cup grated American cheese
⅓ cup seedless raisins
2 egg yolks, well beaten
3 egg whites, beaten stiff but not dry

HAVE READY: 1½-quart soufflé dish, buttered.

Melt butter or margarine in saucepan over low heat. Blend in flour, and cook 1 or 2 minutes. Remove from heat. Gradually add hot milk, and salt, stirring to smooth mixture. Cook and stir over medium heat until sauce boils and thickens. Add horse-radish, grated carrot, grated cheese, and raisins. Stir over low heat until cheese melts and mixture is well blended. Remove from heat and let cool for 10 minutes. Gradually add beaten egg yolks, stirring briskly. Fold in beaten egg whites gently but thoroughly. Pour into prepared 1½-quart soufflé dish. Bake in 325° F. (slow) oven for 50 to 60 minutes.

YIELD: 5 to 6 servings.

CARROT AND CHIVE SOUFFLÉ

6 tablespoons butter or margarine
6 tablespoons flour
1½ cups hot milk
1 teaspoon salt
¼ teaspoon pepper
6 egg yolks, well beaten
2 cups grated raw carrot
1 tablespoon minced chives
6 egg whites, beaten stiff but not dry

HAVE READY: 2-quart soufflé dish, ungreased, set in shallow pan containing 1 inch hot water in 325° F. (slow) oven to heat.

Melt butter or margarine in saucepan over low heat; blend in flour. Cook, stirring frequently, for 3 to 4 minutes, but do not brown. Remove from heat. Gradually add hot milk, then seasonings, stirring until smooth. Cook and stir over medium heat until sauce thickens. Remove from heat, and cool 5 minutes. Beat into beaten egg yolks, using wire whisk or wooden spoon. Stir in grated carrot and minced chives. Fold gently but thoroughly into beaten egg whites. Remove heated 2-quart soufflé dish from oven, and pour soufflé mixture into it. Return to pan of water in oven. Bake in 325° F. (slow) oven for 1½ hours. YIELD: 6 servings.

VARIATION: Use 2 cups chopped raw spinach or thawed and drained frozen chopped spinach and 1 tablespoon minced onion, instead of grated raw carrots and minced chives.

CAULIFLOWER SOUFFLÉ

¼ cup butter or margarine
¼ cup flour
1½ cups hot milk
½ teaspoon salt
¼ teaspoon white pepper
½ teaspoon minced tarragon leaves (⅛ teaspoon if dried)
2 teaspoons minced parsley
5 egg yolks, well beaten
1½ cups tender-crisp cooked cauliflower, coarsely chopped
6 egg whites, beaten stiff but not dry

HAVE READY: 2-quart soufflé dish, buttered, and dusted with fine dry bread crumbs.

Melt butter or margarine in saucepan over low heat. Blend in flour and cook for 3 minutes, stirring occasionally. Remove from heat and gradually add hot milk, stirring to make a smooth mixture. Cook and stir over medium heat until sauce thickens. Remove from heat, add seasonings and herbs, and cool for 10 minutes. Gradually add beaten egg yolks, stirring briskly, then gently stir in chopped cooked cauliflower. Fold in beaten egg whites carefully but thoroughly. Pour into prepared 2-quart soufflé dish. Bake in 325° F. (slow) oven for 50 to 60 minutes. YIELD: 6 servings.

CHEESY BROCCOLI SOUFFLÉ

¼ cup quick-cooking tapioca
½ teaspoon salt
1⅓ cups cold milk
½ cup shredded Cheddar cheese
¼ teaspoon pepper
few grains cayenne pepper
4 egg yolks, well beaten
1 cup cooked chopped broccoli
5 egg whites, beaten stiff but not dry

HAVE READY: 1½-quart soufflé dish, lightly buttered, and dusted with fine dry bread crumbs.

Combine tapioca, salt, and milk in saucepan, and let stand 5 minutes. Cook and stir over medium heat until mixture comes to a full boil. Remove from heat. Stir in shredded cheese and both peppers until cheese melts and blends in. Let cool 10 to 15 minutes. Slowly add beaten egg yolks, stirring briskly. Gently mix in cooked broccoli. Fold into beaten egg whites gently but thoroughly. Pour into prepared 1½-quart soufflé dish set in shallow pan containing 1 inch hot water. Bake in 325° F. (slow) oven for 55 to 60 minutes.

YIELD: 6 servings.

PEANUT CHEESE SOUFFLÉ

¼ cup butter or margarine
¼ cup flour
½ teaspoon salt
1¼ cups cold milk
½ pound sharp Cheddar cheese, shredded
¾ cup finely chopped cocktail peanuts
5 egg yolks, beaten thick and light
6 egg whites, beaten stiff but not dry

HAVE READY: 2-quart soufflé dish, ungreased.

Melt butter or margarine in top of double boiler. Blend in flour and salt. Gradually add cold milk, stirring to smooth mixture. Cook over boiling water, stirring frequently, until sauce is thick and smooth. Stir in shredded cheese, and sprinkle finely chopped peanuts on top. Let stand over low heat until cheese melts, then stir chopped peanuts into cheese mixture until sauce is well blended. Remove top of double boiler from water. Gradually stir hot cheese sauce into beaten egg yolks. Fold cheese mixture into beaten egg whites gently but thoroughly. Pour into 2-quart soufflé dish. Bake in 325° F. (slow) oven for 1¼ hours.

YIELD: 6 to 8 servings.

CALICO CORN SOUFFLÉ

4 tablespoons butter or margarine
4 tablespoons flour
1 cup hot milk
1 teaspoon salt
½ teaspoon pepper
4 drops hot pepper sauce
1 tablespoon minced green pepper
4 egg yolks, well beaten
1 tablespoon minced pimiento, well drained
1 cup canned whole kernel corn, drained well
5 egg whites, beaten stiff but not dry

HAVE READY: 2-quart soufflé dish, buttered, and lightly sprinkled with paprika.

Melt butter or margarine in saucepan over low heat. Blend in flour and cook for 3 minutes. Remove from heat. Gradually stir in hot milk to a smooth mixture, then add next 4 ingredients. Cook and stir over medium heat until sauce is thick. Remove from heat, and let sauce cool 10 minutes. Slowly add beaten egg yolks, stirring briskly. Add minced pimiento and whole kernel corn and mix well. Fold in beaten egg whites gently but thoroughly. Pour into prepared 2-quart soufflé dish. Bake in 350° F. (moderate) oven for 60 to 70 minutes.

YIELD: 6 servings.

NOTE: If desired, 1 cup well-drained canned Mexicorn may be used instead of minced green pepper, minced pimiento, and canned whole kernel corn.

CREAMY CORN SOUFFLÉ

2 tablespoons butter or margarine
2 tablespoons flour
1 teaspoon salt
¼ teaspoon pepper
3 drops hot pepper sauce
¾ cup hot light cream or milk
1 cup canned cream-style corn
4 egg yolks, well beaten
5 egg whites, beaten stiff but not dry

HAVE READY: 1½-quart soufflé dish, buttered.

Melt butter or margarine in saucepan over low heat. Blend in flour and seasonings, and let cook for 1 minute. Remove from heat. Slowly stir in hot light cream or milk to make smooth mixture. Cook and stir over medium heat until sauce thickens. Remove from heat, blend in cream-style corn, and let cool 10 minutes. Slowly add beaten egg yolks, stirring briskly. Fold in beaten egg whites gently but thoroughly. Pour into prepared 1½-quart soufflé dish. Bake in 350° F. (moderate) oven for 40 to 50 minutes.

YIELD: 5 to 6 servings.

FRESH CORN SOUFFLÉ

4 tablespoons butter or margarine
4 tablespoons flour
1 cup hot milk
1 teaspoon salt
½ teaspoon pepper
2 teaspoons minced green pepper
1 teaspoon grated onion
4 egg yolks, well beaten
1 cup fresh corn, cut and scraped from the cob (about 6 ears)
5 egg whites, beaten stiff but not dry

HAVE READY: 2-quart soufflé dish, buttered.

Melt butter or margarine in saucepan over low heat. Blend in flour and cook for 3 minutes. Remove from heat. Gradually stir in hot milk to make a smooth mixture, then add next 4 ingredients. Cook and stir over medium heat until sauce is thick. Remove from heat and cool 10 minutes. Gradually add beaten egg yolks, stirring briskly, then blend in corn. Fold beaten egg whites into soufflé mixture gently but thoroughly. Pour into prepared 2-quart soufflé dish. Bake in 350° F. (moderate) oven for 60 to 70 minutes.

YIELD: 6 servings.

EGGPLANT SOUFFLÉ

2 tablespoons butter or margarine
2 tablespoons flour
1 cup hot light cream
½ teaspoon salt
¼ teaspoon pepper
1 tablespoon grated Parmesan cheese
3 egg yolks, well beaten
1 cup mashed, drained, cooked eggplant
1 cup fresh bread crumbs
4 egg whites, beaten stiff but not dry

HAVE READY: 1½-quart soufflé dish, ungreased.

Melt butter or margarine in saucepan over low heat. Blend in flour and cook for 1 minute. Remove from heat and slowly add hot light cream and seasonings, stirring to make a smooth mixture. Cook and stir over medium heat until sauce thickens. Remove from heat and stir in grated Parmesan cheese. Let cool 8 to 10 minutes. Slowly add beaten egg yolks, stirring briskly. Combine mashed eggplant and soft bread crumbs, mixing thoroughly, then add to sauce mixture and blend well. Fold in beaten egg whites gently but thoroughly. Pour into 1½-quart soufflé dish. Bake in 350° F. (moderate) oven for 50 to 55 minutes.

YIELD: 4 to 5 servings.

HERBED GREEN BEAN SOUFFLÉ

3 tablespoons butter or margarine
3 tablespoons flour
1 teaspoon salt
¼ teaspoon pepper
1 cup hot milk
¼ teaspoon dried savory (1 teaspoon fresh)
2 teaspoons minced chives
1⅓ cups chopped cooked green beans
4 egg yolks, well beaten
5 egg whites, beaten stiff but not dry

HAVE READY: 1½-quart soufflé dish, buttered.

Melt butter or margarine in saucepan over low heat. Blend in flour and seasonings, and cook for 2 minutes. Remove from heat. Gradually add hot milk, stirring to smooth mixture. Cook and stir over medium heat until sauce thickens. Add savory, minced chives, and chopped green beans, mixing well. Remove from heat and cool 10 to 15 minutes. Slowly add beaten egg yolks, stirring briskly. Fold in beaten egg whites gently but thoroughly. Pour into prepared 1½-quart soufflé dish. Bake in 350° F. (moderate) oven for 40 to 50 minutes.

YIELD: 4 to 5 servings.

MUSHROOM SOUFFLÉ

1 pound fresh mushrooms
2 tablespoons butter or margarine
2 teaspoons minced shallots or onions
¼ cup butter or margarine
¼ cup flour
¾ cup hot chicken stock or broth
½ cup hot light cream
1 teaspoon salt
¼ teaspoon pepper
6 egg yolks, well beaten
6 egg whites, beaten stiff but not dry

HAVE READY: 2-quart soufflé dish, buttered, and dusted with fine dry bread crumbs.

Wash, trim, and thinly slice mushrooms. Melt 2 tablespoons of butter or margarine in saucepan or skillet; add mushrooms and minced shallots or onions, and sauté, stirring frequently, for 8 to 10 minutes, but do not allow to brown. Set aside.

Melt ¼ cup butter or margarine in saucepan over low heat. Blend in flour, and cook for 3 minutes, stirring frequently. Remove from heat. Slowly add hot chicken stock or broth and light cream, stirring to make a smooth mixture. Cook and stir over medium heat until sauce thickens. Add seasonings. Remove from heat and cool 10 to 15 minutes. Gradually add beaten egg yolks, stirring briskly. Thoroughly blend in cooked mushroom mixture. Fold in beaten egg whites gently but thoroughly. Pour into prepared 2-quart soufflé dish. Bake in 375° F. (moderate) oven for 40 to 50 minutes.

YIELD: 6 servings.

DELICATE MUSHROOM SOUFFLÉ

1½ pounds fresh mushrooms
¼ cup butter or margarine
¼ cup flour
1½ cups cold medium cream or undiluted evaporated milk
1½ teaspoons salt
¼ teaspoon pepper
few grains cayenne pepper
6 egg yolks, well beaten
6 egg whites, beaten stiff but not dry

HAVE READY: 2-quart soufflé dish, buttered, and dusted with fine dry bread crumbs.

Wash and trim mushrooms. Chop fine. Melt butter or margarine in saucepan or skillet over low heat. Add mushrooms, and sauté, stirring occasionally, for about 10 minutes, but do not let them brown. Blend flour and cream or undiluted evaporated milk to smooth mixture in top of double boiler. Cook and stir over boiling water until thick and smooth. Add seasonings and sautéed mushrooms, and remove from heat to cool 5 minutes. Gradually add about 1 cup of warm sauce to beaten egg yolks, stirring briskly. Return mixture to rest of sauce in double boiler. Cook and stir over hot water until sauce thickens. Remove from heat and let cool 15 to 20 minutes. Fold in beaten egg whites gently but thoroughly. Pour into prepared 2-quart soufflé dish set in pan containing 1 or 2 inches of hot water. Bake in 375° F. (moderate) oven for 50 to 60 minutes.

YIELD: 6 to 8 servings.

GOURMET MUSHROOM SOUFFLÉ

¼ cup butter or margarine
1 tablespoon minced shallots or scallions
1 pound mushrooms, cleaned, trimmed, and finely minced
1 cup light cream
½ cup chicken stock or broth
¼ cup flour
1 teaspoon salt
¼ teaspoon pepper
6 egg yolks, well beaten
6 egg whites, beaten stiff but not dry.

HAVE READY: 2-quart soufflé dish, buttered.

Melt butter or margarine in medium saucepan over low heat. Add minced shallots or scallions and mushrooms, and cook over low heat for 8 to 10 minutes, stirring occasionally. Set aside.

In top of double boiler, slowly add light cream and chicken stock or broth to flour and seasonings, blending to a smooth paste. Cook over hot water, stirring occasionally, until sauce thickens. Combine mushroom mixture and beaten egg yolks, then briskly stir this mixture into sauce, a small amount at a time. Cook and stir over hot water until consistency of smooth soft custard. Remove from over hot water and let cool 15 to 20 minutes. Stir in ⅓ beaten egg whites, then fold in the rest. Pour into prepared 2-quart soufflé dish set in shallow pan containing 1 inch hot water. Bake in 350° F. (moderate) oven for 35 to 45 minutes.

YIELD: 6 servings.

NOODLE SOUFFLÉ

2 tablespoons butter or margarine
1½ cups hot cooked, drained fine noodles
¼ cup butter or margarine
3 tablespoons flour
1 teaspoon salt
¼ teaspoon white pepper
1½ cups hot milk or light cream
½ cup cooked fresh or canned (4 ounces) chopped mushrooms (optional)
4 egg yolks, well beaten
6 egg whites, beaten stiff but not dry

HAVE READY: 2-quart soufflé dish, buttered.

Blend 2 tablespoons butter or margarine into hot drained cooked noodles, and set aside. Melt ¼ cup butter or margarine in saucepan over low heat. Blend in flour and seasonings and cook for 2 minutes, but do not brown. Remove from heat. Gradually add hot milk or cream, stirring to smooth mixture. Cook over medium heat until sauce boils and thickens. Remove from heat. Stir in buttered noodles and chopped mushrooms, if desired. Let cool 10 minutes. Slowly add beaten egg yolks, stirring briskly. Fold in beaten egg whites gently but thoroughly. Pour into prepared 2-quart soufflé dish. Bake in 375° F. (moderate) oven for 30 to 40 minutes.

YIELD: 6 servings.

NOODLE CREAM SOUFFLÉ

4 ounces (½ package) fine noodles
⅓ cup butter or margarine
¼ cup flour
1 teaspoon salt
¼ teaspoon white pepper
1½ cups hot milk
1 small (3 ounces) cake cream cheese
½ pint dairy sour cream
1 tablespoon sugar
4 egg yolks, well beaten
5 egg whites, beaten stiff but not dry

HAVE READY: 2-quart soufflé dish, ungreased.

Cook noodles according to package directions. When done,

remove from heat at once, add about 1 cup cold water to stop cooking; drain noodles and set aside. Melt butter or margarine in saucepan over low heat. Blend in flour and cook for 3 or 4 minutes, stirring occasionally. Remove from heat. Add seasonings, then gradually stir in hot milk to make a smooth mixture. Cook and stir over medium heat until sauce boils and thickens. Remove from heat. Mash cream cheese with fork and blend in sour cream and sugar. Stir cheese mixture into hot sauce until well mixed. Cool 5 to 10 minutes. Gradually add beaten egg yolks, stirring briskly, then stir in cooked noodles. Fold in beaten egg whites gently but thoroughly. Pour into 2-quart soufflé dish. Bake in 350° F. (moderate) oven for 35 to 40 minutes.

YIELD: 6 to 8 servings.

PEAS AND CARROTS SOUFFLÉ

¼ cup butter or margarine
¼ cup flour
1 teaspoon salt
½ teaspoon pepper
1½ cups hot milk
¼ teaspoon crushed dried mint leaves
1 tablespoon minced parsley
5 egg yolks, well beaten
1½ cups cooked fresh, frozen or canned peas and (diced) carrots
5 egg whites, beaten stiff but not dry

HAVE READY: 2-quart soufflé dish, buttered.

Melt butter or margarine in saucepan over low heat. Blend in flour, salt, and pepper, and cook for 3 minutes, stirring occasionally. Remove from heat. Gradually add hot milk, stirring to smooth mixture. Cook and stir over medium heat until sauce boils and thickens. Add dried mint leaves and minced parsley. Remove from heat and let cool 10 minutes. Slowly add beaten egg yolks, stirring briskly. Add cooked peas and carrots, mixing well. Fold in beaten egg whites gently but thoroughly. Pour into prepared 2-quart soufflé dish. Bake in 350° F. (moderate) oven for 45 to 50 minutes.

YIELD: 6 servings.

ONION SOUFFLÉ

4 tablespoons butter or margarine
4 tablespoons flour
1 cup hot milk
1 teaspoon salt
¼ teaspoon pepper
few grains cayenne pepper
6 egg yolks, well beaten
1 tablespoon butter or margarine
½ cup finely chopped onions or scallions
6 egg whites, beaten stiff but not dry

HAVE READY: 2-quart soufflé dish, buttered.

Melt butter or margarine in a saucepan over low heat. Blend in flour, and cook for 3 minutes. Remove from heat. Slowly stir in hot milk and seasonings until mixture is smooth. Cook and stir over medium heat until sauce thickens. Remove from heat and cool 5 minutes. Add beaten egg yolks, stirring briskly. Cook and stir, over low heat, for 2 minutes. Remove from heat, and cool 15 minutes. Meanwhile, melt 1 tablespoon butter or margarine in small saucepan, add chopped onions or scallions, and cook until tender but not browned, about 4 minutes. Add to cooling sauce. Gently but thoroughly stir ⅓ beaten egg whites into cool sauce, then fold in the rest. Pour into prepared 2-quart soufflé dish. Bake in 375° F. (moderate) oven for 35 to 45 minutes.

YIELD: 6 servings.

POTATO SOUFFLÉ

2 tablespoons butter or margarine
2 tablespoons flour
½ cup light cream
1 cup chicken stock or broth
1 teaspoon salt
½ teaspoon pepper
1 tablespoon butter or margarine
1 tablespoon minced onion
1 tablespoon minced chives
1½ cups hot instant mashed potatoes
4 egg yolks, well beaten
4 egg whites, beaten stiff but not dry

HAVE READY: 1½-quart soufflé dish, ungreased.

Melt 2 tablespoons butter or margarine over low heat, blend in 2 tablespoons flour, and cook for 1 minute. Remove from heat. Stir in cream and chicken stock or broth until smooth. Cook and stir over medium heat until thickened. Remove from heat, add seasonings, and set aside to cool. Melt 1 tablespoon butter in small pan, add minced onion and chives, and cook over low heat for 2 minutes. Blend into hot mashed potatoes. Briskly stir beaten egg yolks into cooled sauce, then combine with mashed potatoes, stirring to blend well. Gently but thoroughly fold in beaten egg whites. Pour into prepared 1½-quart soufflé dish. Bake in 375° F. (moderate) oven for 35 to 40 minutes.

YIELD: 4 to 5 servings.

POTATO ALMOND SOUFFLÉ

3 tablespoons butter or margarine
3 tablespoons flour
1½ cups hot milk
1 teaspoon salt
½ teaspoon pepper
few grains cayenne pepper
½ teaspoon grated lemon peel
1 cup hot riced or sieved cooked potato
¼ cup finely chopped toasted blanched almonds
5 egg yolks, well beaten
6 egg whites, beaten stiff but not dry

HAVE READY: 2-quart soufflé dish, buttered, and dusted with finely ground toasted almonds.

Melt butter or margarine in saucepan over low heat. Blend in flour, and cook for 2 minutes. Remove from heat. Gradually add hot milk, salt, and peppers, stirring to smooth mixture. Cook and stir over medium heat until sauce boils and thickens. Remove from heat. Vigorously stir in lemon peel and riced or sieved cooked potato. Add chopped toasted almonds. Let cool 15 minutes. Slowly add beaten egg yolks, stirring briskly. Fold in beaten egg whites gently but thoroughly. Pour into prepared 2-quart soufflé dish. Bake in 375° F. (moderate) oven for 50 to 60 minutes.

YIELD: 6 servings.

RICE SOUFFLÉ

¼ cup butter or margarine
3 tablespoons flour
1 teaspoon salt
¼ teaspoon white pepper
1½ cups hot chicken broth or milk
1 tablespoon minced parsley
1 teaspoon minced chives (optional)
1½ cups cooked rice
4 egg yolks, well beaten
6 egg whites, beaten stiff but not dry

HAVE READY: 2-quart soufflé dish, buttered.

Melt butter or margarine in saucepan over low heat. Blend in flour and seasonings and cook for 2 minutes, but do not brown. Remove from heat. Gradually add hot chicken broth or milk, stirring to smooth mixture. Cook and stir over medium heat until sauce boils and thickens. Remove from heat. Stir in minced parsley, minced chives, if desired, and cooked rice blending thoroughly. Let cool 10 minutes. Slowly add beaten egg yolks, stirring briskly. Fold in beaten egg whites gently but thoroughly. Pour into prepared 2-quart soufflé dish. Bake in 375° F. (moderate) oven for 30 to 40 minutes.

YIELD: 6 servings.

RICE AND MUSHROOM SOUFFLÉ

1 tablespoon butter or margarine
½ cup chopped fresh or canned (4 ounces) mushrooms
1 tablespoon grated onion
¼ cup butter or margarine
3 tablespoons flour
1 teaspoon salt
¼ teaspoon pepper
1½ cups hot chicken broth or milk
1½ cups cooked rice
5 egg yolks, well beaten
6 egg whites, beaten stiff but not dry

HAVE READY: 2-quart soufflé dish, buttered.

Melt 1 tablespoon butter or margarine in small saucepan. Add chopped mushrooms and grated onion. Sauté, stirring occasionally, for 4 or 5 minutes. Remove from heat and set aside. Melt ¼ cup butter or margarine in saucepan over low heat. Blend in flour and seasonings, and cook for 2 minutes. Remove from heat. Gradually add hot broth or milk, stirring to smooth mixture. Cook and stir over medium heat until sauce boils and thickens. Remove from heat. Add chopped mushrooms and cooked rice, mixing well. Let cool 10 minutes. Slowly add beaten egg yolks, stirring briskly. Fold in beaten egg whites gently but thoroughly. Pour into prepared 2-quart soufflé dish. Bake in 375° F. (moderate) oven for 35 to 45 minutes.

YIELD: 6 servings.

SAVORY RICE SOUFFLÉ

¼ cup butter or margarine
¼ cup flour
1 teaspoon salt
¼ teaspoon pepper
2 cups hot milk
½ cup dairy sour cream
½ cup creamed cottage cheese
4 egg yolks, well beaten
1½ cups cooked, drained herbed or curried rice
5 egg whites, beaten stiff but not dry

HAVE READY: 2-quart soufflé dish, buttered.

Melt butter or margarine in saucepan over low heat. Blend in flour and seasonings, and cook for 3 minutes, stirring frequently. Remove from heat. Gradually add hot milk, stirring until mixture is smooth. Cook and stir over medium heat until sauce boils and thickens. Remove from heat. Blend in sour cream and creamed cottage cheese. Cool for 10 to 15 minutes. Slowly add beaten egg yolks, stirring briskly. Mix in cooked herbed or curried rice thoroughly. Fold in beaten egg whites gently but thoroughly. Pour into prepared 2-quart soufflé dish. Bake in 375° F. (moderate) oven for 35 to 45 minutes.

YIELD: 6 servings.

HERBED SPINACH SOUFFLÉ

3 tablespoons butter or margarine
3 tablespoons flour
1 teaspoon salt
¼ teaspoon pepper
1 cup hot milk
1 package frozen chopped spinach, cooked and drained
⅛ teaspoon dried marjoram (½ teaspoon fresh)
¼ teaspoon dried chervil (1 teaspoon fresh)
2 teaspoons minced chives
3 egg yolks, well beaten
4 egg whites, beaten stiff but not dry

HAVE READY: 1½-quart soufflé dish, buttered, and dusted with fine dry bread crumbs.

Melt butter or margarine in saucepan over low heat. Blend in flour, salt, and pepper. Cook and stir for 1 to 2 minutes. Remove from heat. Slowly stir in hot milk to make smooth mixture. Cook and stir over medium heat until sauce boils and thickens. Remove from heat and stir in cooked drained chopped spinach, mixing well. Add marjoram, chervil, and chives. Let cool 10 minutes. Gradually add beaten egg yolks, stirring briskly. Fold in beaten egg whites gently but thoroughly. Pour into prepared 1½-quart soufflé dish. Bake in 350° F. (moderate) oven 35 to 45 minutes.

YIELD: 6 to 8 servings.

SPINACH SOUFFLÉ

1 package frozen chopped spinach
¼ cup butter or margarine
3 tablespoons flour
1½ cups hot milk
1 tablespoon minced onion or shallot
½ teaspoon salt
⅛ teaspoon pepper
few grains ground nutmeg
1 tablespoon dry white wine (optional)
4 egg yolks, well beaten
5 egg whites, beaten stiff but not dry
2 hard-cooked eggs, thinly sliced

HAVE READY: 1½-quart soufflé dish, buttered.

Cook chopped spinach according to package directions, drain well, and set aside. Melt butter or margarine in saucepan over low heat, blend in flour, and cook for 2 or 3 minutes. Remove from heat. Slowly stir in hot milk to make smooth mixture, then add minced onion or shallot, and seasonings. Cook and stir over medium heat until sauce thickens. Remove from heat and let cool for 10 to 15 minutes. Add wine, if desired, then gradually add beaten egg yolks, stirring briskly. Fold in beaten egg whites gently but thoroughly. Pour one third of the soufflé mixture into prepared 1½-quart soufflé dish. Carefully top with a layer of egg slices. Pour on remaining mixture. Bake in 350° F. (moderate) oven for 40 to 45 minutes.

YIELD: 5 to 6 servings.

SPINACH ALMOND SOUFFLÉ

1 package frozen chopped spinach
¼ cup butter or margarine
1 tablespoon minced onion or shallot
1 teaspoon salt
¼ teaspoon pepper
few grains ground nutmeg
¼ cup flour
1½ cups hot chicken broth or milk
¼ cup finely chopped toasted blanched almonds
4 egg yolks, well beaten
5 egg whites, beaten stiff but not dry

HAVE READY: 1½-quart soufflé dish, buttered, and dusted with finely ground toasted almonds.

Cook frozen spinach according to package directions, drain well, and set aside. Melt butter or margarine in saucepan over low heat. Add minced onion or shallot, and cook for 1 minute. Blend in seasonings and flour. Cook, stirring frequently, until mixture is light golden brown. Remove from heat. Gradually add hot chicken broth or milk, stirring to smooth mixture. Cook and stir over medium heat until sauce thickens. Add drained chopped spinach and chopped toasted almonds, mixing well. Remove from heat and cool 10 to 15 minutes. Slowly add beaten egg yolks, stirring briskly. Fold in beaten egg whites gently but thoroughly. Pour into prepared 1½-quart soufflé dish. Bake in 375° F. (moderate) oven for 35 to 45 minutes.

YIELD: 4 to 5 servings.

RAW SPINACH SOUFFLÉ

6 tablespoons butter or margarine
7 tablespoons flour
1½ cups hot milk
1 tablespoon flour
1½ cups chopped raw spinach, firmly packed
4 egg yolks, well beaten
1 tablespoon grated onion
¼ teaspoon pepper
6 egg whites
1 teaspoon salt

HAVE READY: 1½-quart soufflé dish, ungreased, set in shallow pan containing 1 inch hot water in 325° F. (slow) oven to heat.

Melt butter or margarine in saucepan over low heat. Blend in 7 tablespoons flour, and cook for 3 minutes, stirring frequently. Remove from heat, and gradually add hot milk, stirring to smooth mixture. Cook and stir over medium heat until sauce thickens. Remove from heat and let cool 5 minutes. Blend 1 tablespoon flour with chopped raw spinach, and stir into beaten egg yolks. Add grated onion and pepper. Slowly add egg yolk mixture to cooked sauce, stirring briskly. Beat egg whites and salt until stiff, glossy peaks form. Fold spinach mixture, one fourth at a time, into beaten egg whites gently but thoroughly. Pour into heated 1½-quart soufflé dish set in pan containing 1 inch hot water. Bake in 325° F. (slow) oven for 60 to 70 minutes.

YIELD: 5 to 6 servings.

NOTE: If desired, use 1 cup thawed, well-drained, frozen chopped spinach instead of chopped raw spinach.

SQUASH SOUFFLÉ

2 tablespoons butter or margarine
2 tablespoons flour
1 teaspoon salt
¼ teaspoon pepper
¾ cup hot milk
1 cup mashed cooked squash
4 egg yolks, well beaten
5 egg whites, beaten stiff but not dry

HAVE READY: 1½-quart soufflé dish, buttered, and dusted with fine dry bread crumbs.

Melt butter or margarine in saucepan over low heat. Blend in flour and seasonings, and let cook 1 minute. Remove from heat. Slowly stir in hot milk to make smooth mixture. Cook and stir over medium heat until sauce thickens. Remove from heat and blend in mashed squash. Let cool 10 minutes. Gradually add beaten egg yolks, stirring briskly. Fold in beaten egg whites gently but thoroughly. Pour into prepared 1½-quart soufflé dish. Bake in 350° F. (moderate) oven for 40 to 50 minutes.

YIELD: 5 to 6 servings.

SUCCOTASH SOUFFLÉ

1 package frozen succotash
¼ cup butter or margarine
1 tablespoon minced onion or shallot
¼ cup flour
1 teaspoon salt
½ teaspoon pepper
1½ cups hot milk or light cream
5 egg yolks, well beaten
6 egg whites, beaten stiff but not dry

HAVE READY: 2-quart soufflé dish, buttered.

Cook succotash according to package directions. Drain well, chop, and set aside. Melt butter or margarine in saucepan over low heat. Add minced onion or shallot and cook for 1 or 2 minutes. Blend in flour and seasonings and cook for 3 minutes. Remove from heat. Gradually add hot milk, stirring to smooth mixture. Cook and stir over medium heat until sauce boils and thickens. Add chopped cooked succotash, and mix well. Remove from heat and cool 15 minutes. Slowly add beaten egg yolks, stirring briskly. Fold in beaten egg whites gently but thoroughly. Pour into prepared 2-quart soufflé dish. Bake in 350° F. (moderate) oven for 50 to 60 minutes.

YIELD: 6 servings.

SWISS CHARD SOUFFLÉ

¼ cup butter or margarine
1 tablespoon minced onion or shallot
¼ cup flour
1 teaspoon salt
¼ teaspoon pepper
1 cup hot milk
1 cup chopped cooked Swiss chard leaves, drained
¼ to ½ teaspoon Worcestershire sauce (optional)
4 egg yolks, well beaten
5 egg whites, beaten stiff but not dry

HAVE READY: 1½-quart soufflé dish, buttered, and dusted with fine dry bread crumbs.

Melt butter or margarine in saucepan over low heat. Add minced onion or shallot, and cook for 1 minute. Blend in flour and seasonings. Cook, stirring frequently, until mixture is light golden brown. Remove from heat. Gradually add hot milk, stirring to smooth mixture. Cook and stir over medium heat until sauce thickens. Remove from heat, stir in chopped cooked Swiss chard leaves and Worcestershire sauce, if desired. Let sauce cool 10 to 15 minutes. Slowly add beaten egg yolks, stirring briskly. Fold in beaten egg whites gently but thoroughly. Pour into prepared 1½-quart soufflé dish. Bake in 375° F. (moderate) oven for 40 to 50 minutes.

YIELD: 4 to 5 servings.

CREAMY TURNIP SOUFFLÉ

3 tablespoons butter or margarine
3 tablespoons flour
1 teaspoon salt
¼ teaspoon white pepper
¾ cup hot heavy cream
1 cup mashed cooked white turnip
1 tablespoon minced parsley
4 egg yolks, well beaten
5 egg whites, beaten stiff but not dry

HAVE READY: 1½-quart soufflé dish, buttered.

Melt butter or margarine in saucepan over low heat. Blend in flour and seasonings, and cook for 2 minutes. Do not let flour brown. Remove from heat, and gradually add hot cream, stirring to smooth mixture. Cook and stir until sauce thickens. Stir in mashed turnips and minced parsley. Remove from heat and cool 10 minutes. Slowly add beaten egg yolks, stirring briskly. Fold in beaten egg whites gently but thoroughly. Pour into prepared 1½-quart soufflé dish. Bake in 350° F. (moderate) oven for 35 to 45 minutes.

YIELD: 4 to 5 servings.

VEGETABLE SOUFFLÉ

3 tablespoons butter or margarine
2 tablespoons cornstarch
½ teaspoon salt
¼ teaspoon pepper
1 cup cold milk
1 cup any finely chopped cooked vegetable
4 egg yolks, well beaten
5 egg whites, beaten stiff but not dry

HAVE READY: 2-quart soufflé dish, buttered.

Melt butter or margarine in saucepan over low heat. Remove from heat. Blend in cornstarch and seasonings; slowly stir in cold milk until mixture is smooth. Cook and stir over medium heat until sauce boils and thickens, about 5 or 6 minutes. Remove from heat. Add chopped cooked vegetable, and stir to blend. Slowly add beaten egg yolks, stirring vigorously. Cool sauce for 10 minutes. Fold in beaten egg whites gently but thoroughly. Pour into prepared 2-quart soufflé dish set in shallow pan containing 1 inch of hot water. Bake in 350° F. (moderate) oven for 1¼ hours.

YIELD: 5 to 6 servings.

NOTE: This soufflé can be repuffed. Leave in soufflé dish; set dish in shallow pan with 1 inch hot water. Reheat in 350° F. (moderate) oven until puffed—about 25 to 30 minutes.

WILD RICE AND MUSHROOM SOUFFLÉ

¼ cup butter or margarine
¼ cup flour
1 teaspoon salt
¼ teaspoon pepper
1½ cups hot chicken broth
1 cup cooked or canned cooked wild rice
½ cup chopped cooked fresh or canned (3 ounces) mushrooms
4 egg yolks, well beaten
5 egg whites, beaten stiff but not dry

HAVE READY: 1½-quart soufflé dish, buttered.

Melt butter or margarine in saucepan over low heat. Blend in flour and seasonings. Cook for 3 minutes, stirring occasionally. Remove from heat and gradually add hot chicken broth, stirring to smooth mixture. Cook and stir over medium heat until sauce boils and thickens. Add cooked wild rice and mushrooms, mixing well, and cook for about 2 minutes. Remove from heat and cool 15 minutes. Slowly add beaten egg yolks, stirring briskly. Fold in beaten egg whites gently but thoroughly. Pour into prepared 1½-quart soufflé dish. Bake in 350° F. (moderate) oven for 40 to 50 minutes.

YIELD: 5 to 6 servings.

4

DESSERT SOUFFLÉS

These hot soufflés provide truly elegant finishing touches to lunch or dinner. Some are baked, some steamed, many flavored with dessert favorites such as fruits, nuts, liqueurs, or brandies. Though perfect in themselves they may be accompanied by a bit of fruit, dessert sauce, or whipped cream.

ALMOND SOUFFLÉ

1/3 cup flour
2 tablespoons sugar
1 cup cold light cream
1/4 cup butter or margarine
5 egg yolks
1/4 cup sugar
1/2 teaspoon vanilla extract
1/8 teaspoon almond extract
1/4 cup chopped toasted blanched almonds
5 egg whites, beaten stiff but not dry

HAVE READY: 1½-quart soufflé dish, buttered, and dusted with sugar or very finely ground almonds.

Blend together flour and 2 tablespoons sugar in saucepan. Gradually add cream, stirring to smooth mixture. Add butter or margarine and cook and stir over low heat until sauce comes to a boil and thickens. Remove from heat and let cool 10 minutes. Beat egg yolks and 1/4 cup sugar together until thick and light. Slowly add to cooled sauce, stirring briskly. Blend in vanilla and almond extracts and chopped almonds. Fold in beaten egg whites gently but thoroughly. Pour into prepared 1½-quart soufflé dish. Bake in 325° F. (slow) oven for 45 to 55 minutes.

YIELD: 5 to 6 servings.

DELICATE ALMOND SOUFFLÉ

1 cup cold milk
2 tablespoons cornstarch
4 egg yolks
¼ cup sugar
¼ teaspoon salt
½ teaspoon almond extract
½ teaspoon vanilla extract
5 egg whites
¼ cup sugar
1 tablespoon ground almonds

HAVE READY: 2-quart soufflé dish, buttered, and dusted with fine dry macaroon crumbs or sugar.

In a saucepan, slowly add milk to cornstarch to make a smooth mixture. Bring to a boil over medium heat, stirring frequently, and let boil 1 minute. Combine egg yolks, ¼ cup sugar, and salt and beat until thick and light. Slowly pour in hot milk mixture, stirring briskly. Cool for 10 to 15 minutes. Add flavoring extracts. Beat egg whites to soft peaks; gradually add ¼ cup sugar, and continue beating until stiff glossy peaks form. Fold into egg yolk mixture gently but thoroughly. Pour into prepared 2-quart soufflé dish set in shallow pan containing 1 inch hot water. Sprinkle top lightly with ground almonds. Bake in 325° F. (slow) oven for 40 to 45 minutes.

YIELD: 6 servings.

ALMOND DOUBLE BOILER SOUFFLÉ

⅓ cup butter or margarine
¼ cup granulated sugar
6 egg yolks, well beaten
⅛ teaspoon salt
1 teaspoon vanilla extract
1½ tablespoons Falernum or Orgeat syrup
1 cup finely ground or grated blanched almonds
6 egg whites
2 tablespoons confectioners' sugar

HAVE READY: 2-quart double boiler or chafing dish, top section buttered including inside of cover.

Cream butter until soft, gradually add granulated sugar, creaming together until light and fluffy. Slowly cream in beaten egg yolks, salt, vanilla extract, and Falernum or Orgeat syrup. Beat in ground or grated blanched almonds. Beat egg whites to soft peaks. Gradually add confectioners' sugar, beating continuously until stiff glossy peaks form. Fold beaten egg whites into almond mixture gently but thoroughly. Pour into prepared double boiler top or chafing dish pan. Cover. Cook over hot, not boiling, water for 1 to 1¼ hours. Do not let water touch top pan. Turn out on warm plate to serve, or serve directly from chafing dish.

YIELD: 6 servings.

APPLENUT SOUFFLÉ

¼ cup sugar
¼ cup flour
¼ teaspoon salt
4 egg yolks, well beaten
1¼ cups hot milk or light cream
¼ cup butter or margarine
1 cup finely diced peeled apples
⅓ cup finely chopped California walnuts
5 egg whites, beaten stiff but not dry

HAVE READY: 1½-quart soufflé dish, buttered, and dusted with sugar.

Blend together sugar, flour, and salt in top of double boiler. Add beaten egg yolks, beating all together until smooth. Gradually beat in hot milk or light cream. Add butter. Cook and stir over hot water until sauce thickens like soft custard. Remove from heat and let cool 10 minutes. Stir in finely diced apples and finely chopped walnuts. Let cool 5 or 10 minutes more. Fold in beaten egg whites gently but thoroughly. Pour into prepared 1½-quart soufflé dish. Bake in 325° F. (slow) oven for 35 to 45 minutes.

YIELD: 4 to 5 servings.

SPICED APPLE EGG WHITE SOUFFLÉ

4 egg whites
1/8 teaspoon salt
1/4 teaspoon cream of tartar
1/3 cup sugar
1 cup thick applesauce
1/2 teaspoon cinnamon
1/4 teaspoon nutmeg
1 teaspoon grated lemon peel

HAVE READY: 1-quart soufflé dish or deep baking dish, buttered on bottom only.

Combine egg whites, salt, and cream of tartar, and beat to soft peaks. Gradually add sugar, beating continuously until stiff glossy peaks form. Blend together applesauce, spices, and grated lemon peel. Fold into beaten egg whites gently but thoroughly. Pour into prepared 1-quart soufflé dish or baking dish set in shallow pan containing 1 inch hot water. Bake in 325° F. (slow) oven for 40 to 50 minutes.

YIELD: 4 to 5 servings.

APPLE BRANDY SOUFFLÉ

1 1/2 cups applesauce
1/4 to 1/3 cup sugar, to taste
1 tablespoon lemon juice
1 teaspoon grated lemon peel
1 to 2 tablespoons Calvados (apple brandy)
4 egg yolks, well beaten
4 egg whites, beaten stiff but not dry

HAVE READY: 1 1/2-quart soufflé dish, buttered, and dusted with finely ground nuts.

Combine applesauce, sugar, lemon juice, and grated lemon peel in saucepan. Bring to a boil over low heat, stirring constantly. Remove from heat and stir in apple brandy. Let cool 10 minutes. Slowly add beaten egg yolks, stirring constantly. Fold in beaten egg whites gently but thoroughly. Pour into prepared 1 1/2-quart soufflé dish set in shallow pan containing

1 to 2 inches of water. Bake in 375° F. (moderate) oven for 30 to 40 minutes.

YIELD: 4 to 5 servings.

APRICOT SOUFFLÉ

3 tablespoons cornstarch
½ cup sugar
⅛ teaspoon salt
¾ cup cold milk
3 egg yolks, well beaten
½ cup puréed canned peeled apricots
1 teaspoon grated orange or lemon peel
1 tablespoon Apry liqueur (optional)
4 egg whites, beaten stiff but not dry

HAVE READY: 1½-quart soufflé dish, buttered, and dusted with sugar.

Combine cornstarch, sugar, and salt in saucepan, blending well. Gradually add cold milk, stirring to smooth mixture. Cook and stir over medium heat until sauce comes to a boil. Let boil 1 or 2 minutes. Remove from heat and let cool 10 minutes. Slowly add beaten egg yolks, stirring briskly. Add puréed apricots, grated orange or lemon peel, and liqueur, if desired. Fold into beaten egg whites gently but thoroughly. Pour into prepared 1½-quart soufflé dish. Bake in 325° F. (slow) oven for 45 to 55 minutes.

YIELD: 6 servings.

APRICOT EGG WHITE SOUFFLÉ

4 egg whites
few grains salt
⅛ teaspoon cream of tartar
¼ cup sugar
1 cup puréed cooked dried apricots
¼ teaspoon almond extract
½ teaspoon grated lemon peel

HAVE READY: 1½-quart soufflé dish or deep casserole, buttered, and dusted with sugar.

Beat egg whites and salt until frothy; add cream of tartar

and beat to soft peaks. Gradually add sugar, beating continuously until stiff glossy peaks are formed. Blend together puréed apricots, almond extract, and grated lemon peel. Fold into beaten egg whites gently but thoroughly. Pour into prepared 1½-quart soufflé dish or deep casserole set in shallow pan containing 1 or 2 inches of hot water. Bake in 350° F. (moderate) oven for 40 to 45 minutes.

YIELD: 6 servings.

APRICOT LIQUEUR SOUFFLÉ

3 tablespoons butter or margarine
3 tablespoons flour
¾ cup hot milk
¼ cup sugar
4 egg yolks, well beaten
¼ cup apricot liqueur
5 egg whites, beaten stiff but not dry

HAVE READY: 1½-quart soufflé dish, buttered, and dusted with sugar or fine dry macaroon crumbs.

Melt butter or margarine in saucepan over low heat. Blend in flour and cook 2 minutes. Remove from heat. Gradually stir in hot milk to make smooth mixture, then add sugar. Cook and stir over medium heat until sauce thickens. Remove from heat and cool 10 minutes. Gradually add beaten egg yolks, stirring briskly, then stir in liqueur. Fold in beaten egg whites gently but thoroughly. Pour into prepared 1½-quart soufflé dish. Bake in 375° F. (moderate) oven 25 to 35 minutes.

YIELD: 6 servings.

DELICATE B AND B SOUFFLÉ

8 egg yolks
¾ cup sugar
½ cup Brandy and Benedictine liqueur
8 egg whites, beaten stiff but not dry

HAVE READY: 1½-quart soufflé dish, buttered, and dusted with fine dry macaroon crumbs.

Beat egg yolks until thick and light. Slowly add sugar, beating constantly until sugar is dissolved. Cook and stir in double boiler over hot, not boiling, water until thickened, about 8 to 10 minutes. Pour into bowl set in crushed ice and beat with electric or rotary beater until cool. Add liqueur. Fold beaten egg whites into egg yolk mixture gently but thoroughly. Pour into prepared 1½-quart soufflé dish. Bake in 400° F. (hot) oven for 15 to 20 minutes.

YIELD: 6 servings.

BRANDYBERRY SOUFFLÉ

1½ cups puréed fresh or frozen strawberries or raspberries
¼ to ⅓ cup sugar, to taste
2 teaspoons lemon juice
½ teaspoon grated lemon peel
2 tablespoons strawberry or raspberry brandy
4 egg yolks, well beaten
5 egg whites, beaten stiff but not dry

HAVE READY: 1½-quart soufflé dish, lightly buttered, and dusted with sugar.

Combine puréed berries and sugar to taste. (If raspberries are used, strain out seeds before measuring purée.) Add lemon juice and grated lemon peel. Bring to a boil over low heat, stirring constantly. Remove from heat and stir in strawberry or raspberry brandy. Let cool 10 minutes. Slowly add beaten egg yolks, stirring briskly. Fold in beaten egg whites gently but thoroughly. Pour into 1½-quart soufflé dish set in shallow pan containing 1 to 2 inches hot water. Bake in 375° F. (moderate) oven for 30 to 40 minutes.

YIELD: 4 to 5 servings.

BRANDIED PEACH SOUFFLÉ

1½ cups fresh, frozen, or canned sliced peaches
¼ to ⅓ cup sugar, to taste
1 tablespoon lemon juice
1 teaspoon grated lemon peel
1 to 2 tablespoons peach-flavored brandy
4 egg yolks, well beaten
5 egg whites, beaten stiff but not dry

HAVE READY: 1½-quart soufflé dish, buttered, and dusted with sugar or fine dry macaroon crumbs.

Press peach slices through sieve or whirl in blender until smooth pulp. Combine peach pulp, sugar, lemon juice, and grated lemon peel in saucepan. Bring to a boil over low heat, stirring constantly. Remove from heat and stir in peach-flavored brandy. Let cool 10 minutes. Slowly add beaten egg yolks, stirring briskly. Fold in beaten egg whites gently but thoroughly. Pour into prepared 1½-quart soufflé dish set in shallow pan containing 1 to 2 inches of hot water. Bake in 375° F. (moderate) oven for 30 to 40 minutes.

YIELD: 4 to 5 servings.

BUTTERCRUNCH SOUFFLÉ

¼ cup butter or margarine
¼ cup flour
⅛ teaspoon salt
1 cup hot light cream
¼ cup sugar
2 teaspoons vanilla extract
1 tablespoon coffee-flavored liqueur, if desired
4 egg yolks, well beaten
½ cup finely crushed buttercrunch candy
5 egg whites
2 tablespoons sugar (additional)

HAVE READY: 1½-quart soufflé dish, buttered, and dusted with sugar or finely ground nuts.

Melt butter or margarine in saucepan over low heat. Blend in flour and salt and cook for 1 minute. Remove from heat.

Gradually add hot cream, stirring to smooth mixture, then add sugar. Cook and stir over medium heat until sauce is thick and smooth. Remove from heat. Blend in vanilla extract and coffee liqueur, if desired. Let cool 10 minutes. Slowly add beaten egg yolks, stirring briskly. Stir in crushed buttercrunch candy. Beat egg whites to soft peaks. Gradually add 2 tablespoons sugar, beating continuously until stiff glossy peaks form. Fold beaten egg whites into cooled sauce mixture. Pour into prepared 1½-quart soufflé dish. Bake in 375° F. (moderate) oven for 35 to 40 minutes.

YIELD: 4 to 5 servings.

CAMEMBERT OR BRIE DESSERT SOUFFLÉ

3 tablespoons butter or margarine
3 tablespoons flour
¾ cup hot milk
⅛ teaspoon salt
few grains cayenne pepper
¾ cup sieved Camembert or Brie cheese
2 tablespoons dry white wine
4 egg yolks, well beaten
5 egg whites, beaten stiff but not dry

HAVE READY: 1½-quart soufflé dish, ungreased.

Melt butter or margarine in saucepan over low heat. Blend in flour and cook 2 minutes, but do not allow to brown. Remove from heat. Gradually add hot milk and seasonings, stirring to smooth mixture. Cook and stir over medium heat until sauce is thick. Remove from heat. Stir in cheese and wine until cheese melts and is well blended. Let sauce cool 10 minutes. Slowly add beaten egg yolks, stirring briskly. Fold in beaten egg whites gently but thoroughly. Pour into 1½-quart soufflé dish. Bake in 375° F. (moderate) oven for 30 to 35 minutes. When served, accompany each portion with chilled fresh fruit.

YIELD: 4 to 5 servings.

CACAO SOUFFLÉ

3 tablespoons butter or margarine
3 tablespoons flour
¾ cup hot milk
3 tablespoons sugar
4 egg yolks, well beaten
3 tablespoons crème de cacao or cacao mit nuss liqueur
5 egg whites, beaten stiff but not dry

HAVE READY: 1½-quart soufflé dish, buttered, and dusted with finely ground nuts.

Melt butter or margarine in saucepan over low heat. Blend in flour and cook 2 minutes. Remove from heat. Gradually stir in hot milk to make smooth mixture, then add sugar. Cook and stir over medium heat until sauce thickens. Remove from heat and cool 10 minutes. Gradually add beaten egg yolks, stirring briskly, then stir in liqueur. Fold in beaten egg whites gently but thoroughly. Pour into prepared 1½-quart soufflé dish. Bake in 375° F. (moderate) oven 25 to 35 minutes.

YIELD: 6 servings.

CHARTREUSE SOUFFLÉ

3 tablespoons butter or margarine
3 tablespoons flour
¾ cup hot milk
¼ cup sugar
4 egg yolks, well beaten
3 tablespoons green Chartreuse liqueur
5 egg whites, beaten stiff but not dry
1 tablespoon chopped pistachio nuts

HAVE READY: 1½-quart soufflé dish, buttered, and dusted with finely ground pistachio nuts.

[1] Basic Cheese Soufflé, its hearty flavor sparked with a touch of hot liquid pepper.

[2] Cheese and Bacon Soufflé, made with quick-cooking tapioca, holds its puff an extra long time. Here's a special for buffet service.

[3] Spinach Soufflé, dainty accompaniment for any choice of meat, poultry, or fish.

[4] Raisin Angel Puff blends sweet angel food and raisins with tangy orange peel and lemon juice to make an airy, refreshing dessert.

[5] Potato Puff, light as a cloud but satisfyingly hearty too.

[6] Quick Mushroom Soufflé is one for the cook in a hurry. Canned soup and canned mushrooms from the emergency shelf are the principal basic ingredients.

Melt butter or margarine in saucepan over low heat. Blend in flour and cook for 2 minutes. Remove from heat. Gradually add hot milk, stirring to smooth mixture. Cook and stir over medium heat until sauce thickens. Add sugar and stir until dissolved. Remove from heat; let sauce cool 10 minutes. Gradually add beaten egg yolks, stirring briskly, then add liqueur. Fold in beaten egg whites gently but thoroughly. Pour into prepared 1½-quart soufflé dish. Top with 1 tablespoon chopped pistachio nuts. Bake in 375° F. (moderate) oven for 25 to 35 minutes.

YIELD: 6 servings.

CHERRY CORDIAL SOUFFLÉ

3 tablespoons butter or margarine
3 tablespoons flour
¾ cup hot milk
⅓ cup sugar
4 egg yolks, well beaten
3 to 4 tablespoons Cherry Heering or Edelkirsch liqueur
5 egg whites, beaten stiff but not dry

HAVE READY: 1½-quart soufflé dish, buttered, and dusted with sugar.

Melt butter or margarine in saucepan over low heat. Blend in flour, and cook 2 minutes. Remove from heat. Gradually stir in hot milk to make smooth mixture, then add sugar. Cook and stir over medium heat until sauce thickens. Remove from heat and cool 10 minutes. Gradually add beaten egg yolks, stirring briskly, then stir in liqueur. Fold in beaten egg whites gently but thoroughly. Pour into prepared 1½-quart soufflé dish. Bake in 375° F. (moderate) oven 25 to 35 minutes.

YIELD: 6 servings.

CHESTNUT OR MARRON SOUFFLÉ

1 cup puréed cooked chestnuts or canned, unsweetened chestnut or marron purée
½ cup sugar
1 cup hot milk
3 tablespoons butter or margarine
2 tablespoons flour
½ teaspoon vanilla extract
4 egg yolks, well beaten
5 egg whites
2 tablespoons sugar (additional)

HAVE READY: 1½-quart soufflé dish, well buttered, and dusted with sugar.

Blend together chestnut or marron purée and ½ cup sugar in saucepan. Gradually beat in hot milk, using wire whisk or rotary beater. Cook and stir over low heat until mixture has thickened. Remove from heat. In another saucepan, melt butter or margarine over low heat. Blend in flour and cook for 1 minute. Gradually add hot chestnut mixture. Cook and stir for 2 minutes. Remove from heat, add vanilla extract, and let cool 10 minutes. Slowly add beaten egg yolks, stirring briskly. Let cool 10 more minutes. Beat egg whites to soft peaks. Gradually add 2 tablespoons sugar, beating continuously until stiff glossy peaks form. Fold beaten egg whites into chestnut mixture gently but thoroughly. Pour into prepared 1½-quart soufflé dish, set in shallow pan containing 1 to 2 inches hot water. Bake in 375° F. (moderate) oven for 45 to 55 minutes.

YIELD: 6 servings.

CHOCOLATE SOUFFLÉ

2 squares (2 ounces) unsweetened chocolate, broken up
¾ cup cold milk
3 tablespoons cornstarch
½ cup sugar
½ teaspoon salt
3 tablespoons cold milk
1 teaspoon vanilla extract
3 egg yolks, well beaten
4 egg whites, beaten stiff but not dry

HAVE READY: 1½-quart soufflé dish, buttered, and dusted with sugar.

Melt chocolate with ¾ cup milk over hot water. Blend together cornstarch, sugar, and salt in saucepan. Stir in 3 tablespoons cold milk to make a smooth mixture. Add hot chocolate mixture gradually, stirring so that no lumps form. Cook and stir over medium heat until sauce boils and thickens. Remove from heat, add vanilla extract, and let cool 10 to 15 minutes. Gradually add beaten egg yolks, stirring briskly. Fold in beaten egg whites gently but thoroughly. Pour into 1½-quart soufflé dish set in shallow pan containing 1 inch hot water. Bake in 350° F. (moderate) oven for 45 to 55 minutes.

YIELD: 6 servings.

CHOCOLATE DOUBLE BOILER SOUFFLÉ

1 cup (6 ounce package) semi-sweet chocolate pieces
4 egg whites
¼ teaspoon salt
¼ teaspoon cream of tartar
¼ cup light brown sugar, firmly packed
½ teaspoon vanilla extract

HAVE READY: 2-quart double boiler or chafing dish, top section buttered including inside of cover.

Melt semi-sweet chocolate pieces in saucepan or bowl over hot (not steaming) water. Remove from water and set aside. Combine egg whites, salt, and cream of tartar. Beat to soft peaks. Gradually add brown sugar, beating continuously until stiff glossy peaks form. Gently but thoroughly fold in melted chocolate and vanilla extract. Pour into buttered top of 2-quart double boiler or chafing dish. Cover. Cook over hot water for 1 to 1¼ hours. Do not let water touch bottom of top pan. If service is delayed, turn off heat and leave soufflé, covered, over hot water until ready to serve.

YIELD: 6 servings.

CHOCOLATE CACAO SOUFFLÉ

¼ cup butter or margarine
¼ cup flour
½ teaspoon salt
½ cup sugar
1¼ cups hot milk or light cream
1½ squares (1½ ounces) unsweetened chocolate
½ cup crème de cacao liqueur
5 egg yolks, well beaten
6 egg whites, beaten stiff but not dry

HAVE READY: 2-quart soufflé dish, buttered, and dusted with sugar or fine dry cookie crumbs.

Melt butter or margarine in saucepan over low heat. Blend in flour, and cook for 3 or 4 minutes. Remove from heat. Mix in salt and sugar. Gradually add hot milk or light cream, stirring to smooth mixture. Cook and stir over medium heat until sauce is thick and smooth. Remove from heat. Stir in chocolate and crème de cacao until chocolate is melted. Let cool 10 to 15 minutes. Slowly add beaten egg yolks, stirring briskly. Fold in beaten egg whites gently but thoroughly. Pour into prepared 2-quart soufflé dish. Bake in 350° F. (moderate) oven for 55 to 65 minutes. YIELD: 8 servings.

DOUBLE CHOCOLATE SOUFFLÉ

1 square (1 ounce) unsweetened chocolate
½ package (2 ounces) German's sweet chocolate
¾ cup hot milk
⅓ cup sugar
3 tablespoons cornstarch
¼ teaspoon salt
2 tablespoons cold milk
3 egg yolks, well beaten
1 teaspoon vanilla extract
4 egg whites, beaten stiff but not dry

HAVE READY: 1½-quart soufflé dish, buttered, and dusted with sugar.

Break up unsweetened and sweet chocolate and melt in hot

milk over hot water. Blend together sugar, cornstarch, and salt in saucepan. Slowly add 2 tablespoons cold milk, mixing to smooth paste. Gradually stir in chocolate milk mixture. Cook and stir over medium heat until sauce comes to a boil and thickens. Remove from heat and let cool 10 minutes. Slowly add beaten egg yolks, stirring briskly, then stir in vanilla extract. Fold gently but thoroughly into beaten egg whites. Pour into prepared 1½-quart soufflé dish set in shallow pan containing 1 inch hot water. Bake in 350° F. (moderate) oven for 45 to 55 minutes.

YIELD: 6 servings.

DELICATE CHOCOLATE SOUFFLÉ

1 tablespoon cornstarch
⅔ cup cold milk
3 tablespoons butter or margarine
1½ squares (1½ ounces) unsweetened chocolate
1 teaspoon vanilla extract
4 egg yolks
2 tablespoons sugar
4 egg whites
⅛ teaspoon salt
3 tablespoons sugar

HAVE READY: 1½-quart soufflé dish, buttered, and dusted with sugar.

Measure cornstarch into saucepan. Gradually blend in milk until mixture is smooth, then add butter or margarine. Cook and stir over medium heat until sauce comes to a boil. Let boil 1 minute. Remove from heat. Add chocolate and vanilla extract, stirring until chocolate melts. Let cool 10 minutes. Beat egg yolks with 2 tablespoons sugar until light and thick. Gradually add to cooled chocolate mixture, stirring briskly. Beat egg whites and salt to soft peaks. Gradually add 3 tablespoons sugar, beating continuously to stiff glossy peaks. Gently but thoroughly fold chocolate mixture into beaten egg whites. Pour into prepared 1½-quart soufflé dish. Bake in 350° F. (moderate) oven for 45 to 50 minutes. YIELD: 6 servings.

CHOCOLATE LIQUEUR SOUFFLÉ

2 tablespoons butter or margarine
2 tablespoons flour
few grains salt
¾ cup hot milk
1½ squares (1½ ounces) unsweetened chocolate
⅓ cup sugar
¼ cup crème de cacao liqueur
3 egg yolks, well beaten
4 egg whites, beaten stiff but not dry

HAVE READY: 1½-quart soufflé dish, buttered, and dusted with sugar or fine dry macaroon crumbs.

Melt butter or margarine in saucepan over low heat. Blend in flour and salt and cook for 1 minute. Remove from heat. Slowly add hot milk, stirring to smooth mixture. Cook and stir over medium heat until sauce comes to a boil and thickens. Reduce heat. Add chocolate and sugar and stir until chocolate melts and sugar dissolves. Remove from heat, stir in crème de cacao, and cool 10 to 15 minutes. Gradually add beaten egg yolks, stirring briskly. Fold in beaten egg whites gently but thoroughly. Pour into prepared 1½-quart soufflé dish. Bake in 350° F. (moderate) oven for 40 to 50 minutes.

YIELD: 6 servings.

CHOCOLATE ORANGE SOUFFLÉ

2 tablespoons butter or margarine
2 tablespoons flour
1 cup hot milk
2½ squares (2½ ounces) unsweetened chocolate
½ cup sugar
1 teaspoon grated orange peel
5 egg yolks, well beaten
2 tablespoons Cointreau or Curaçao liqueur
6 egg whites, beaten stiff but not dry

HAVE READY: 2-quart soufflé dish, lightly buttered, and dusted with sugar.

Melt butter or margarine in saucepan over low heat. Blend in flour and cook for 1 minute. Remove from heat and slowly add hot milk, stirring to smooth mixture. Cook and stir over medium heat until sauce thickens. Add chocolate and sugar. Stir until chocolate melts. Remove from heat. Add grated orange peel, and let sauce cool 15 to 20 minutes. Slowly add beaten egg yolks, stirring briskly, then stir in liqueur. Fold in beaten egg whites gently but thoroughly. Pour into prepared 2-quart soufflé dish. Bake in 350° F. (moderate) oven for 40 to 50 minutes.

YIELD: 6 servings.

CHOCOLATE CREAM SOUFFLÉ

1 cup medium or heavy cream
3 squares (3 ounces) unsweetened chocolate, broken up
⅓ cup flour
½ teaspoon salt
¼ cup sugar
⅓ cup cold milk
1 teaspoon vanilla extract
¼ teaspoon almond extract
5 egg yolks, well beaten
6 egg whites
¼ cup sugar

HAVE READY: 2-quart soufflé dish, lightly buttered, and dusted with sugar.

Heat cream and chocolate together in top of double boiler over direct low heat until chocolate melts. Remove from heat and beat with wire whisk. Combine flour, salt, and ¼ cup sugar in bowl. Slowly add cold milk, stirring to smooth mixture. Add to chocolate mixture. Cook and stir over boiling water until sauce is thick and smooth. Remove from heat, and add vanilla and almond extracts. Cool 10 to 12 minutes. Slowly add beaten egg yolks, stirring briskly. Beat egg whites to soft peaks. Gradually add ¼ cup sugar, beating continuously until stiff glossy peaks form. Fold chocolate mixture into beaten egg whites gently but thoroughly. Pour into prepared 2-quart soufflé dish. Bake in 400° F. (hot) oven for 30 to 40 minutes.

YIELD: 8 servings.

CHOCOLATE LAYER SOUFFLÉ

¾ cup sugar
½ cup sifted flour
1 teaspoon salt
1⅓ cups cold milk
1 teaspoon vanilla extract
1 cup (6-ounce package) semi-sweet chocolate pieces
6 egg yolks, beaten thick and light
7 egg whites, beaten stiff but not dry

HAVE READY: 2-quart soufflé dish, ungreased.

Blend sugar, flour, and salt together thoroughly in saucepan. Gradually add milk, stirring to make smooth mixture. Cook and stir over medium heat until sauce boils and thickens. Remove from heat and add vanilla extract. Set aside about ⅔ of sauce mixture. To remaining ⅓ add semi-sweet chocolate pieces, stirring until melted and well blended. Add half of beaten egg yolks to white sauce mixture, then fold in half of beaten egg whites. Add remaining egg yolks to chocolate mixture, then fold in remaining egg whites. Spoon alternate layers of white and chocolate mixtures into 2-quart soufflé dish, beginning and ending with a white layer. Bake in 325° F. (slow) oven for 65 to 75 minutes.

YIELD: 8 servings.

CHOCOLATE RUM SOUFFLÉ

2 squares (2 ounces) unsweetened chocolate, broken up
3 tablespoons butter or margarine
2 tablespoons flour
¼ teaspoon salt
½ cup sugar
1 cup hot milk
1 teaspoon vanilla extract
2 tablespoons light or dark rum
4 egg yolks, well beaten
5 egg whites, beaten stiff but not dry

HAVE READY: 1½-quart soufflé dish, buttered, and dusted with sugar or fine dry macaroon crumbs.

Melt chocolate in custard cup over hot water. Melt butter or margarine in saucepan over low heat. Blend in flour and salt, and cook 1 minute. Remove from heat. Blend in sugar thoroughly, then slowly add hot milk, stirring to smooth mixture. Cook and stir over medium heat until sauce thickens. Remove from heat, and add vanilla extract and melted chocolate, mixing well. Let cool 10 minutes. Stir in rum, then gradually add beaten egg yolks, stirring briskly. Fold in beaten egg whites gently but thoroughly. Pour into prepared 1½-quart soufflé dish set in shallow pan containing 1 inch hot water. Bake in 350° F. (moderate) oven for 45 to 55 minutes.

YIELD: 5 to 6 servings.

SWEET CHOCOLATE SOUFFLÉ

1 package (¼ pound) German's sweet chocolate, broken
1 cup hot milk or light cream
3 tablespoons sugar
3 tablespoons flour
4 egg yolks, well beaten
2 teaspoons butter or margarine
1 teaspoon vanilla extract
5 egg whites, beaten stiff but not dry

HAVE READY: 1½-quart soufflé dish, buttered, and dusted with sugar.

Add broken sweet chocolate to hot milk in saucepan and stir over low heat until chocolate melts. Remove from heat. Blend together sugar and flour. Beat into beaten egg yolks until mixture is thick and light. Slowly add to hot milk mixture, stirring briskly. Cook and stir over low heat until sauce is thick and smooth. Remove from heat, add butter and vanilla extract, and let cool 15 minutes. Fold in beaten egg whites gently but thoroughly. Pour into prepared 1½-quart soufflé dish. Bake in 350° F. (moderate) oven for 35 to 40 minutes.

YIELD: 4 to 5 servings.

COCONUT SOUFFLÉ

2 tablespoons butter or margarine
2 tablespoons flour
½ cup hot milk
2 tablespoons sugar
4 egg yolks, well beaten
½ teaspoon vanilla extract
¼ teaspoon almond extract
½ cup toasted flaked coconut
5 egg whites, beaten stiff but not dry

HAVE READY: 1½-quart soufflé dish, buttered, and dusted with sugar.

Melt butter or margarine in saucepan over low heat. Blend in flour, and cook for 1 minute. Remove from heat and gradually stir in hot milk until smooth. Cook and stir over medium heat until sauce is thickened. Remove from heat. Stir in sugar; cool for 5 minutes. Gradually add beaten egg yolks, stirring vigorously. Stir in flavoring extracts and toasted coconut. Cool 10 to 15 minutes more. Stir in ⅓ beaten egg whites, then fold in the rest gently but thoroughly. Pour into prepared 1½-quart soufflé dish set in shallow pan containing 1 inch hot water. Bake in 350° F. (moderate) oven for 35 to 40 minutes.

YIELD: 4 to 5 servings.

COTTAGE CHEESE DESSERT SOUFFLÉ

2 tablespoons cornstarch
½ cup sugar
½ teaspoon salt
¾ cup cold light cream
½ cup creamed cottage cheese
4 egg yolks, well beaten
1 teaspoon vanilla extract
1 teaspoon grated orange or lemon peel
¼ cup chopped seedless raisins
3 tablespoons finely chopped almonds
5 egg whites, beaten stiff but not dry

HAVE READY: 1½-quart soufflé dish, buttered, and dusted with sugar or ground almonds.

Combine cornstarch, sugar, and salt in saucepan, blending well. Gradually add cold light cream, stirring to smooth mixture. Cook and stir over medium heat until sauce comes to a boil. Let boil 1 or 2 minutes. Remove from heat. Cool 10 minutes. Stir in cottage cheese, then slowly add beaten egg yolks, stirring briskly. Add vanilla extract, grated orange or lemon peel, chopped raisins, and finely chopped almonds. Mix well. Fold in beaten egg whites gently but thoroughly. Pour into prepared 1½-quart soufflé dish. Bake in 350° F. (moderate) oven for 45 to 55 minutes.

YIELD: 5 to 6 servings.

FROZEN CHEESY CHOCOLATE SOUFFLÉ

1 cup (8 ounces) cream cheese
½ cup light cream
1 cup (6 ounces) semi-sweet chocolate pieces
4 egg yolks, well beaten
1 teaspoon vanilla extract
4 egg whites
¼ teaspoon cream of tartar
¼ cup confectioners' sugar

HAVE READY: 1½-quart soufflé dish, lined with two 16½-inch lengths of aluminum foil joined with a firm fold to make a center seam. Foil should extend 2 inches above edge of dish all around. Cut circle of foil to fit top of dish, and reserve until soufflé has frozen.

Mash cream cheese with a fork in saucepan, blend in light cream, and cook, stirring occasionally, over low heat, until mixture is heated through. Meanwhile, melt chocolate pieces over hot (not boiling) water. Combine chocolate with cheese mixture, and remove from heat. Slowly add beaten egg yolks, stirring vigorously, then stir in vanilla extract. Beat egg whites until foamy. Sprinkle on cream of tartar and continue beating, gradually adding confectioners' sugar until stiff but glossy peaks form. Fold beaten egg whites into chocolate mixture gently but thoroughly. Pour into foil-lined 1½-quart soufflé dish. Freeze.

When soufflé has frozen, lift it from soufflé dish by grasping foil liner. Cover with circle of foil; fold down extended edges to secure it. Return to freezer for storage up to 4 weeks.

To bake, replace foil-wrapped soufflé in baking dish; remove foil from top; fold overhanging foil at edge of dish to form a sort of collar. Place soufflé immediately in 300° F. (slow) oven. Bake for 1½ hours.

YIELD: 4 to 6 servings.

NOTE: To bake without freezing, pour soufflé as soon as made into ungreased 1½-quart soufflé dish. Bake in 300° F. (slow) oven for 50 to 55 minutes.

FRUITED DOUBLE BOILER SOUFFLÉ

4 egg whites
⅛ teaspoon salt
¼ teaspoon cream of tartar
¼ cup sugar
1 jar puréed peaches, plums, prunes, or apricots for infants
½ teaspoon grated lemon peel
2 teaspoons Cointreau or Curaçao liqueur (optional)

HAVE READY: 2-quart double boiler, top section buttered including inside of cover.

Beat egg whites and salt together until foamy, sprinkle on cream of tartar, and beat to soft peaks. Gradually add sugar, beating continuously until stiff glossy peaks form and sugar is dissolved. Fold in puréed fruit of choice, grated lemon peel, and liqueur, if desired, gently but thoroughly. Pour into prepared 2-quart double boiler, and set cover in place. Cook over hot, not boiling, water for 50 minutes. Do not let water touch top pan of double boiler. If not served at once, leave cover in place, turn heat as low as possible, and hold for 20 to 40 minutes. This is one type of soufflé that very successfully waits for the guests. Turn out on warm plate to serve.

YIELD: 4 to 5 servings.

NOTE: This soufflé may be made in a covered chafing dish, and served directly from the chafing dish pan.

The recipe may be doubled, using 1 jar chopped fruit for juniors instead of fruits puréed for infants, and cooked in a covered 2½-quart chafing dish for 1¼ hours or longer.

BAKED FRUITED EGG WHITE SOUFFLÉ

4 egg whites
⅛ teaspoon salt
¼ teaspoon cream of tartar
⅓ to ½ cup sugar, to taste
1¼ cups thick puréed cooked dried prunes, apricots, peaches or pears
1 teaspoon grated lemon peel
1 tablespoon lemon juice
⅛ teaspoon almond extract

HAVE READY: 1-quart soufflé dish or deep baking dish, lightly buttered on bottom only.

Sprinkle egg whites with salt and cream of tartar, and beat to soft peaks. Gradually add sugar, beating continuously until stiff glossy peaks form. Blend together puréed cooked dried fruit of choice, grated lemon peel, lemon juice, and almond extract. Fold into beaten egg whites gently but thoroughly. Pour into prepared 1-quart soufflé dish or deep baking dish. Bake in 325° F. (slow) oven for 40 to 45 minutes.

YIELD: 6 servings.

FRUIT AND KIRSCH EGG WHITE SOUFFLÉ

2 cups puréed fresh or frozen strawberries or peaches
2 to 3 tablespoons kirsch brandy
¼ to ⅓ cup sugar, to taste
6 egg whites
¼ teaspoon cream of tartar
½ cup confectioners' sugar

HAVE READY: 1½-quart soufflé dish, buttered, and dusted with sugar.

Blend together puréed strawberries or peaches, kirsch, and sugar to taste in a large bowl. Beat egg whites until foamy, sprinkle on cream of tartar, and beat to soft peaks. Gradually add confectioners' sugar, beating continuously until stiff glossy peaks form. Fold beaten egg whites into fruit sauce gently but thoroughly. Pour into prepared 1½-quart soufflé dish. Bake in 350° F. (moderate) oven for 20 to 25 minutes.

YIELD: 4 to 5 servings.

GRAND MARNIER SOUFFLÉ

3 tablespoons butter or margarine
3 tablespoons flour
¾ cup hot milk
¼ cup sugar
4 egg yolks, well beaten
¼ cup Grand Marnier liqueur
⅛ teaspoon salt
5 egg whites
1 tablespoon sugar (additional)
2 teaspoons confectioners' sugar

HAVE READY: 1½-quart soufflé dish, well buttered, and dusted with sugar.

Melt butter or margarine in saucepan over low heat; blend in flour, and cook for 1 minute. Remove from heat; gradually add hot milk, stirring until mixture is smooth, then add ¼ cup sugar. Cook and stir over medium heat until sauce has thickened, about 3 to 4 minutes. Remove from heat and cool 5 minutes. Gradually add beaten egg yolks, stirring vigorously. Stir and cook over low heat for 2 minutes. Remove from heat and cool 15 to 20 minutes. Stir in liqueur. Sprinkle salt on egg whites and beat to soft peaks. Gradually add 1 tablespoon sugar, continuously beating until egg whites are stiff but glossy.

Place cooked sauce in large bowl and mix in ⅓ of beaten egg whites gently but thoroughly. Fold in remaining beaten egg whites. Pour into prepared 1½-quart soufflé dish. Bake in 375° F. (moderate) oven for 30 minutes. Open oven door, quickly sprinkle top of soufflé with 2 teaspoons confectioners' sugar without moving the soufflé. Close door gently, and continue baking for 8 to 10 minutes to glaze the soufflé.

YIELD: 6 servings.

GINGER SOUFFLÉ

3 tablespoons butter or margarine
3 tablespoons flour
1 cup hot milk
⅓ cup sugar
½ cup minced crystalline candied ginger
1 tablespoon ginger-flavored brandy (optional)
4 egg yolks, well beaten
5 egg whites, beaten stiff but not dry

HAVE READY: 2-quart soufflé dish, lightly buttered, and dusted with sugar.

Melt butter or margarine in saucepan, blend in flour, and cook for 2 minutes. Remove from heat. Gradually add hot milk, stirring to a smooth mixture. Cook and stir over medium heat until sauce boils and thickens. Remove from heat. Stir in sugar, minced ginger, and ginger-flavored brandy, if desired. Let cool 10 to 15 minutes. Add beaten egg yolks slowly, stirring briskly. Fold in beaten egg whites gently but thoroughly. Pour into prepared 2-quart soufflé dish. Bake in 375° F. (moderate) oven for 40 to 50 minutes.

YIELD: 6 to 8 servings.

BRANDIED GINGER SOUFFLÉ

3 tablespoons butter or margarine
3 tablespoons flour
1 cup hot light cream or evaporated milk
6 egg yolks, well beaten
¼ cup ginger-flavored brandy
½ cup minced preserved ginger
6 egg whites, beaten stiff but not dry

HAVE READY: 2-quart soufflé dish, buttered, and dusted with sugar.

Melt butter or margarine in saucepan over low heat. Blend in flour and cook 2 minutes. Remove from heat. Gradually add hot cream or evaporated milk, stirring to smooth mixture. Cook and stir over medium heat until sauce thickens. Remove from heat and cool 10 minutes. Slowly add beaten egg yolks, stirring briskly, then stir in brandy and minced ginger. Fold in beaten egg whites gently but thoroughly. Pour into prepared 2-quart soufflé dish. Bake in 375° F. (moderate) oven for 25 to 35 minutes.

YIELD: 6 to 8 servings.

HOT GINGER SOUFFLÉ

¼ cup butter or margarine
¼ cup flour
¾ cup hot milk or light cream
¼ teaspoon salt
¼ teaspoon ground ginger
3 egg yolks
⅓ cup sugar
1½ teaspoons vanilla extract
⅓ cup chopped candied ginger
5 egg whites, beaten stiff but not dry

HAVE READY: 1½-quart soufflé dish, lightly buttered, and dusted with sugar.

Melt butter or margarine in saucepan over low heat. Blend in flour, and cook, stirring, for 3 or 4 minutes. Remove from heat. Gradually add hot milk or cream, salt, and ground ginger, stirring to smooth mixture. Cook and stir over medium heat until sauce thickens. Remove from heat and let cool 10 minutes. Beat egg yolks until light. Gradually add sugar and continue beating until thick. Stir in vanilla extract. Slowly add beaten egg yolks to cooled sauce, stirring briskly. Blend in chopped candied ginger. Fold sauce mixture into beaten egg whites gently but thoroughly. Pour into prepared 1½-quart soufflé dish. Bake in 350° F. (moderate) oven for 40 to 45 minutes.

YIELD: 5 to 6 servings.

LEMON VELVET SOUFFLÉ

¼ cup butter or margarine
¼ cup flour
⅛ teaspoon salt
1 cup hot milk or light cream
⅓ cup sugar
4 egg yolks, well beaten
½ teaspoon vanilla extract
2 teaspoons grated lemon peel
2 tablespoons lemon juice
5 egg whites
2 tablespoons sugar (additional)

HAVE READY: 1½-quart soufflé dish, buttered, and dusted with sugar and, if desired, ½ teaspoon grated lemon peel.

Melt butter or margarine in saucepan over low heat. Blend in flour and salt, and cook for 1 minute, but do not brown. Remove from heat. Gradually stir in hot milk or light cream to make smooth mixture, then add ⅓ cup sugar. Cook and stir over medium heat until sauce is smooth and thickened. Remove from heat and cool for 10 minutes. Slowly add beaten egg yolks, stirring briskly. Blend in vanilla extract, grated lemon peel, and lemon juice. Beat egg whites to soft peaks. Gradually add 2 tablespoons sugar, beating continuously until stiff glossy peaks form. Fold beaten egg whites into cooled sauce mixture gently but thoroughly. Pour into prepared 1½-quart soufflé dish. Bake in 375° F. (moderate) oven for 30 to 40 minutes.

YIELD: 4 to 5 servings.

LIQUEUR OR BRANDY EGG WHITE SOUFFLÉ

3 egg yolks
1 tablespoon sugar
3 tablespoons any fruit-flavored liqueur or brandy
8 egg whites
⅛ teaspoon salt
2 tablespoons sugar (additional)

HAVE READY: 1½-quart soufflé dish, ungreased.

Beat egg yolks with 1 tablespoon sugar until thick and light.

Gradually beat in fruit-flavored liqueur or brandy of choice. Beat egg whites and salt to soft peaks. Gradually add 2 tablespoons sugar, beating continuously until stiff glossy peaks form and sugar is dissolved. Fold beaten egg whites gently but thoroughly into egg-yolk mixture. Pour into 1½-quart soufflé dish. Bake in 400° F. (hot) oven for 15 to 20 minutes.

YIELD: 6 servings.

LIQUEUR OR BRANDY SOUFFLÉ

⅓ cup butter or margarine
⅔ cup flour
½ teaspoon salt
1½ cups hot milk or light cream
5 egg yolks, well beaten
7 egg whites
1 cup sugar
1 tablespoon lemon juice
1 teaspoon grated lemon peel
⅓ cup fruit-flavored liqueur
or
¼ cup fruit-flavored brandy

HAVE READY: 2- or 2½-quart soufflé dish, buttered, and dusted with sugar or fine dry macaroon crumbs.

Melt butter or margarine in saucepan over low heat. Blend in flour and salt. Cook and stir for 3 or 4 minutes. Remove from heat. Slowly stir in hot milk or cream to make smooth mixture. Cook and stir over medium heat until sauce is thick and smooth. Remove from heat. Gradually add hot sauce to beaten egg yolks, beating vigorously. Let mixture cool 15 minutes. Beat egg whites to soft peaks. Gradually add sugar, beating continuously until stiff glossy peaks form and sugar is dissolved. Beat in lemon juice a little at a time. Add grated lemon peel and liqueur or brandy to cool sauce, mixing thoroughly. Fold sauce into beaten egg white gently but thoroughly.

Pour into prepared 2- or 2½-quart soufflé dish set in shallow pan containing 1 inch hot water. Bake in 350° F. (moderate) oven for 60 to 70 minutes.

YIELD: 8 servings.

FRENCH-STYLE LIQUEUR SOUFFLÉ

- *4 egg yolks, beaten thick and light*
- *¼ cup confectioners' sugar*
- *¼ cup hot milk*
- *½ teaspoon vanilla extract*
- *¼ cup chopped mixed glacé fruits*
- *1 to 2 tablespoons kirsch brandy or fruit-flavored liqueur*
- *½ cup heavy cream, whipped*
- *5 egg whites*
- *½ cup granulated sugar*

HAVE READY: 1½-quart soufflé dish, lightly buttered, and dusted with sugar.

Blend beaten egg yolks and confectioners' sugar together in saucepan. Gradually stir in hot milk. Cook and stir over low heat until sauce thickens. Remove from heat, add vanilla extract, and let cool 10 minutes. Combine chopped glacé fruits and kirsch or liqueur, then add to cooled sauce. Carefully stir in whipped cream. Beat egg whites to soft peaks. Gradually add granulated sugar, beating continuously until stiff glossy peaks form. Fold creamy sauce mixture into beaten egg whites gently but thoroughly. Pour into prepared 1½-quart soufflé dish. Bake in 400° F. (hot) oven for 30 to 40 minutes.

YIELD: 4 to 6 servings.

CLASSIC LIQUEUR SOUFFLÉ

- *6 to 8 ladyfingers*
- *1½ to 2 tablespoons any fruit-flavored liqueur*
- *2 tablespoons butter or margarine*
- *1 tablespoon flour*
- *½ cup hot milk or light cream*
- *½ teaspoon vanilla extract*
- *5 egg yolks*
- *¼ cup sugar*
- *¼ cup liqueur (same as used to moisten lady fingers)*
- *6 egg whites*
- *2 tablespoons sugar (additional)*

HAVE READY: 1½-quart soufflé dish, buttered, and dusted with sugar.

Moisten ladyfingers with 1½ to 2 tablespoons of liqueur of choice, sprinkled on. Set aside. Melt butter or margarine in small saucepan over low heat, and blend in flour. Cook and stir for 1 minute. Remove from heat and slowly add hot milk or cream to make a smooth mixture. Cook and stir over medium heat until sauce boils and thickens slightly, about 4 minutes. Remove from heat and let cool slightly. Add vanilla extract. Beat egg yolks and ¼ cup sugar together until light and thick. Slowly add to warm sauce, stirring briskly. Blend in ¼ cup liqueur. Beat egg whites to soft peaks. Gradually add 2 tablespoons sugar, beating continuously until stiff glossy peaks form. Fold beaten egg whites into sauce gently but thoroughly.

Pour about half of soufflé mixture into prepared 1½-quart soufflé dish. Cover with moistened ladyfingers arranged in a layer. Top with remaining soufflé mixture. Bake in 375° F. (moderate) oven 20 to 25 minutes. If desired, quickly sprinkle top of soufflé with a little confectioners' sugar two minutes before removing soufflé from oven, to form a delicate glaze.

YIELD: 6 servings.

MACAROON LIQUEUR SOUFFLÉ

4 almond macaroons, coarsely broken
1 to 1½ tablespoons coffee or orange-flavored liqueur
¼ cup butter or margarine
¼ cup flour
⅛ teaspoon salt
1 cup hot milk or light cream
⅓ cup sugar
1 teaspoon vanilla extract
¼ teaspoon almond extract
4 egg yolks, well beaten
5 egg whites
2 tablespoons sugar (additional)

HAVE READY: 1½-quart soufflé dish, buttered, and dusted with sugar or fine dry macaroon crumbs.

Spread coarsely broken macaroons on bottom of prepared 1½-quart soufflé dish, and sprinkle with liqueur of choice.

Melt butter or margarine in saucepan over low heat. Blend

in flour and salt, and cook for 1 minute, but do not brown. Remove from heat. Gradually stir in hot milk or cream to make smooth mixture, then add ⅓ cup sugar. Cook and stir over medium heat until sauce is smooth and thickened. Remove from heat, add vanilla and almond extracts and let cool 10 minutes. Slowly add beaten egg yolks, stirring briskly. Let cool 10 to 15 more minutes. Beat egg whites to soft peaks. Gradually add 2 tablespoons sugar, beating continuously until stiff glossy peaks form. Fold beaten egg whites into cooled sauce mixture gently but thoroughly. Pour on top of liqueur-moistened macaroon crumbs in soufflé dish. Bake in 375° F. (moderate) oven for 30 to 40 minutes.

YIELD: 5 to 6 servings.

MARRON LIQUEUR SOUFFLÉ

¼ cup butter or margarine
¼ cup flour
⅛ teaspoon salt
1 cup hot milk or light cream
⅓ cup sugar
1 teaspoon vanilla extract
1 to 1½ tablespoons chocolate or coffee-flavored liqueur
4 egg yolks, well beaten
1 cup puréed drained marrons preserved in vanilla syrup
5 egg whites
2 tablespoons sugar (additional)

HAVE READY: 1½-quart soufflé dish, buttered, and dusted with sugar.

Melt butter or margarine in saucepan over low heat. Blend in flour and salt, and cook for 1 minute, but do not brown. Remove from heat. Gradually add hot milk or cream, stirring to smooth mixture. Add ⅓ cup sugar. Cook and stir over medium heat until sauce is smooth and thick. Remove from heat. Stir in vanilla extract and liqueur of choice, then cool for 10 minutes. Slowly add beaten egg yolks, stirring briskly. Blend in puréed preserved marrons. Beat egg whites to soft peaks. Gradually add 2 tablespoons sugar, beating continuously until stiff glossy peaks form. Fold beaten egg whites into cooled sauce mixture gently but thoroughly. Pour into prepared 1½-quart soufflé dish. Bake in 375° F. (moderate) oven for 30 to 40 minutes. YIELD: 4 to 5 servings.

BAKED MARMALADE SOUFFLÉ

3 tablespoons butter or margarine
3 tablespoons flour
¼ teaspoon salt
¾ cup hot milk
2 tablespoons sugar
1 tablespoon grated lemon peel
2 tablespoons grated orange peel
3 egg yolks, well beaten
¼ cup orange marmalade, sweet or bitter, to taste
5 egg whites
1 tablespoon sugar (additional)

HAVE READY: 1½-quart soufflé dish, buttered, and dusted with sugar or finely ground nuts.

Melt butter or margarine in saucepan over low heat. Blend in flour and salt, and cook for 1 minute, but do not brown. Remove from heat. Gradually add hot milk, then sugar, stirring to smooth mixture. Cook and stir over medium heat until sauce is thick and smooth. Remove from heat, add grated lemon and orange peel, and let cool 10 minutes. Slowly add beaten egg yolks, stirring briskly. Blend in orange marmalade. Beat egg whites to soft peaks. Gradually add 1 tablespoon sugar, beating continuously until stiff glossy peaks form. Fold beaten egg whites into cooled sauce mixture. Pour into prepared 1½-quart soufflé dish. Bake in 375° F. (moderate) oven for 35 to 40 minutes. YIELD: 4 to 5 servings.

OLD-FASHIONED MARMALADE SOUFFLÉ

4 egg whites
⅛ teaspoon salt
¼ teaspoon cream of tartar
2 tablespoons sugar
½ cup orange marmalade
1 teaspoon grated orange or lemon peel (optional)

HAVE READY: 2-quart double boiler, top section buttered including inside of cover.

Beat egg whites and salt until foamy, sprinkle on cream of tartar, and beat to soft peaks. Gradually add sugar, beating continuously until stiff glossy peaks form and sugar is dissolved. Fold in marmalade, one tablespoonful at a time, gently but thoroughly. Add grated orange or lemon peel, if desired. Pour into prepared 2-quart double boiler and set cover in place. Cook over hot, not boiling, water for 50 minutes. Do not let water touch top pan of double boiler. If not served at once, leave cover in place, turn heat as low as possible, and hold for 20 to 40 minutes. This is one type of soufflé that very successfully waits for the guests. Turn out on warm plate or platter to serve.

YIELD: 4 to 5 servings.

NOTE: This soufflé may be made in a covered chafing dish, and served directly from the chafing dish pan.

MOCHA SOUFFLÉ

2 squares (2 ounces) unsweetened chocolate, broken up
¼ cup butter or margarine
3 tablespoons flour
⅓ cup sugar
1 teaspoon instant coffee
1 cup hot milk
1 teaspoon vanilla extract
3 egg yolks, well beaten
4 egg whites
¼ teaspoon salt
⅓ cup sugar

HAVE READY: 1½-quart soufflé dish, ungreased, set in shallow pan containing 1 inch hot water and heated in 350° F. (moderate) oven.

Melt chocolate in custard cup over hot water. Melt butter or margarine in saucepan over low heat. Blend in flour, and cook for 2 to 3 minutes. Remove from heat. Add ⅓ cup sugar and instant coffee, mixing well, then slowly add hot milk, stirring to smooth mixture. Cook and stir over medium heat until sauce thickens and comes to a boil. Remove from heat, blend in melted chocolate and vanilla extract, and let cool 10 minutes. Gradually add beaten egg yolks, stirring briskly. Combine egg whites and salt and beat to soft peaks. Gradually add ⅓ cup sugar beating continuously until stiff glossy peaks form. Fold into chocolate mixture gently but thoroughly. Pour into warmed 1½-quart soufflé dish set in shallow pan containing 1 inch hot water. Bake in 350° F. (moderate) oven for 60 to 70 minutes.

YIELD: 6 servings.

NUT DESSERT SOUFFLÉ

¼ cup butter or margarine
¼ cup flour
½ teaspoon salt
1 cup hot milk
¼ teaspoon grated lemon peel
3 egg yolks, well beaten
½ cup sugar
½ cup finely chopped pecans or filberts
1 teaspoon vanilla extract
4 egg whites, beaten stiff but not dry

HAVE READY: 1-quart soufflé dish, well buttered, and dusted with sugar.

Melt butter or margarine in saucepan over low heat. Blend in flour and salt, and cook for 3 minutes, stirring occasionally. Remove from heat and gradually stir in hot milk to make a smooth mixture. Cook and stir over medium heat until sauce thickens. Stir in grated lemon peel, and set aside to cool slightly. In large bowl, combine beaten egg yolks, sugar, chopped nuts, and vanilla extract. Stir to blend, then gradually add the cooked sauce, stirring vigorously. Gently but thoroughly fold in beaten egg whites. Pour into prepared 1-quart soufflé dish set in shallow pan containing 1 inch hot water. Bake in 350° F. (moderate) oven for 35 to 40 minutes.

YIELD: 4 servings.

TOASTED NUT SOUFFLÉ

3 tablespoons cornstarch
½ cup sugar
⅛ teaspoon salt
¾ cup cold milk
3 egg yolks, well beaten
½ cup finely chopped toasted almonds, filberts, pecans, or California walnuts
1 teaspoon vanilla extract
1 tablespoon coffee-flavored liqueur (optional)
4 egg whites, beaten stiff but not dry

HAVE READY: 1½-quart soufflé dish, buttered, and dusted with sugar or very finely ground nuts.

Combine cornstarch, sugar, and salt in saucepan. Gradually add cold milk, stirring to smooth mixture. Cook and stir over medium heat until sauce comes to a boil. Let boil 1 or 2 minutes. Remove from heat and let cool 10 minutes. Slowly add beaten egg yolks, stirring briskly. Add chopped almonds, filberts, pecans, or walnuts, vanilla extract, and coffee liqueur, if desired. Fold into beaten egg whites gently but thoroughly. Pour into prepared 1½-quart soufflé dish. Bake in 325° F. (slow) oven for 45 to 55 minutes.

YIELD: 6 servings.

DAINTY ORANGE TAPIOCA SOUFFLÉ

⅓ cup quick-cooking tapioca
¼ teaspoon salt
⅔ cup sugar
1 cup water
2 tablespoons butter or margarine
2 teaspoons grated orange peel
1 cup strained orange juice
1 teaspoon lemon juice
3 egg yolks, well beaten
4 egg whites, beaten stiff but not dry

HAVE READY: 2-quart soufflé dish, ungreased.

Combine tapioca, salt, and sugar in saucepan. Add water,

and let stand 5 minutes. Cook and stir over medium heat until mixture comes to a full boil. Remove from heat. Add butter or margarine, stirring until melted, then add grated orange peel, strained orange juice, and lemon juice. Gradually stir into beaten egg yolks, blending well. Fold in beaten egg whites gently but thoroughly. Pour into 2-quart soufflé dish set in shallow pan containing 1 inch hot water. Bake in 350° F. (moderate) oven for 45 to 55 minutes.

YIELD: 6 servings.

PIQUANT ORANGE SOUFFLÉ

½ cup butter or margarine
½ cup flour
1½ cups hot milk
½ teaspoon salt
2 teaspoons grated orange peel
6 egg yolks
⅔ cup sugar
1 tablespoon Curaçao or Cointreau liqueur
8 egg whites, beaten stiff but not dry
peeled sections of 2 or 3 oranges

HAVE READY: 2-quart soufflé dish, buttered, and dusted with sugar or flour.

Melt butter or margarine in saucepan over low heat. Blend in flour, and cook, stirring, for 3 or 4 minutes. Remove from heat. Gradually add hot milk, salt, and orange peel, stirring to smooth mixture. Cook and stir over medium heat until sauce thickens. Remove from heat. Beat egg yolks and sugar together until very thick. Beat in warm sauce a little at a time. Return mixture to saucepan and cook and stir over low heat for 4 minutes. Remove from heat, add liqueur, and let cool 15 to 20 minutes. Fold in beaten egg whites gently but thoroughly. Arrange orange sections on bottom of prepared 2-quart soufflé dish. Pour soufflé mixture on top carefully. Bake in 375° F. (moderate) oven for 55 to 60 minutes.

YIELD: 8 servings.

CANNED PEAR SOUFFLÉ

6 tablespoons butter
6 tablespoons flour
1½ cups milk
¼ cup pear syrup (from canned pears)
6 egg yolks, slightly beaten
¾ cup chopped drained canned Bartlett pears
1 tablespoon pear or ginger brandy (optional)
6 egg whites
¼ cup sugar

HAVE READY: 2-quart soufflé dish, well buttered, and dusted with sugar.

Melt butter in saucepan over low heat. Blend in flour to smooth mixture. Cook and stir for 1 minute. Remove from heat. Slowly stir in milk and pear syrup. Cook and stir over medium heat until sauce comes to a boil and thickens. Remove from heat and let cool 10 minutes. Gradually add beaten egg yolks, stirring briskly. Gently fold in chopped pears, and add pear or ginger brandy, if desired. Beat egg whites and sugar to stiff glossy peaks; then fold into sauce gently but thoroughly. Pour into prepared 2-quart soufflé dish set in shallow pan containing 1 inch hot water. Bake in 375° F. (moderate) oven for 50 to 60 minutes.

YIELD: 6 to 8 servings.

PEACH ALMOND DOUBLE BOILER SOUFFLÉ

2 tablespoons butter or margarine
3 tablespoons flour
⅛ teaspoon salt
⅔ cup hot milk
1 jar puréed peaches for infants
½ teaspoon vanilla extract
¼ teaspoon almond extract
3 egg yolks, well beaten
3 egg whites
¼ cup sugar

HAVE READY: 1½- or 2-quart double boiler, top section well buttered including inside of cover.

Melt butter or margarine in saucepan over low heat. Blend

in flour and salt and cook for 1 or 2 minutes. Remove from heat. Gradually add hot milk, stirring to smooth mixture. Cook and stir over medium heat until sauce thickens. Remove from heat. Stir in puréed peaches, vanilla and almond extracts, and let cool 10 minutes. Slowly add beaten egg yolks, stirring briskly. Beat egg whites to soft peaks. Gradually add sugar, beating continuously to stiff glossy peaks. Fold beaten egg whites into peach sauce gently but thoroughly. Pour into prepared 1½- or 2-quart double boiler top. Cover. Cook over simmering (not boiling) water for 1 hour. If not served at once, turn off heat and let stand for 15 to 30 more minutes. Do not remove cover until ready to serve, then turn out onto warm plate or platter.

YIELD: 4 to 6 servings.

PISTACHIO SOUFFLÉ

3 tablespoons cornstarch
½ cup sugar
few grains salt
¾ cup cold milk
3 egg yolks, well beaten
½ cup finely chopped pistachio nuts
1 teaspoon vanilla extract
½ teaspoon almond extract
3 or 4 drops green liquid vegetable coloring
4 egg whites, beaten stiff but not dry

HAVE READY: 1½-quart soufflé dish, buttered, and dusted with sugar or fine dry macaroon crumbs.

Combine cornstarch, sugar, and salt in saucepan. Gradually add cold milk, stirring to smooth mixture. Cook and stir over medium heat until sauce comes to a boil. Let boil 1 or 2 minutes. Remove from heat and let cool 10 minutes. Slowly add beaten egg yolks, stirring briskly. Add chopped nuts, flavoring extracts, and green vegetable coloring. Fold into beaten egg whites gently but thoroughly. Pour into prepared 1½-quart soufflé dish. Bake in 325° F. (slow) oven for 45 to 55 minutes.

YIELD: 6 servings.

PLUM JAM SOUFFLÉ

3 tablespoons cornstarch
1/3 to 1/2 cup sugar, to taste
1/8 teaspoon salt
3/4 cup cold milk
4 egg yolks, well beaten
1/2 cup plum jam
1 to 2 tablespoons plum brandy or orange juice
5 egg whites, beaten stiff but not dry

HAVE READY: 1½-quart soufflé dish, buttered, and dusted with sugar.

Combine cornstarch, sugar, and salt in saucepan, blending well. Gradually add cold milk, stirring to smooth mixture. Cook and stir over medium heat until sauce comes to a boil. Let boil 1 or 2 minutes, then remove from heat and let cool 10 minutes. Slowly add beaten egg yolks, stirring briskly. Blend together plum jam and plum brandy or orange juice. Stir into sauce, mixing well. Fold sauce into beaten egg whites gently but thoroughly. Pour into prepared 1½-quart soufflé dish. Bake in 325° F. (slow) oven for 45 to 55 minutes.

YIELD: 5 to 6 servings.

NOTE: For variety, use instead of plum jam and plum brandy, similar amounts of apricot jam and apricot brandy or liqueur, peach jam and peach brandy, strawberry jam and strawberry brandy.

PRUNE EGG WHITE SOUFFLÉ

4 egg whites
few grains salt
1/8 teaspoon cream of tartar
1/4 cup sugar
1 cup puréed cooked pitted dried prunes
1/8 teaspoon almond extract
1 teaspoon grated orange or lemon peel

HAVE READY: 1½-quart soufflé dish or deep casserole, buttered, and dusted with sugar.

Beat egg whites and salt until frothy; add cream of tartar and beat to soft peaks. Gradually add sugar, beating constantly until stiff glossy peaks are formed. Blend together puréed prunes, almond extract, and grated orange or lemon peel. Fold into beaten egg whites gently but thoroughly. Pour into prepared 1½-quart soufflé dish or deep casserole set in shallow pan containing 1 or 2 inches of hot water. Bake in 350° F. (moderate) oven for 40 to 45 minutes. YIELD: 6 servings.

PRUNE AND WALNUT SOUFFLÉ

3 tablespoons cornstarch
½ cup sugar
⅛ teaspoon salt
¾ cup cold milk
4 egg yolks, well beaten
½ cup puréed cooked pitted dried prunes
1 teaspoon grated orange or lemon peel
⅓ cup finely chopped California walnuts
5 egg whites, beaten stiff but not dry

HAVE READY: 1½-quart soufflé dish, buttered, and dusted with sugar or very finely ground walnuts.

Combine cornstarch, sugar, and salt in saucepan. Gradually add cold milk, stirring to smooth mixture. Cook and stir over medium heat until sauce comes to a boil. Let boil 1 or 2 minutes. Remove from heat and let cool 10 minutes. Slowly add beaten egg yolks, stirring briskly. Add puréed prunes, grated orange or lemon peel, and chopped walnuts. Fold into beaten egg whites gently but thoroughly. Pour into prepared 1½-quart soufflé dish. Bake in 325° F. (slow) oven for 45 to 55 minutes. YIELD: 6 servings.

VANILLA CREAM SOUFFLÉ

½ cup flour
½ cup sugar
1½ cups cold light cream
1½ teaspoons vanilla extract
6 egg yolks, well beaten
6 egg whites, beaten stiff but not dry

HAVE READY: 1½-quart soufflé dish, buttered, and dusted with sugar or finely ground nuts.

Blend together flour and sugar in top of double boiler, mixing well. Gradually stir in cold light cream to make a smooth mixture. Cook over boiling water, stirring frequently, until sauce thickens. Remove from heat, add vanilla extract, and let cool about 30 minutes, covered to keep skin from forming. Add beaten egg yolks, stirring briskly. Fold in beaten egg whites gently but thoroughly. Pour into prepared 1½-quart soufflé dish. Bake in 325° F. (slow) oven for 35 to 45 minutes.

YIELD: 6 servings.

VANILLA DOUBLE BOILER SOUFFLÉ

2 tablespoons butter or margarine
2 tablespoons flour
⅛ teaspoon salt
⅔ cup hot milk
1½ teaspoons vanilla extract
⅛ teaspoon almond extract
2 egg yolks, well beaten
3 egg whites
⅓ cup sugar

HAVE READY: 1½- or 2-quart double boiler, top section buttered including buttering inside of cover.

Melt butter or margarine in saucepan over low heat. Blend in flour and salt and cook for 1 minute. Remove from heat and gradually stir in hot milk to make smooth mixture. Cook and stir over medium heat until sauce thickens. Remove from heat, cool 5 or 10 minutes, and add vanilla and almond extracts. Gradually add beaten egg yolks, stirring briskly. Beat egg whites to soft peaks. Gradually add sugar, beating continuously until stiff glossy peaks form. Fold beaten egg whites into sauce gently but thoroughly. Pour into prepared 1½- or 2-quart double boiler top. Cover. Cook over simmering (not boiling) water for 1 hour. If not served at once, turn off heat and let stand for 15 to 30 more minutes. Do not remove cover until ready to serve; then turn out on warm plate or platter.

YIELD: 4 to 6 servings.

VANILLA CUSTARD SOUFFLÉ

3 tablespoons butter or margarine
3 tablespoons flour
1½ cups hot milk
¼ teaspoon salt
6 egg yolks, well beaten
⅓ cup sugar
1½ teaspoons vanilla extract
6 egg whites, beaten stiff but not dry

HAVE READY: 1½-quart soufflé dish, buttered, and dusted with sugar or fine dry macaroon crumbs.

Cream butter or margarine and flour together in saucepan. Slowly add hot milk and salt, stirring constantly to make smooth mixture. Cook and stir over low heat until sauce comes just to a boil and thickens slightly. Remove from heat and cool for 5 minutes. Combine beaten egg yolks, sugar, and vanilla extract. Gradually add egg yolk mixture to sauce, stirring briskly. Fold in beaten egg whites gently but thoroughly. Pour into prepared 1½-quart soufflé dish set in shallow pan containing 1 inch hot water. Bake in 350° F. (moderate) oven for 50 to 60 minutes.

YIELD: 6 servings.

DELICATE VANILLA SOUFFLÉ

2 teaspoons cornstarch
1 tablespoon water
3 tablespoons butter or margarine
3 tablespoons flour
¾ cup hot milk or light cream
4 egg yolks
½ cup sugar
1½ teaspoons vanilla extract
5 egg whites
⅛ teaspoon salt

HAVE READY: 1½-quart soufflé dish, buttered, and dusted with sugar.

Combine cornstarch and water to make smooth paste, and set aside. Melt butter or margarine in saucepan over low heat.

Blend in flour, and let cook for 2 minutes. Remove from heat. Gradually add hot milk or cream, stirring it to a smooth mixture. Cook and stir over medium heat until sauce comes to a boil. Stir in cornstarch paste and let boil for 1 minute. Remove from heat and let cool 10 minutes. Beat egg yolks with ½ cup sugar until thick and light. Slowly add to warm sauce, stirring vigorously. Add vanilla extract. Beat egg whites and salt to stiff glossy peaks. Add half of beaten egg whites to sauce, beating them in thoroughly. Fold in remaining beaten egg white gently but thoroughly. Pour into prepared 1½-quart soufflé dish. Bake in 350° F. (moderate) oven for 35 to 40 minutes.

YIELD: 6 servings.

RICE AND FRUIT SOUFFLÉ

2 tablespoons cornstarch
½ cup sugar
½ teaspoon salt
1 cup cold milk or light cream
5 egg yolks, beaten thick and light
½ teaspoon vanilla extract
1 teaspoon grated orange or lemon peel
½ cup cooked rice
½ cup finely diced peeled apples, peaches, or apricots
6 egg whites, beaten stiff but not dry

HAVE READY: 2-quart soufflé dish, buttered, and dusted with sugar.

Combine cornstarch, sugar, and salt in saucepan, blending well. Gradually add cold milk or light cream, stirring to smooth mixture. Cook and stir over medium heat until sauce comes to a boil. Let boil 1 or 2 minutes, then remove from heat. Cool for 10 minutes. Slowly add beaten egg yolks, stirring briskly. Blend in vanilla extract, grated orange or lemon peel, cooked rice, and finely diced fruit of choice. Fold in beaten egg whites gently but thoroughly. Pour into prepared 2-quart soufflé dish. Bake in 350° F. (moderate) oven for 60 to 70 minutes.

YIELD: 6 servings.

CLASSIC SOUFFLÉ ROTHSCHILD

¼ pound minced mixed glacé fruits
½ cup brandy
2 tablespoons butter or margarine
2 tablespoons flour
⅔ cup hot milk
¼ teaspoon salt
4 egg yolks
½ cup sugar
1 teaspoon vanilla extract
5 egg whites, beaten stiff but not dry

HAVE READY: 1½-quart soufflé dish, ungreased.

Stir minced glacé fruits and brandy together in a small bowl and set aside. Melt butter or margarine in saucepan over low heat. Blend in flour, and cook 1 minute. Remove from heat. Slowly add hot milk, then salt, stirring to smooth mixture. Cook and stir over medium heat until sauce thickens. Remove from heat and cool 10 minutes. Beat egg yolks until light, gradually add sugar, and continue beating until thick. Slowly add to cooled sauce, stirring briskly, then stir in vanilla extract. Fold in egg whites gently but thoroughly. Pour half of soufflé mixture into 1½-quart soufflé dish. Lightly drain glacé fruit by removing it from bowl with a slotted spoon, and spread it in a layer on top of the soufflé in the dish. Cover with remaining soufflé mixture. Bake in 375° F. (moderate) oven for 25 to 30 minutes. The soft center of the baked soufflé serves as a sauce for served portions.

YIELD: 5 to 6 servings.

TANGERINE LIQUEUR SOUFFLÉ

3 tablespoons butter or margarine
3 tablespoons flour
¾ cup hot milk
¼ cup sugar
4 egg yolks, well beaten
3 tablespoons crème de mandarine liqueur
5 egg whites, beaten stiff but not dry
1 tablespoon chopped toasted filberts (optional)

HAVE READY: 1½-quart soufflé dish, buttered, and dusted with finely ground toasted filberts.

Melt butter or margarine in saucepan over low heat. Blend in flour and cook 2 minutes. Remove from heat. Gradually stir in hot milk to make smooth mixture, then add sugar. Cook and stir over medium heat until sauce thickens. Remove from heat and cool 10 minutes. Gradually add beaten egg yolks, stirring briskly, then stir in liqueur. Fold in beaten egg whites gently but thoroughly. Pour into prepared 1½-quart soufflé dish. Top with 1 tablespoon chopped toasted filberts, if desired. Bake in 375° F. (moderate) oven for 25 to 35 minutes.

YIELD: 6 servings.

STRAWBERRY SOUFFLÉ

¼ cup butter or margarine
¼ cup flour
⅛ teaspoon salt
1 cup hot milk or light cream
⅓ cup sugar
1 to 1½ tablespoons kirsch brandy
4 egg yolks, well beaten
5 egg whites
2 tablespoons sugar (additional)
1 cup sweetened sliced fresh or frozen strawberries, well drained

HAVE READY: 1½-quart soufflé dish, buttered, and dusted with sugar.

Melt butter or margarine in saucepan over low heat. Blend in flour and salt and cook for 2 minutes, but do not brown. Remove from heat. Gradually stir in hot milk or cream to make smooth mixture, then add ⅓ cup sugar. Cook and stir over medium heat until sauce is smooth and thickened. Remove from heat, add brandy, and let cool for 10 minutes. Slowly add beaten egg yolks, stirring briskly. Let cool 10 to 15 more minutes. Beat egg whites to soft peaks. Gradually add 2 tablespoons sugar, beating continuously until stiff glossy peaks form. Fold beaten egg whites into cooled sauce mixture. Spoon sweetened sliced strawberries into prepared 1½-quart soufflé dish.

Pour soufflé mixture on top of berries. Bake in 375° F. (moderate) oven for 30 to 40 minutes.

YIELD: 5 to 6 servings.

NOTE: If desired, 1 cup sweetened fresh or frozen raspberries, well drained, can be used instead of strawberries.

DAINTY SPICED SOUFFLÉ

¼ cup butter or margarine
¼ cup flour
¼ teaspoon salt
1 cup hot milk
4 egg yolks
½ cup sugar
½ teaspoon ground cardamom, nutmeg, mace, or cinnamon
1 teaspoon grated lemon peel
1 teaspoon vanilla extract
5 egg whites, beaten stiff but not dry

HAVE READY: 1½-quart soufflé dish, buttered, and dusted with sugar.

Melt butter or margarine in saucepan over low heat. Blend in flour and salt, and cook, stirring, for 3 minutes, but do not brown. Remove from heat. Gradually add hot milk, stirring to smooth mixture. Cook and stir over medium heat until sauce boils and thickens. Remove from heat and cool 10 minutes. Beat egg yolks until thick and light. Gradually beat in sugar, ground spice of choice, grated lemon peel, and vanilla extract. Add yolk mixture slowly to sauce, stirring briskly. Fold in beaten egg whites gently but thoroughly. Pour into prepared 1½-quart soufflé dish set in shallow pan containing 1 inch hot water. Bake in 350° F. (moderate) oven for 1 hour.

YIELD: 6 servings.

5

COLD SOUFFLÉS

Though these are not true soufflés, and are more American than Continental in character, they take this name from the shape of the finished mold which closely resembles a baked soufflé. Their great advantage to the hostess is that they not only can, but must, be made well ahead of mealtime. They're perfect, too, for buffet service.

COLD AVOCADO CREAM SOUFFLÉ

1 envelope unflavored gelatine
¼ cup cold water
3 egg yolks, lightly beaten
¼ cup sugar
¼ cup fresh lime or lemon juice
1 teaspoon grated lime or lemon peel
½ cup canned crushed pineapple, drained
2 large ripe avocados, peeled, seeded, and mashed smoothly
3 egg whites
¼ cup sugar
½ cup heavy cream, whipped

HAVE READY: 1-quart soufflé dish with collar rising 1½ to 2 inches above rim, lightly oiled, including collar.

Sprinkle gelatine on cold water and set aside to soften. Blend together beaten egg yolks, ¼ cup sugar, lime or lemon juice, and grated lime or lemon peel in saucepan or top of double boiler. Cook, stirring constantly, over hot water until sauce is slightly thickened and smooth like soft custard. Remove from heat and stir in softened gelatine until it dissolves. Add crushed pineapple and mashed avocado, blending well. Refrigerate, stirring occasionally, until mixture mounds up slightly.

Beat egg whites in large bowl to soft peaks. Gradually add ¼ cup sugar, beating continuously until stiff glossy peaks form and sugar is dissolved. Pile whipped cream on beaten egg whites. Fold in cold avocado mixture gently but thoroughly. Pour into collared 1-quart soufflé dish. Chill 3 to 4 hours until firm. Carefully remove collar before serving.

YIELD: 6 servings.

COLD BRANDIED CHOCOLATE SOUFFLÉ

1 envelope unflavored gelatine
½ cup light brown sugar, firmly packed
¼ cup water
1 cup (6-ounce package) semi-sweet chocolate pieces
4 egg yolks, slightly beaten
¼ cup brandy
4 egg whites
¼ teaspoon salt
¼ cup light brown sugar, firmly packed
1 cup heavy cream, whipped

HAVE READY: 1-quart soufflé dish with collar rising 2 inches above rim, or 6 half-pint individual soufflé dishes with collars rising 1 inch above rims, lightly oiled, including collars.

Combine first 4 ingredients in saucepan. Cook and stir over very low heat until gelatine and sugar dissolve and chocolate pieces melt. Remove from heat. Gradually add egg yolks, beating chocolate mixture briskly with wire whisk or spoon. Stir in brandy. Beat egg whites and salt to soft peaks. Gradually add ¼ cup light brown sugar, continuously beating until stiff and glossy peaks form. Fold in chocolate mixture gently but thoroughly. Fold in whipped cream until no streaks remain. Pour or spoon into prepared 1-quart soufflé dish or 6 individual soufflé dishes. Refrigerate to chill until firm, about 3 hours. Loosen and peel off collar before serving.

YIELD: 6 servings.

NOTE: If desired, ¼ cup light or dark rum may be substituted for the brandy.

COLD CHOCOLATE SOUFFLÉ

1 envelope unflavored gelatine
¼ cup water
¾ cup milk
¼ cup sugar
⅛ teaspoon salt
2 egg yolks
1 cup (6-ounce package) semi-sweet chocolate pieces
½ teaspoon vanilla extract
2 egg whites
¼ cup sugar
1 cup heavy cream, whipped

HAVE READY: 1-quart soufflé dish with collar rising 2 inches above rim, lightly oiled, including inside of collar.

Sprinkle gelatine on water in medium saucepan and let stand 4 or 5 minutes to soften. Add milk, ¼ cup sugar, salt, egg yolks, and chocolate pieces. Mix well. Cook and stir over low heat until gelatine dissolves and chocolate melts, about 6 minutes. Remove from heat. Beat with rotary beater or wire whisk until chocolate is thoroughly blended in. Add vanilla extract. Chill, stirring occasionally, until mixture mounds up slightly when dropped from spoon (about 20 minutes in refrigerator).

Beat egg whites to soft peaks. Gradually add ¼ cup sugar, beating continuously until stiff glossy peaks form. Fold into chocolate mixture gently but thoroughly; then fold in whipped cream so that no streaks remain. Pour into prepared 1-quart soufflé dish. Refrigerate to chill until firm for about 3 hours. Loosen and peel away collar before serving.

YIELD: 4 to 5 servings.

NOTE: In the interest of calorie saving, 1 envelope whipped topping mix (prepared according to package directions) can be substituted for the whipped cream.

COLD CHOCOLATE BAVARIAN SOUFFLÉ

2 envelopes unflavored gelatine
½ cup cold water
½ cup sugar
2 tablespoons flour
½ cup dark cocoa
½ teaspoon salt
4 eggs, slightly beaten
2 cups cold milk
1 teaspoon vanilla extract
⅛ teaspoon almond extract
5 egg whites, beaten stiff but not dry
1 cup heavy cream, whipped

HAVE READY: 1½-quart soufflé dish with collar rising 3 inches above rim, lightly oiled, including collar.

Sprinkle gelatine on ½ cup cold water and set aside to soften. Blend together sugar, flour, cocoa, and salt in top of double boiler. Mix in beaten egg yolks thoroughly, then gradually stir in milk to make a smooth mixture. Cook and stir over hot water until mixture clings to spoon like soft custard. Remove from heat. Stir in softened gelatine until it dissolves. Add vanilla and almond extracts. Refrigerate sauce, and chill, stirring occasionally, until it mounds up. Fold in beaten egg whites gently but thoroughly, then fold in whipped cream. Pour into collared 1½-quart soufflé dish. Chill 3 to 4 hours until firm. Carefully remove collar before serving.

YIELD: 8 servings.

COLD CHOCOLATE CREAM SOUFFLÉ

1 envelope unflavored gelatine
¼ cup cold water
2 squares (2 ounces) unsweetened chocolate
½ cup confectioners' sugar
1 cup hot milk
¾ cup granulated sugar
⅛ teaspoon salt
2 teaspoons noisette or crème de cacao liqueur
2 cups heavy cream, whipped

HAVE READY: 1½-quart soufflé dish with collar rising 2 to 3 inches above rim, lightly oiled, including collar.

Sprinkle gelatine on cold water and set aside to soften. Melt chocolate in small saucepan over hot water. Blend in confectioners' sugar, then stir in hot milk to make smooth mixture. Cook and stir over low heat until thoroughly hot, but do not allow to boil. Remove from heat. Stir in softened gelatine and granulated sugar until both are dissolved. Add salt and liqueur. Refrigerate and chill, stirring occasionally, until mixture is as thick as raw egg white. Beat with electric or rotary beater until light and fluffy. Fold in whipped cream gently but thoroughly. Pour into collared 1½-quart soufflé dish. Chill for 2½ to 3 hours until firm. Carefully remove collar before serving.

YIELD: 6 to 8 servings.

COLD SWEET CHOCOLATE CREAM SOUFFLÉ

2 envelopes unflavored gelatine
¼ cup cold water
1 package (¼ pound) German's sweet chocolate
¼ cup hot water
5 egg yolks
3 tablespoons noisette or cacao mit nuss liqueur or rum
⅓ cup sugar
5 egg whites, beaten stiff but not dry
1 cup heavy cream, whipped

HAVE READY: 1-quart soufflé dish with collar rising 3 inches above rim, or 1½-quart soufflé dish with collar rising 2 inches above rim, lightly oiled, including collar.

Sprinkle gelatine on ¼ cup cold water, and set aside to soften. Break up sweet chocolate and melt it in ¼ cup hot water over low heat. Remove from heat and set aside to cool. Beat egg yolks until thick and light in top of double boiler over hot, not boiling, water. Gradually beat in liqueur of choice or rum, and sugar, continuing beating for 5 minutes. Remove from heat and let cool 10 minutes. Dissolve softened gelatine over a small amount of hot water. Add dissolved gelatine and cooled chocolate to egg mixture, beating vigorously. Fold in beaten egg whites gently but thoroughly, then fold in whipped cream. Pour into collared 1- or 1½-quart soufflé dish. Chill 3 to 4 hours until firm. Carefully remove collar before serving.

YIELD: 6 to 8 servings.

COLD CREAMY COTTAGE CHEESE SOUFFLÉ

2 envelopes unflavored gelatine
½ cup cold water
2 cups creamed cottage cheese
¾ cup sugar
1¼ cups boiling water
1 tablespoon lemon juice
1 teaspoon grated lemon peel
1 cup heavy cream, whipped

HAVE READY: 1-quart soufflé dish with collar rising 1½ to 2 inches above rim, lightly oiled, including collar.

Sprinkle gelatine on cold water and set aside to soften. Beat creamed cottage cheese and sugar together to make a smooth mixture. Dissolve softened gelatine in boiling water, then gradually stir into sweetened cottage cheese. Blend in lemon juice and grated lemon peel. Refrigerate and cool, stirring occasionally, until mixture mounds up slightly. Fold in whipped cream gently but thoroughly. Pour into collared 1-quart soufflé dish. Chill 3 to 4 hours until firm. Carefully remove collar before serving.

YIELD: 6 servings.

COLD COFFEE CREAM SOUFFLÉ

1 envelope unflavored gelatine
¼ cup cold water
½ cup strong coffee
½ cup sugar
½ teaspoon salt
4 egg yolks, slightly beaten
2 to 3 teaspoons coffee liqueur
4 egg whites
½ cup sugar (additional)
1 cup heavy cream, whipped

HAVE READY: 2-quart soufflé dish with collar rising 2 inches above rim, lightly oiled, including collar.

Sprinkle gelatine on cold water and set aside to soften. Heat coffee in top of double boiler. Briskly stir in ½ cup sugar, salt, and beaten egg yolks. Cook, stirring constantly, over hot water until sauce is slightly thickened and smooth like soft custard. Remove top of double boiler from heat. Stir in softened gelatine until dissolved, then add coffee liqueur. Refrigerate until cool. Beat egg whites in large bowl to soft peaks. Gradually add ½ cup sugar, beating continuously until stiff glossy peaks form. Pile whipped cream on beaten egg whites. Gently but thoroughly fold in cool coffee custard. Pour into collared 2-quart soufflé dish. Chill for 2½ to 3 hours until firm. Carefully remove collar before serving.

YIELD: 8 servings.

COLD CONTINENTAL CUSTARD SOUFFLÉ

3 egg yolks
¼ cup sugar
⅛ teaspoon salt
2 cups hot milk
1 tablespoon cherry or raspberry liqueur
1½ cups heavy cream, whipped
1 envelope unflavored gelatine
¼ cup water
candied cherries or fresh raspberries, if desired

HAVE READY: 1-quart soufflé dish, lightly coated with apricot or strained raspberry jam, and with lightly oiled collar rising 2 inches above rim.

Beat eggs lightly in top of double boiler, stir in sugar and salt, then gradually add hot milk. Cook and stir over hot (not boiling) water until mixture coats a spoon. Remove from heat and let cool. Stir in cherry or raspberry liqueur, then fold in whipped cream gently but thoroughly. Sprinkle gelatine on cold water and let stand 3 or 4 minutes to soften. Set over hot water until gelatine dissolves. Stir dissolved gelatine lightly but thoroughly into custard cream mixture. Pour into prepared

1-quart soufflé dish. Refrigerate for 3 to 4 hours to chill until firm. If desired, garnish with candied cherries or fresh raspberries. Carefully remove collar before serving.

YIELD: 4 to 6 servings.

COLD SMOKED FISH SOUFFLÉ

2 envelopes unflavored gelatine
¼ cup cold water
¼ cup butter or margarine
¼ cup flour
½ teaspoon salt
1½ cups hot light cream or diluted evaporated milk
1 small cake (3 ounces) cream cheese, softened
few grains cayenne pepper
3 egg yolks, well beaten
½ pound smoked salmon, sturgeon, or black cod
4 egg whites, beaten stiff but not dry
1 cup heavy cream, whipped

HAVE READY: 1½-quart soufflé dish with collar rising 2 inches above rim, lightly oil including collar.

Sprinkle gelatine on cold water and set aside to soften. Melt butter or margarine in saucepan over low heat; blend in flour and salt. Cook and stir for 2 minutes, but do not brown. Remove from heat and slowly add hot cream or evaporated milk, stirring to smooth mixture. Cook and stir over medium heat until sauce boils and thickens. Remove from heat. Stir in softened gelatine until dissolved, then blend in softened cream cheese and cayenne pepper. Slowly add beaten egg yolks, stirring briskly. Let sauce cool 15 minutes. Flake smoked fish with fork, then mince very fine. Fold into cooled sauce. Gently but thoroughly fold in beaten egg whites and whipped cream. Pour into collared 1½-quart soufflé dish. Chill for 3 to 4 hours until firm. Carefully remove collar before serving.

YIELD: 6 servings.

GRASSHOPPER SOUFFLÉ

1 envelope unflavored gelatine
½ cup water
¼ cup sugar
⅛ teaspoon salt
3 egg yolks
¼ cup green crème de menthe liqueur
¼ cup white crème de cacao liqueur
3 egg whites
¼ cup sugar (additional)
1 cup heavy cream, whipped
2 tablespoons finely chopped pistachio nuts

HAVE READY: 1½-quart soufflé dish with collar rising 1 inch above rim, lightly oiled, including collar.

Sprinkle gelatine on water in medium saucepan, and let stand to soften about 4 minutes. Add next 3 ingredients and mix well. Cook and stir over low heat until gelatine dissolves and mixture thickens slightly, about 5 minutes. Remove from heat; stir in crème de menthe and crème de cacao. Chill, stirring occasionally, until mixture mounds up slightly when dropped from spoon, about 20 minutes. Beat egg whites to soft peaks; gradually add ¼ cup sugar, beating continuously until stiff glossy peaks form. Fold liqueur mixture into beaten egg whites, then fold in whipped cream, gently but thoroughly. Pour into prepared 1½-quart soufflé dish. Garnish top with chopped pistachio nuts. Refrigerate to chill until firm, about 3 to 4 hours. Loosen and peel away collar before serving.

YIELD: 6 servings.

COLD LEMON SOUFFLÉ

1 envelope unflavored gelatine
¾ cup water
¾ cup lemon juice
1 cup sugar
¼ teaspoon salt
3 egg yolks
1 teaspoon grated lemon peel
3 egg whites
⅓ cup sugar

HAVE READY: 1½-quart soufflé dish with collar rising 1 inch above rim, lightly oiled, including collar.

Sprinkle gelatine on water in medium saucepan, and let stand to soften, about 4 minutes. Add next 4 ingredients and mix well. Cook and stir over low heat until gelatine dissolves and mixture thickens slightly, about 5 minutes. Remove from heat and add grated lemon peel. Chill, stirring occasionally, until mixture mounds up slightly when dropped from a spoon, about 20 to 30 minutes. Beat egg whites to soft peaks; gradually add ⅓ cup sugar, beating continuously until stiff glossy peaks form. Fold into lemon mixture gently but thoroughly. Pour into prepared 1½-quart soufflé dish. Refrigerate to chill until firm, about 3 to 4 hours. Loosen and peel away collar before serving. YIELD: 4 to 5 servings.

COLD LEMON CREAM SOUFFLÉ

1 envelope unflavored gelatine
¼ cup cold water
4 egg yolks, slightly beaten
½ cup lemon juice
½ cup sugar
½ teaspoon salt
1 teaspoon grated lemon peel
4 egg whites
½ cup sugar (additional)
1 cup heavy cream, whipped

HAVE READY: 2-quart soufflé dish with collar rising 2 inches above rim, lightly oiled, including collar.

Sprinkle gelatine on cold water and set aside to soften. Blend together beaten egg yolks, lemon juice, ½ cup sugar, and salt in top of double boiler. Cook, stirring constantly, over hot water, until sauce is slightly thickened and smooth like soft custard. Remove top of double boiler from heat. Stir in softened gelatine until dissolved, then add grated lemon peel. Refrigerate until cool but not set. Beat egg whites in large bowl to soft peaks. Gradually add ½ cup sugar, beating continuously until stiff glossy peaks form. Pile whipped cream on beaten egg whites. Gently but thoroughly fold in lemon custard. Pour into collared 2-quart soufflé dish. Chill for 2½ to 3 hours until firm. Carefully remove collar before serving.

YIELD: 8 servings.

COLD LEMON VELVET SOUFFLÉ

1 envelope unflavored gelatine
⅓ cup sugar
¼ teaspoon salt
4 egg yolks, slightly beaten
½ cup lemon juice
¼ cup water
1 teaspoon grated lemon peel
4 egg whites
⅓ cup sugar (additional)

HAVE READY: 1½-quart soufflé dish with collar rising 1½ inches above rim, lightly oiled, including collar.

Mix gelatine, ⅓ cup sugar, and the salt together well in top of double boiler. Combine egg yolks, lemon juice, and water, and add to gelatine mixture. Cook and stir over hot water until gelatine dissolves and mixture thickens, about 8 minutes. Add grated lemon peel, and remove from heat. Chill, stirring occasionally, until mixutre mounds up slightly when dropped from spoon, about 20 to 30 minutes. Beat egg whites to soft peaks. Gradually add ⅓ cup sugar, beating continuously until stiff glossy peaks form. Fold in gelatine mixture gently but thoroughly. Pour into prepared 1½-quart soufflé dish. Refrigerate to chill for 3 or 4 hours until firm. Loosen and peel off collar before serving.

YIELD: 5 to 6 servings.

COLD MACAROON LAYER SOUFFLÉ

10 almond macaroons
¼ to ⅓ cup coffee liqueur or light rum
2 envelopes unflavored gelatine
¼ cup cold water
5 egg yolks
1 cup sugar
2 cups hot milk
⅛ teaspoon salt
5 egg whites, beaten stiff but not dry
½ cup heavy cream, whipped

HAVE READY: 1½-quart soufflé dish with collar rising 1½ to 2 inches above rim, lightly oiled, including collar.

Crumble macaroons onto shallow dish and moisten evenly

with liqueur or rum. Sprinkle gelatine on cold water and set aside to soften. Beat egg yolks and sugar together until thick and light. Very slowly beat in hot milk. Add salt. Cook, stirring constantly, in saucepan over low heat until mixture is slightly thickened and smooth like soft custard. Remove from heat, add softened gelatine and stir until it is dissolved. Let cool 15 minutes. Gently but thoroughly fold in beaten egg whites, then whipped cream.

Spread half of soaked macaroon crumbs on bottom of prepared 1½-quart soufflé dish. Pile on about ½ of soufflé mixture. Gently scatter remaining macaroon crumbs on top, then spoon in rest of soufflé mixture. Chill 3 or 4 hours until firm. Carefully remove collar before serving. If desired, unmold soufflé to serve.

YIELD: 6 to 8 servings.

COLD MACAROON CRUMB SOUFFLÉ

1 envelope unflavored gelatine
¼ cup cold water
3 egg yolks, lightly beaten
⅓ cup sugar
⅛ teaspoon salt
2 cups hot milk
1 teaspoon vanilla extract
⅛ teaspoon almond extract
1 cup coarse almond macaroon crumbs
3 egg whites, beaten stiff but not dry

HAVE READY: 1-quart soufflé dish with collar rising 1 to 1½ inches above rim, lightly oiled, including collar.

Sprinkle gelatine on cold water and set aside to soften. Blend together beaten egg yolks, sugar, and salt in top of double boiler. Slowly add hot milk, stirring briskly. Cook and stir over hot water until mixture coats a spoon like soft custard. Add softened gelatine and stir until dissolved. Pour into a bowl, add vanilla and almond extracts, and let cool 20 to 30 minutes. Stir in macaroon crumbs until they are well moistened and sauce has thickened slightly. Fold in beaten egg whites gently but thoroughly. Pour into collared 1-quart soufflé dish. Chill 3 hours until firm. Carefully remove collar before serving.

YIELD: 4 to 6 servings.

MOCHA SOUFFLÉ

1 envelope unflavored gelatine
¼ cup cold water
1 package (4 ounces) sweet cooking chocolate, broken up
1 teaspoon instant coffee
¼ cup hot water
6 egg yolks, unbeaten
¼ cup sugar
6 egg whites, beaten stiff but not dry
1 cup heavy cream, whipped

HAVE READY: 1-quart soufflé dish, with collar extending 2 inches above rim, lightly oiled, including collar.

Sprinkle gelatine on cold water and let stand 4 or 5 minutes to soften. Combine chocolate, instant coffee, and hot water in saucepan. Cook and stir over low heat until chocolate melts. Add softened gelatine and stir until dissolved. Remove from heat. Combine egg yolks and sugar in top of double boiler over hot, not boiling, water. Beat until egg is thick and very light, and sugar is dissolved. Stir in chocolate mixture and, when well blended, pour into a large bowl. Let cool 10 minutes. Fold in beaten egg whites gently but thoroughly. Let cool 10 minutes more. Fold in whipped cream until no streaks remain. Pour into prepared 1-quart soufflé dish. Refrigerate to chill for 3 or 4 hours. Loosen and peel collar away before serving.

YIELD: 6 servings.

NOTE: In the interest of calorie saving, 1 envelope whipped topping mix (prepared according to package directions) can be substituted for the whipped cream.

COLD ORANGE LIQUEUR SOUFFLÉ

2 envelopes unflavored gelatine
½ cup sugar
1 cup cold milk
6 egg yolks, lightly beaten
1 cup orange juice
1 tablespoon grated orange or lemon peel
6 egg whites
½ cup sugar (additional)
3 to 4 tablespoons Curaçao, Cointreau, or Grand Marnier liqueur
1 cup heavy cream, whipped

HAVE READY: 1½-quart soufflé dish with collar rising 1 inch above rim, lightly oiled including collar.

Combine gelatine and ½ cup sugar thoroughly in saucepan. Blend in cold milk and beaten egg yolks. Cook and stir over medium heat until well heated and slightly thickened, but do not allow to boil. Remove from heat. Refrigerate until cool. Add orange juice and grated orange or lemon peel. Chill, stirring occasionally, until mixture mounds up slightly. Beat egg whites to soft peaks. Gradually add ½ cup sugar, beating continuously until stiff glossy peaks form. Fold into chilled gelatine mixture gently but thoroughly. Fold in liqueur of choice and whipped cream. Pour into collared 1½-quart soufflé dish. Chill for 3 to 4 hours until firm. Remove collar before serving.

YIELD: 8 servings.

COLD ORANGE SOUFFLÉ

1 envelope unflavored gelatine
½ cup water
2 egg yolks
¼ teaspoon salt
1 can (6 ounces) frozen orange juice concentrate, thawed
¼ cup sugar
2 egg whites
¼ cup sugar (additional)
½ cup heavy cream, whipped

HAVE READY: 1-quart soufflé dish with collar rising 1½ inches above rim, lightly oiled, including collar.

Sprinkle gelatine on water in top of double boiler. Beat together egg yolks, salt, ½ can frozen orange juice concentrate, and ¼ cup sugar. Stir into gelatine mixture. Place over hot water and cook, stirring constantly, until gelatine dissolves and mixture thickens slightly, about 8 to 10 minutes. Remove from heat, add remaining ½ can frozen orange juice concentrate; pour into bowl. Chill, stirring occasionally, until mixture mounds up slightly when dropped from spoon, about 20 to 30 minutes. Beat egg whites to soft peaks; gradually add ¼ cup sugar, beating continuously until stiff glossy peaks form. Fold in gelatine mixture, then fold in whipped cream gently but thoroughly. Pour into prepared 1-quart soufflé dish. Refrigerate to chill until firm, about 3 to 4 hours. Carefully remove collar before serving.

YIELD: 5 to 6 servings.

COLD PEACH SOUFFLÉ

1 package (12 ounces) frozen sliced peaches
1 envelope unflavored gelatine
4 egg yolks
¼ cup cold water
1 tablespoon lemon juice or peach brandy
⅛ teaspoon salt
⅛ teaspoon almond extract
4 egg whites
½ cup sugar
1 cup heavy cream, whipped

HAVE READY: 1½-quart soufflé dish with collar rising 2 to 3 inches above rim, or 2-quart soufflé dish with collar rising 1 inch above rim, lightly oiled, including collar.

Thaw and drain frozen sliced peaches, reserving syrup. Measure syrup, add cold water, if necessary, to make ½ cup, and place in top of double boiler. Sprinkle on gelatine and let stand 5 minutes to soften. Beat egg yolks and ¼ cup cold water together and add to gelatine mixture. Cook, stirring constantly, over hot water until gelatine dissolves and sauce thickens slightly. Remove top of double boiler from heat. Stir in lemon juice or peach brandy, salt, and almond extract. Refrigerate. Push drained peaches through sieve or whirl in blender until smooth. Stir into gelatine mixture and chill in refrigerator until mixture mounds up slightly. Beat egg whites to soft peaks; gradually add sugar, beating continuously until stiff glossy peaks form and sugar is dissolved. Fold in chilled gelatine mixture gently but thoroughly, then fold in whipped cream. Pour into collared 1½-quart or 2-quart soufflé dish. Chill for 2½ to 3 hours until firm. Carefully remove collar before serving.

YIELD: 6 to 8 servings.

COLD PINEAPPLE SOUFFLÉ

4 egg yolks, well beaten
1 can (1 pound, 4½ ounces) crushed pineapple, undrained
2 envelopes unflavored gelatine
2 tablespoons sugar
1 teaspoon salt
2 tablespoons lemon juice
1 teaspoon vanilla extract
¼ teaspoon almond extract
4 egg whites
3 tablespoons sugar
1 cup heavy cream, whipped

HAVE READY: 1-quart soufflé dish, with collar rising 3 inches above rim.

Combine beaten egg yolks and undrained crushed pineapple, beating together thoroughly. Blend gelatine with 2 tablespoons sugar and salt, then stir into pineapple mixture. Cook and stir over medium heat until sauce is hot and gelatine thoroughly dissolved. Remove from heat. Stir in lemon juice and vanilla and almond extracts. Refrigerate to chill, stirring occasionally, until mixture mounds up slightly. Beat egg whites to soft peaks. Gradually add 3 tablespoons sugar, beating continuously until stiff glossy peaks form. Fold pineapple mixture into beaten egg whites gently but thoroughly, then fold in whipped cream. Pour into collared 1-quart soufflé dish. Chill until firm, about 3 to 4 hours. Carefully peel off collar before serving.

YIELD: 6 servings.

COLD RASPBERRY SOUFFLÉ

1 envelope unflavored gelatine
¼ cup cold water
4 egg yolks, lightly beaten
½ cup sugar
few grains salt
1 cup strained puréed raspberries (fresh or frozen)
1 tablespoon framboise liqueur (optional)
4 egg whites
¼ cup sugar (additional)
1 cup heavy cream

HAVE READY: 1½-quart soufflé dish with collar rising 2 inches above rim, or 2-quart soufflé dish with collar rising 1 inch above rim, lightly oiled, including collar.

Sprinkle gelatine on cold water and set aside to soften. Combine beaten egg yolks with ½ cup of sugar and the salt in saucepan or top of double boiler. Cook and stir over hot (not boiling) water until thick, about 10 minutes. Remove from heat. Stir in softened gelatine until dissolved. Refrigerate mixture to cool for 15 minutes. Blend in puréed raspberries, and framboise liqueur, if desired. Refrigerate while preparing remaining ingredients. Beat egg whites to soft peaks. Gradually add ¼ cup sugar, beating continuously until stiff glossy peaks form. Whip cream until just stiff. Pile whipped cream onto beaten egg whites. Fold in raspberry mixture gently but thoroughly. Pour into collared 1½- or 2-quart soufflé dish. Chill for 2½ to 3 hours until firm. Carefully remove collar before serving.

YIELD: 6 to 8 servings.

COLD RASPBERRY CREAM SOUFFLÉ

2 envelopes unflavored gelatine
½ cup cold water
1 package (10 ounces) frozen raspberries, thawed
1 package (8 ounces) cream cheese
½ cup sugar
1¾ cups boiling water
1 tablespoon lemon juice
1 cup heavy cream, whipped

HAVE READY: 1-quart soufflé dish with collar rising 2 inches above rim, lightly oiled, including collar.

Sprinkle gelatine on cold water and set aside to soften. Drain thawed raspberries and reserve juice. Soften cream cheese by beating with a fork, then gradually beat in sugar. Dissolve softened gelatine in boiling water, then add, gradually, to cream cheese mixture. Blend in lemon juice and juice from drained raspberries. Refrigerate and cool, stirring occasionally, until mixture mounds up slightly. Carefully fold in raspberries, then fold in whipped cream gently but thoroughly. Pour into collared 1-quart soufflé dish. Chill 3 to 4 hours until firm. Carefully remove collar before serving.

YIELD: 6 servings.

COLD STRAWBERRY SOUFFLÉ

1 envelope unflavored gelatine
¼ cup cold water
1 package (10 ounces) frozen sliced strawberries, thawed
4 egg yolks, lightly beaten
½ cup sugar
few grains salt
1 tablespoon fraise or framboise liqueur, or kirsch brandy
4 egg whites
¼ cup sugar (additional)
1 cup heavy cream, whipped

HAVE READY: 2-quart soufflé dish with collar rising 1 to 2 inches above rim, lightly oiled, including collar.

Sprinkle gelatine on cold water and set aside to soften. Push thawed strawberries through sieve or whirl in blender until smooth. Set aside. Combine beaten egg yolks, ½ cup sugar, and salt in top of double boiler. Cook and stir over hot water until sauce is slightly thickened and smooth like soft custard. Remove top of double boiler from heat. Add softened gelatine and liqueur and stir until gelatine dissolves. Refrigerate until cool. Beat egg whites in large bowl to soft peaks. Gradually add ¼ cup sugar, beating continuously until stiff glossy peaks form. Blend puréed strawberries into cooled custard. Pile whipped cream on beaten egg whites, then fold in strawberry custard gently but thoroughly. Pour into collared 2-quart soufflé dish. Chill 2½ to 3 hours until firm. Carefully remove collar before serving.

YIELD: 8 servings.

COLD STRAWBERRY CHEESE SOUFFLÉ

1 package (10 ounces) frozen sliced strawberries, thawed
2 envelopes unflavored gelatine
¼ cup cold water
1 cup creamed cottage cheese
⅔ cup sugar
1½ cups boiling water
1 tablespoon lemon juice
1 cup heavy cream, whipped

HAVE READY: 1-quart soufflé dish with collar rising 1½ to 2 inches above rim, lightly oiled, including collar.

Drain thawed strawberries, reserving juice. Sprinkle gelatine on cold water and set aside to soften. Blend creamed cottage cheese and sugar together thoroughly to make a smooth mixture. Dissolve softened gelatine in boiling water, then gradually add to sweetened cottage cheese. Blend in lemon juice and reserved juice from drained strawberries. Refrigerate and chill, stirring occasionally, until mixture mounds up slightly. Lightly fold in drained strawberry slices. Gently but thoroughly fold in whipped cream. Pour into collared 1-quart soufflé dish. Chill 3 to 4 hours until firm. Carefully peel off collar before serving.

YIELD: 6 servings.

COLD WINE CREAM SOUFFLÉ

2 envelopes unflavored gelatine
½ cup cold water
½ cup medium sweet sherry or dessert wine
¾ cup sugar
2 cups orange juice
1 to 2 tablespoons lemon juice, to taste
1 cup heavy cream, whipped

HAVE READY: 1½-quart soufflé dish with collar rising 2 inches above rim, lightly oiled, including collar.

Sprinkle gelatine on cold water in small bowl, and let stand for about 5 minutes to soften. Place bowl over hot water to dissolve gelatine. Combine wine, sugar, and fruit juices in large bowl. Add dissolved gelatine and mix well. Refrigerate until mixture thickens to egg-white consistency. Beat with rotary or electric beater until very light and fluffy. Fold in whipped cream gently but thoroughly. Pour into prepared collared 1½-quart soufflé dish. Chill 2½ to 3 hours until firm. Carefully remove collar before serving.

YIELD: 6 servings.

6

SOUFFLÉS FOR TWO OR THREE SERVINGS

Here are properly proportioned and correctly timed soufflés and soufflélike dishes for small families. They're specially designed for the couple or for live-alone cook or couple with one guest.

ALMOND SOUFFLÉ

3 tablespoons flour
2 tablespoons sugar
½ cup cold light cream
2 tablespoons butter or margarine
3 egg yolks
2 tablespoons sugar (additional)
½ teaspoon vanilla extract
few drops almond extract
3 tablespoons finely chopped toasted blanched almonds
3 egg whites, beaten stiff but not dry

HAVE READY: 1½-pint or 1-quart soufflé dish, buttered, and dusted with sugar or very finely ground almonds.

Blend together flour and 2 tablespoons sugar in small saucepan. Gradually add cream, stirring to smooth mixture. Add butter or margarine and cook, stirring, over low heat until sauce comes to a boil and thickens. Remove from heat and let cool 5 to 10 minutes. Beat egg yolks and additional 2 tablespoons sugar together until thick and light. Slowly add to cooled sauce, stirring briskly. Blend in vanilla and almond extracts and finely chopped almonds. Fold in beaten egg whites gently but thoroughly. Pour into prepared 1½-pint or 1-quart soufflé dish. Bake in 325° F. (slow) oven for 25 to 35 minutes.

YIELD: 3 servings.

APRICOT OR PEACH LIQUEUR SOUFFLÉ

1 tablespoon cornstarch
2 tablespoons sugar
few grains salt
⅓ cup cold milk
2 egg yolks, well beaten
¼ cup canned "baby food" strained apricots or peaches
¼ teaspoon grated lemon peel
1 to 2 teaspoons apricot or peach liqueur or brandy
2 egg whites
1 tablespoon sugar

HAVE READY: Two 12-ounce or three 8-ounce soufflé dishes, buttered, and dusted with sugar.

Combine cornstarch, sugar, and salt in small saucepan. Gradually add cold milk, stirring to smooth mixture. Cook and stir over medium heat until sauce boils for 1 minute. Remove from heat and let cool 5 to 8 minutes. Slowly add beaten egg yolks, stirring briskly. Add strained apricots or peaches, grated lemon peel, and liqueur or brandy. Beat egg whites to soft peaks. Gradually add 1 tablespoon sugar, beating continuously to stiff glossy peaks. Fold beaten egg whites into fruit mixture gently but thoroughly. Pour into prepared 12-ounce or 8-ounce soufflé dishes. Bake in 325° F. (slow) oven for 25 to 30 minutes.

YIELD: 2 or 3 servings.

BEEF SOUFFLÉ FOR TWO

1 tablespoon cornstarch
¼ cup cold milk
⅓ cup hot milk
½ teaspoon salt
⅛ teaspoon pepper
1 tablespoon tomato sauce (optional)
⅔ cup ground or minced leftover cooked beef
2 egg yolks, well beaten
3 egg whites, beaten stiff but not dry

HAVE READY: Two 8-ounce or 10-ounce soufflé dishes, buttered.

Measure cornstarch into saucepan. Slowly stir in cold milk to make a smooth paste. Gradually add hot milk, stirring constantly to prevent lumps. Cook and stir over medium heat until mixture boils for 3 minutes. Remove from heat. Blend in seasonings and tomato sauce, if desired. Add ground or minced beef. Slowly add beaten egg yolks, stirring briskly. Fold in beaten egg whites. Divide equally into two 8- or 10-ounce prepared soufflé dishes. Bake in 350° F. (moderate) oven for 20 to 25 minutes.

YIELD: 2 servings.

CARROT PUFF

1¼ cups hot mashed cooked carrots
½ teaspoon salt
⅛ teaspoon pepper
2 tablespoons butter or margarine, melted
2 egg yolks, well beaten
3 egg whites, beaten stiff but not dry

HAVE READY: 1-quart soufflé dish or deep casserole, buttered.

Combine first 4 ingredients and beat together with wire whisk or spoon until well blended. Let cool 5 minutes. Slowly add beaten egg yolks, stirring briskly. Fold in beaten egg whites gently but thoroughly. Pour into prepared 1-quart soufflé dish or deep casserole. Bake in 375° F. (moderate) oven for 25 to 35 minutes.

YIELD: 3 servings.

COLD BERRY CREAM SOUFFLÉ

1 envelope unflavored gelatine
¼ cup cold water
1 small package (3 ounces) cream cheese
¼ cup sugar
1 cup boiling water
1 teaspoon lemon juice
¾ cup fresh or frozen raspberries or sliced strawberries, mashed
½ cup heavy cream, whipped

HAVE READY: 1-pint soufflé dish with collar rising 2 inches above rim, lightly oiled, including collar.

Sprinkle gelatine on cold water and set aside to soften. Soften cream cheese by beating with a fork, then beat in sugar. Dissolve softened gelatine in boiling water, then add gradually to cream cheese mixture. Blend in lemon juice. Cool in refrigerator, stirring occasionally, until mixture mounds up slightly. Carefully fold in mashed berries. Fold in whipped cream gently but thoroughly. Pour into collared 1-pint soufflé dish. Chill 1½ to 2 hours until firm. Carefully remove collar before serving.

YIELD: 2 to 3 servings.

BROCCOLI AND CHEESE SOUFFLÉ

2 tablespoons quick-cooking tapioca
¼ teaspoon salt
⅔ cup cold milk
⅓ cup shredded Cheddar cheese
⅛ teaspoon pepper
few grains cayenne pepper
2 egg yolks, well beaten
⅔ cup cooked chopped broccoli
3 egg whites, beaten stiff but not dry

HAVE READY: Two 12-ounce or three 8-ounce soufflé dishes, buttered, and dusted with fine dry bread crumbs.

Combine tapioca, salt, and milk in saucepan, and let stand 5 minutes. Cook and stir over medium heat until mixture comes to a full boil. Remove from heat. Stir in shredded cheese and both peppers until cheese melts and blends in. Let cool 10 minutes. Slowly add beaten egg yolks, stirring briskly. Gently mix in cooked broccoli. Fold into beaten egg whites gently but thoroughly. Divide evenly into two 12-ounce or three 8-ounce prepared soufflé dishes. Bake in 325° F. (slow) oven for 30 to 40 minutes.

YIELD: 2 or 3 servings.

FRENCH-STYLE CHEESE SOUFFLÉ

¼ cup butter or margarine
2 tablespoons flour
1 cup hot milk
¼ teaspoon salt
⅛ teaspoon white pepper
few grains ground nutmeg
3 egg yolks, well beaten
⅓ cup grated Gruyère cheese
3 egg whites, beaten stiff but not dry

HAVE READY: 1-quart soufflé dish or 2 pint-sized soufflé dishes, buttered.

Melt butter or margarine in saucepan over low heat. Blend in flour, and cook for 2 minutes. Remove from heat. Slowly stir in hot milk until mixture is smooth. Cook and stir over medium heat until sauce thickens. Add seasonings, remove from heat, and cool for 10 minutes. Combine beaten egg yolks and grated cheese. Gradually add to sauce, stirring briskly. Fold in beaten egg whites. Pour into buttered 1-quart dish or 2 pint-sized soufflé dishes. Bake in 400° F. (hot) oven for 20 to 25 minutes.

YIELD: 2 or 3 servings.

HUNGARIAN-STYLE CHEESE SOUFFLÉ

1 cup soft bread crumbs
½ cup grated sharp Cheddar cheese
⅛ teaspoon pepper
⅛ teaspoon paprika
⅓ to ½ cup milk
2 egg yolks, well beaten
2 egg whites, beaten stiff but not dry

HAVE READY: Two 8-ounce or 10-ounce soufflé dishes, lightly buttered, and dusted with fine dry bread crumbs.

Combine soft bread crumbs, grated cheese, and seasonings. Stir with a fork while adding just enough milk to moisten mixture. Add beaten egg yolks, stirring briskly. Gently but thoroughly fold in beaten egg whites. Divide equally into two prepared 8- or 10-ounce soufflé dishes. Bake in 350° F. (moderate) oven for 25 to 30 minutes.

YIELD: 2 servings.

INDIVIDUAL CHEESE SOUFFLÉS

1 tablespoon butter or margarine
2 tablespoons flour
¼ teaspoon salt
⅛ teaspoon pepper
⅛ teaspoon dry mustard
½ cup hot milk
¾ cup grated Cheddar or Swiss cheese
3 egg yolks, well beaten
3 egg whites, beaten stiff but not dry

HAVE READY: Two pint-sized or three half-pint-sized soufflé dishes, ungreased.

Melt butter or margarine in small saucepan. Blend in flour and seasonings, and cook for 1 minute. Remove from heat. Slowly stir in hot milk until mixture is smooth. Cook and stir over medium heat until sauce thickens. Reduce heat, add grated cheese, and stir until cheese melts and is blended in. Cool for 5 minutes. Slowly add beaten egg yolks, stirring vigorously. Gently but thoroughly fold in beaten egg whites. Pour into individual soufflé dishes, filling each to within 1 inch of top. Bake in 300° F. (slow) oven for 30 to 35 minutes.

YIELD: 2 or 3 servings.

NOTE: If desired, these soufflés may be frozen in foil-lined soufflé dishes as described in recipe for Freeze-and-Bake Cheese Soufflé (see Index). Bake frozen individual soufflés in 300° F. (slow) oven for 50 to 60 minutes.

CHEESE AND WINE SOUFFLÉ

2 tablespoons quick-cooking tapioca
¼ teaspoon salt
⅔ cup milk
½ cup grated Cheddar cheese, lightly packed
1 tablespoon dry white wine
2 egg yolks, well beaten
3 egg whites, beaten stiff but not dry

HAVE READY: 1-quart soufflé dish or deep casserole, ungreased.

Combine tapioca, salt, and milk in saucepan, and let stand 5 minutes. Cook and stir over medium heat until mixture comes to a full boil. Remove from heat, add cheese, and stir until cheese melts. Blend in wine. Cool for 5 to 10 minutes. Add tapioca mixture to beaten egg yolks, mixing well. Fold into beaten egg whites gently but thoroughly. Pour into 1-quart soufflé dish or deep casserole set in shallow pan containing 1 inch hot water. Bake in 350° F. (moderate) oven for 35 to 40 minutes.

YIELD: 2 to 3 servings.

NOTE: If desired, soufflé may be baked in 2 pint-sized soufflé dishes, with baking time reduced to 25 to 30 minutes.

QUICK CREAMY CHEESE PUFF

½ cup instant-blending flour
¼ teaspoon salt
¼ to ½ teaspoon white pepper
¾ cup dairy sour cream
2 tablespoons grated Parmesan cheese
3 egg yolks
3 egg whites, beaten to soft peaks
¼ cup butter or margarine, melted
2 teaspoons grated Parmesan cheese (additional)

HAVE READY: 1-quart soufflé dish, well buttered, and sprinkled lightly with grated Parmesan cheese.

Combine first 3 ingredients in bowl. Blend in sour cream and 2 tablespoons grated Parmesan cheese; beat with wire whisk or spoon until thick and creamy. Add egg yolks and beat vigorously until mixture is ivory colored. Gently fold in beaten egg whites. Pour into prepared 1-quart soufflé dish set in shallow pan containing 1 inch hot water. Bake in 350° F. (moderate) oven for 35 to 40 minutes until puffed and browned. Serve at once with sauce made of ¼ cup melted butter or margarine combined with 2 teaspoons grated Parmesan cheese.

YIELD: 2 to 3 servings.

CHICKEN SOUFFLÉ MADEIRA

1 tablespoon butter or margarine
1 tablespoon flour
½ cup hot light cream
½ teaspoon salt
¼ teaspoon pepper
2 to 3 teaspoons Madeira wine
2 egg yolks, well beaten
⅔ cup minced cooked chicken
3 egg whites, beaten stiff but not dry

HAVE READY: 1-quart soufflé dish, ungreased.

Melt butter or margarine in saucepan over low heat. Blend in flour and cook for about 1 minute. Remove from heat.

Gradually add hot cream and seasonings, stirring to smooth mixture. Cook and stir over medium heat until sauce thickens. Remove from heat, add wine, and cool 10 minutes. Slowly add beaten egg yolks, stirring briskly, then mix in chicken. Fold in beaten egg whites gently but thoroughly. Pour into 1-quart soufflé dish. Bake in 350° F. (moderate) oven for 35 to 40 minutes.

YIELD: 3 servings.

CHICKEN MUSHROOM SOUFFLÉ

2 tablespoons butter or margarine
1 can (3 ounces) chopped mushrooms, drained
2 tablespoons flour
½ cup hot medium cream
½ cup hot chicken broth
¼ teaspoon salt
⅛ teaspoon pepper
¼ cup grated Swiss cheese
1 tablespoon sherry (optional)
2 egg yolks, well beaten
½ cup cooked drained spaghetti or rice
½ cup minced cooked chicken
3 egg whites, beaten stiff but not dry

HAVE READY: 1-quart soufflé dish, buttered.

Melt butter or margarine in saucepan over low heat; add chopped mushrooms, and sauté for 2 minutes. Blend in flour. Cook and stir for 2 more minutes. Remove from heat. Gradually add hot cream and chicken broth, stirring to smooth mixture; add salt and pepper. Cook and stir over medium heat until sauce thickens. Remove from heat, add grated cheese, stir until cheese melts, and add sherry, if desired. Cool 10 minutes. Slowly add beaten egg yolks, stirring briskly. Thoroughly mix in spaghetti or rice and minced chicken. Fold in beaten egg whites gently but thoroughly. Pour into prepared 1-quart soufflé dish. Bake in 350° F. (moderate) oven for 40 to 50 minutes.

YIELD: 3 servings.

CHOCOLATE SOUFFLÉ I

1 square (1 ounce) unsweetened chocolate, broken up
⅓ cup hot milk
1½ tablespoons cornstarch
¼ cup sugar
⅛ teaspoon salt
2 tablespoons cold milk
½ teaspoon vanilla extract
2 egg yolks, well beaten
2 egg whites, beaten stiff but not dry

HAVE READY: 1½-pint or 1-quart soufflé dish, buttered and dusted with sugar.

Melt chocolate in hot milk over hot water. Blend together cornstarch, sugar, and salt in saucepan. Add cold milk and stir to smooth paste. Stir in hot chocolate mixture gradually so that no lumps form. Cook and stir over medium heat until sauce boils and thickens. Remove from heat, add vanilla extract, and let cool 10 minutes. Gradually add beaten egg yolks, stirring briskly. Fold in beaten egg whites gently but thoroughly. Pour into prepared 1½-pint or 1-quart soufflé dish set in shallow pan containing about 1 inch hot water. Bake in 350° F. (moderate) oven for 30 to 40 minutes.

YIELD: 3 servings.

CHOCOLATE SOUFFLÉ II

2 teaspoons cornstarch
⅓ cup cold milk
1 tablespoon butter or margarine
1 square (1 ounce) unsweetened chocolate
½ teaspoon vanilla extract
2 egg yolks
1 tablespoon sugar
3 egg whites
few grains salt
2 tablespoons sugar (additional)

HAVE READY: 1-quart soufflé dish, buttered, and dusted with sugar.

Measure cornstarch into small saucepan. Slowly stir in cold

milk to make smooth mixture. Add butter or margarine and cook, stirring, over medium heat until sauce comes to a boil. Let boil 1 minute. Remove from heat. Add chocolate and vanilla extract, stirring until chocolate melts. Let cool 5 to 10 minutes. Beat egg yolks with 1 tablespoon sugar until thick and light. Slowly add to cooled sauce, stirring briskly. Beat egg whites and salt to soft peaks. Gradually add 2 tablespoons sugar, beating continuously until stiff glossy peaks form. Gently but thoroughly fold chocolate mixture into beaten egg whites. Pour into prepared 1-quart soufflé dish. Bake in 350° F. (moderate) oven for 30 to 40 minutes.

YIELD: 3 servings.

COLD CHOCOLATE BAVARIAN SOUFFLÉ

1 envelope unflavored gelatine
¼ cup cold water
¼ cup sugar
1 tablespoon flour
¼ cup dark cocoa
¼ teaspoon salt
2 egg yolks, lightly beaten
1 cup cold milk
½ teaspoon vanilla extract
few drops almond extract
3 egg whites, beaten stiff but not dry
½ cup heavy cream, whipped

HAVE READY: 1½-pint soufflé dish with collar rising 3 inches above rim.

Sprinkle gelatine on cold water and set aside to soften. Blend together sugar, flour, cocoa, and salt in top of double boiler. Thoroughly mix in beaten egg yolks, then gradually stir in cold milk to make smooth mixture. Cook and stir over hot water until mixture clings to spoon like soft custard. Remove from heat. Stir in softened gelatine and vanilla and almond extracts until gelatine dissolves. Refrigerate to cool, stirring occasionally, until mixture mounds up slightly. Fold in beaten egg whites gently but thoroughly, then fold in whipped cream. Pour into collared 1½-pint soufflé dish. Chill 2 or 3 hours until firm. Carefully remove collar before serving.

YIELD: 3 servings.

CHOCOLATE CREAM SOUFFLÉ

½ cup medium or heavy cream
1½ squares (1½ ounces) unsweetened chocolate
3 tablespoons flour
¼ teaspoon salt
2 tablespoons sugar
¼ cup cold milk
½ teaspoon vanilla extract
⅛ teaspoon almond extract
3 egg yolks, well beaten
3 egg whites
2 tablespoons sugar (additional)

HAVE READY: 1½-pint or 1-quart soufflé dish, lightly buttered, and dusted with sugar.

Heat cream and chocolate together in top of double boiler over direct low heat until chocolate melts. Remove from heat and beat together with a wire whisk. Combine flour, salt, and 2 tablespoons sugar in a bowl. Slowly stir in cold milk to make smooth mixture. Blend in chocolate mixture, and cook, stirring, over boiling water until sauce is thick and smooth. Remove from heat, add vanilla and almond extracts, and cool 10 minutes. Slowly add beaten egg yolks, stirring briskly. Beat egg whites to soft peaks. Gradually add 2 tablespoons sugar, beating continuously, until stiff glossy peaks form. Fold chocolate mixture into beaten egg whites gently but thoroughly. Pour into prepared 1½-pint or 1-quart soufflé dish. Bake in 400° F. (hot) oven for 25 to 30 minutes.

YIELD: 3 servings.

CHOCOLATE DOUBLE BOILER SOUFFLÉ

½ cup (3 ounces) semi-sweet chocolate pieces
2 egg whites
⅛ teaspoon salt
⅛ teaspoon cream of tartar
2 tablespoons light brown sugar
1 teaspoon vanilla extract

HAVE READY: 1- or 1½-quart double boiler, top section buttered, including inside of cover.

Melt semi-sweet chocolate pieces in cup over hot, not steaming, water. Remove from water and set aside. Combine egg whites, salt, and cream of tartar. Beat to soft peaks. Gradually add brown sugar, beating continuously until stiff, glossy peaks form. Gently but thoroughly fold in melted chocolate and vanilla extract. Pour into buttered top of 1- or 1½-quart double boiler. Cover. Cook over hot water for 45 to 60 minutes. If service is delayed, turn off heat and leave soufflé, covered, over hot water for 15 to 20 minutes more.

YIELD: 3 servings.

CHOCOLATE PUDDING SOUFFLÉ

1 package chocolate pudding mix
⅛ teaspoon salt
1¼ cups milk
3 egg yolks
½ teaspoon vanilla extract
⅛ teaspoon almond extract
3 egg whites, beaten to soft peaks

HAVE READY: 1-quart soufflé dish or deep casserole, buttered and dusted with sugar.

Carefully blend together chocolate pudding mix, salt, and milk in saucepan. Cook and stir over medium heat until pudding begins to boil. Remove from heat. Beat egg yolks in 2-quart bowl until light and thick. Gradually beat in hot pudding until mixture is smooth. Add vanilla and almond extracts. Fold pudding mixture into beaten egg whites gently but thoroughly. Pour into prepared 1-quart soufflé dish or deep casserole. Bake in 350° F. (moderate) oven for about 1 hour.

YIELD: 3 to 4 servings.

CORN PUFF

2 egg yolks, well beaten
½ cup undiluted evaporated milk
1 tablespoon butter or margarine, melted
1½ cups canned whole kernel corn
½ teaspoon salt
few grains cayenne pepper
⅛ teaspoon nutmeg
2 egg whites, beaten stiff but not dry
paprika

HAVE READY: 1½-pint or 1-quart soufflé dish or deep casserole, buttered.

Blend first 3 ingredients together well in bowl. Stir in corn and seasonings. Fold in beaten egg whites gently but thoroughly. Pour into prepared 1½-pint or 1-quart soufflé dish or deep casserole. Sprinkle paprika on top. Bake in 350° F. (moderate) oven for 30 to 40 minutes.

YIELD: 3 servings.

CREAMY CORN SOUFFLÉ

1½ tablespoons butter or margarine
1½ tablespoons flour
½ teaspoon salt
⅛ teaspoon pepper
few grains cayenne pepper
½ cup hot light cream or diluted evaporated milk
½ cup canned cream-style corn
2 egg yolks, well beaten
3 egg whites, beaten stiff but not dry

HAVE READY: 1½-pint or 1-quart soufflé dish, buttered.

Melt butter or margarine in saucepan over low heat. Blend in flour and seasonings, and cook 1 minute. Remove from heat.

Slowly stir in hot light cream or evaporated milk to make smooth mixture. Cook and stir over medium heat until sauce thickens. Remove from heat, blend in cream-style corn, and let cool 10 minutes. Slowly add beaten egg yolks, stirring briskly. Fold in beaten egg whites gently but thoroughly. Pour into prepared 1½-pint or 1-quart soufflé dish. Bake in 350° F. (moderate) oven for 35 to 45 minutes.

YIELD: 3 servings.

PIQUANT EGG SOUFFLÉ

2 tablespoons butter or margarine
2 tablespoons flour
½ teaspoon salt
½ cup hot milk or tomato juice
4 drops hot pepper sauce
⅛ teaspoon dry mustard (optional)
2 egg yolks, well beaten
2 egg whites, beaten stiff but not dry
2 hard-cooked eggs, sliced

HAVE READY: 1½-pint souffle dish or two 10- or 12-ounce soufflé dishes, buttered, and dusted with fine dry bread crumbs.

Melt butter or margarine in saucepan over low heat. Blend in flour and salt, and cook for 1 minute. Remove from heat. Gradually add hot milk or tomato juice, stirring to smooth mixture. Cook and stir over medium heat until sauce thickens. Remove from heat. Add hot pepper sauce and dry mustard, if desired. Let sauce cool 10 minutes. Slowly add beaten egg yolks, stirring briskly. Fold in beaten egg whites gently but thoroughly. Pour about half of soufflé mixture into prepared 1½-pint or individual soufflé dishes. Top with layer of sliced hard-cooked eggs. Cover with remaining soufflé mixture. Bake in 350° F. (moderate) oven for 25 to 30 minutes (1½ pint) or 20 to 25 minutes (individual).

YIELD: 2 servings.

FISH PUFF

½ cup hot milk
1¼ cups soft bread crumbs
¼ teaspoon salt
⅛ teaspoon pepper
¾ cup flaked cooked fish, well mashed
1 teaspoon minced parsley
2 egg yolks, well beaten
2 egg whites, beaten stiff but not dry

HAVE READY: 1½-pint soufflé dish or two 10- or 12-ounce soufflé dishes, buttered.

Combine hot milk and soft bread crumbs in saucepan. Cook and stir over medium heat until hot and smooth, about 4 minutes. Add seasonings and remove from heat. Add mashed fish and minced parsley and mix well. Slowly add beaten egg yolks, stirring briskly. Fold in beaten egg whites gently but thoroughly. Pour into prepared 1½-pint or individual soufflé dishes. Bake in 350° F. (moderate) oven for 35 to 40 minutes (1½ pint) or 25 to 35 minutes (individual).

YIELD: 2 servings.

BAKED FRUITED EGG WHITE SOUFFLÉ

2 egg whites
few grains salt
⅛ teaspoon cream of tartar
¼ to ⅓ cup sugar, to taste
⅔ cup thick puréed cooked dried prunes, apricots, peaches or pears
½ teaspoon grated lemon peel
2 teaspoons lemon juice
few drops almond extract

HAVE READY: 1½-pint soufflé dish or three 8-ounce soufflé dishes, lightly buttered on bottom only.

Sprinkle egg whites with salt and cream of tartar, and beat

[7] Toasted Nut Soufflé gets its special flavor from finely chopped and lightly browned California walnuts.

[8] Easy Frozen Caramel Nut Soufflé is a dainty make-ahead dessert for any occasion.

[9] Cold Orange Soufflé,
made with fresh orange juice
and grated peel brings
a refreshing finishing touch
to a hearty meal.

[10] Vanilla Pudding Soufflé P
fluffy cornstarch pudding
in a pastry shell, has
a special trick to offer.
Bake it early, then
repuff it for serving.

[11] Easy Frozen Chocolate Soufflé makes use of packaged pudding mix to save steps in preparation. Currant jelly garnish on the whipped cream topping is a bright color note.

[12] Cold Mocha Soufflé uses a blend of sweet cooking chocolate and instant coffee to produce this popular flavor.

[13] Cold Pineapple Soufflé, made with canned crushed pineapple, has a distinctive crisply cool taste. Strawberries to garnish lend color and pleasant flavor contrast.

to soft peaks. Gradually add sugar, beating continuously until stiff glossy peaks form. Blend together puréed cooked dried fruit of choice, grated lemon peel, lemon juice, and almond extract. Fold into beaten egg whites gently but thoroughly. Pour into prepared 1½-pint or individual 8-ounce soufflé dishes. Bake in 325° F. (slow) oven for 35 to 40 minutes (1½ pint) or 25 to 30 minutes (individual).

YIELD: 3 servings.

GINGER CREAM SOUFFLÉ

3 egg yolks, slightly beaten
3 tablespoons confectioners' sugar
3 tablespoons cold milk
½ teaspoon vanilla extract
2 tablespoons finely chopped preserved ginger
1 tablespoon syrup from ginger or ginger-flavored brandy
3 egg whites
3 tablespoons granulated sugar
½ cup heavy cream, whipped

HAVE READY: 1-quart soufflé dish, buttered, and dusted with sugar.

Combine beaten egg yolks, confectioners' sugar, and milk in small saucepan, stirring to smooth mixture. Cook and stir over low heat until sauce thickens. Remove from heat and pour into a bowl. Add vanilla extract, chopped preserved ginger, and ginger syrup or brandy, mixing well. Let cool about 5 minutes. Beat egg whites to soft peaks. Gradually add granulated sugar, beating continuously until stiff glossy peaks form. Fold whipped cream into beaten egg whites. Fold this mixture into ginger sauce gently but thoroughly. Pour into prepared 1-quart soufflé dish. Bake in 350° F. (moderate) oven for 25 to 35 minutes.

YIELD: 3 servings.

HAM SOUFFLÉ

2 tablespoons butter or margarine
2 tablespoons flour
½ teaspoon pepper
½ cup hot milk
2 egg yolks, well beaten
⅔ cup ground cooked ham
½ teaspoon dry mustard
3 egg whites, beaten stiff but not dry

HAVE READY: 1-quart soufflé dish, buttered.

Melt butter or margarine in saucepan over low heat. Blend in flour and pepper, and cook for 1 minute. Remove from heat. Slowly add hot milk, stirring to smooth mixture. Cook and stir over medium heat until sauce is very thick. Remove from heat and cool 5 minutes. Slowly add beaten egg yolks, stirring briskly. Mix in ground ham and mustard thoroughly. Fold beaten egg whites into ham mixture gently but thoroughly. Pour into prepared 1-quart soufflé dish. Bake in 350° F. (moderate) oven for 30 to 35 minutes.

YIELD: 3 servings.

JAM SOUFFLÉ

2 tablespoons cornstarch
¼ to ⅓ cup sugar, to taste
few grains salt
½ cup cold milk
2 egg yolks, well beaten
¼ cup plum, apricot, peach, or strawberry jam
1 tablespoon plum, apricot, peach, or strawberry brandy, or orange juice
3 egg whites, beaten stiff but not dry

HAVE READY: 1-quart soufflé dish or three 10-ounce soufflé dishes, buttered and dusted with sugar.

Combine first 3 ingredients in saucepan, blending well. Slowly add cold milk, stirring to smooth mixture. Cook and stir over medium heat until mixture boils 1 or 2 minutes. Remove from heat and cool 10 minutes. Slowly add beaten egg yolks, stirring briskly. Blend in jam of choice with complementary brandy or with orange juice. Stir into sauce, mixing well. Fold sauce into beaten egg whites gently but thoroughly. Pour into prepared 1-quart or individual 10-ounce soufflé dishes. Bake in 325° F. (slow) oven for 35 to 45 minutes (1 quart) or 25 to 35 minutes (individual).

YIELD: 3 servings.

LEMON SOUFFLÉ PUFF

2 egg yolks
3 tablespoons confectioners' sugar
1 tablespoon lemon juice
1 teaspoon grated lemon peel
2 egg whites
few grains salt

HAVE READY: 1½-pint or 1-quart soufflé dish or deep baking dish, buttered, and dusted with sugar.

Beat egg yolks until thick and light. Gradually beat in confectioners' sugar, lemon juice, and grated lemon peel. Beat egg whites and salt to stiff glossy peaks. Fold lemon mixture into beaten egg whites gently but thoroughly. Pour into prepared 1½-pint or 1-quart soufflé dish or deep baking dish set in shallow pan containing about 1 inch hot water. Bake in 350° F. (moderate) oven for 30 to 40 minutes.

YIELD: 2 to 3 servings.

LIQUEUR SOUFFLÉ

¼ cup sugar
¼ cup flour
few grains salt
3 egg yolks, well beaten
1 cup hot medium cream
2 tablespoons any liqueur
3 egg whites, beaten stiff but not dry

HAVE READY: 1½-pint soufflé dish or three 8-ounce soufflé dishes, buttered, and dusted with sugar.

Blend sugar, flour, and salt together well in top of double

boiler. Add beaten egg yolks, mixing well. Slowly add hot cream, stirring to smooth mixture. Cook and stir over hot water until sauce is smooth and thickened like custard. Remove from heat, add liqueur, and let cool 15 minutes, stirring occasionally. Fold in beaten egg whites gently but thoroughly. Pour into prepared 1½-pint or individual 8-ounce soufflé dishes. Bake in 350° F. (moderate) oven for 20 to 25 minutes.

YIELD: 3 servings.

BAKED LIQUEUR EGG WHITE SOUFFLÉ

2 egg yolks
2 teaspoons sugar
1 to 1½ tablespoons any fruit-flavored liqueur or brandy
4 egg whites
few grains salt
1 tablespoon sugar (additional)

HAVE READY: 1½-pint soufflé dish or two 10-ounce soufflé dishes, ungreased.

Beat egg yolks with 2 teaspoons sugar until light and thick. Gradually beat in fruit-flavored liqueur or brandy of choice. Beat egg whites and salt to soft peaks. Gradually add 1 tablespoon sugar, beating continuously until stiff glossy peaks form. Fold beaten egg whites gently but thoroughly into egg-yolk mixture. Pour into 1½-pint or two 10-ounce soufflé dishes. Bake in 400° F. (hot) oven for 12 to 15 minutes.

YIELD: 2 servings.

MARMALADE SOUFFLÉ

2 egg whites
few grains salt
⅛ teaspoon cream of tartar
1 tablespoon sugar
⅓ cup orange marmalade
½ teaspoon grated orange or lemon peel

HAVE READY: 1- or 1½-quart double boiler, top section buttered, including inside of cover.

Beat egg whites and salt until foamy, sprinkle on cream of

tartar, and beat to soft peaks. Gradually add sugar, beating continuously until stiff glossy peaks form. Fold in marmalade a little at a time, gently but thoroughly, then fold in grated orange or lemon peel. Pour into prepared 1- or 1½-quart double boiler and set cover in place. Cook over hot, not boiling, water for 35 to 40 minutes. Do not let water touch top pan of double boiler. If not served at once, turn heat as low as possible, leave cover in place, and hold for 15 to 20 minutes. This soufflé successfully waits for the guests. Turn out on warm plate or platter to serve.

YIELD: 2 or 3 servings.

NUT DESSERT SOUFFLÉ

1 tablespoon cornstarch
2 tablespoons sugar
few grains salt
⅓ cup cold milk
2 egg yolks, well beaten
¼ cup finely chopped toasted almonds, filberts, pecans, or walnuts
¼ teaspoon vanilla extract
⅛ teaspoon almond extract
2 egg whites
1 tablespoon sugar

HAVE READY: Two 12-ounce or three 8-ounce soufflé dishes, buttered, and dusted with sugar or very finely ground nuts.

Combine cornstarch, sugar, and salt in small saucepan. Gradually add cold milk, stirring to a smooth mixture. Cook and stir over medium heat until sauce boils for 1 minute. Remove from heat and let cool 5 to 8 minutes. Slowly add beaten egg yolks, stirring briskly. Add chopped almonds, filberts, pecans, or walnuts, and flavoring extracts. Beat egg whites to soft peaks. Gradually add 1 tablespoon sugar, beating continuously to stiff glossy peaks. Fold beaten egg whites into nut mixture gently but thoroughly. Pour into prepared 12-ounce or 8-ounce soufflé dishes. Bake in 325° F. (slow) oven for 25 to 30 minutes.

YIELD: 2 or 3 servings.

COLD ORANGE CREAM SOUFFLÉ

1 package (3 ounces) orange-flavored gelatin
1 cup boiling water
1 small package (3 or 4 ounces) cream cheese
2 tablespoons sugar
½ cup orange juice
½ teaspoon grated orange peel
½ cup heavy cream, whipped

HAVE READY: 1½-pint soufflé dish with collar rising 2 inches above rim.

Stir gelatin into boiling water until dissolved, then set aside. Soften cream cheese by beating with a fork, then beat in sugar thoroughly. Gradually add gelatin mixture, orange juice and grated orange peel, stirring until smooth. Refrigerate to cool, stirring occasionally, until mixture mounds up slightly. Fold in whipped cream gently but thoroughly. Pour into collared 1½-pint soufflé dish. Chill 2 to 3 hours until firm. Carefully peel off collar before serving.

YIELD: 3 servings.

COLD ORANGE LIQUEUR SOUFFLÉ

1 envelope unflavored gelatine
¼ cup sugar
½ cup cold milk or light cream
3 egg yolks, slightly beaten
½ cup orange juice
1 teaspoon grated orange peel
3 egg whites
¼ cup sugar (additional)
1 to 2 tablespoons Curaçao, Cointreau, or Grand Marnier liqueur
½ cup heavy cream, whipped

HAVE READY: 1½-pint or 1-quart soufflé dish with collar rising 2 inches above rim, oiled lightly, including collar.

Blend gelatine and sugar together thoroughly in saucepan. Gradually add cold milk or cream and beaten egg yolks, mixing well. Cook and stir over low heat until well heated, but do not boil. Remove from heat and refrigerate until cool. Add orange juice and grated orange peel. Chill, stirring occasionally, until mixture mounds up slightly. Beat egg whites to soft peaks. Gradually add sugar, beating continuously until stiff glossy peaks form. Fold into chilled gelatine mixture gently but thoroughly. Similarly fold in liqueur of choice, then whipped cream. Pour into collared 1½-pint or 1-quart soufflé dish. Chill for 2 to 2½ hours until firm. Carefully remove collar before serving.

YIELD: 3 servings.

ORANGE TAPIOCA SOUFFLÉ

3 tablespoons quick-cooking tapioca
⅛ teaspoon salt
⅓ cup sugar
½ cup water
1 tablespoon butter or margarine
1 teaspoon grated orange peel
½ cup strained orange juice
½ teaspoon lemon juice
2 egg yolks, well beaten
2 egg whites, beaten stiff but not dry

HAVE READY: 1½-pint or 1-quart soufflé dish, ungreased.

Combine tapioca, salt, and sugar in saucepan. Add water, and let stand 5 minutes. Cook and stir over medium heat until mixture comes to a full boil. Remove from heat. Stir in butter or margarine until melted, then add grated orange peel, orange and lemon juices. Gradually stir into beaten egg yolks, blending well. Fold in beaten egg whites gently but thoroughly. Pour into 1½-pint or 1-quart soufflé dish set in shallow pan containing 1 inch hot water. Bake in 350° F. (moderate) oven for 30 to 40 minutes.

YIELD: 3 servings.

POTATO SOUFFLÉ

1 tablespoon butter or margarine
1 cup hot instant mashed potato
¼ cup hot milk
¼ teaspoon salt
⅛ teaspoon white pepper
few grains ground nutmeg
1 teaspoon minced parsley
2 egg yolks, well beaten
2 egg whites, beaten stiff but not dry

HAVE READY: 1-pint soufflé dish, buttered.

Beat butter or margarine into hot mashed potato, using wire whisk or fork. Gradually add hot milk, then salt, pepper, nutmeg, and minced parsley, beating well. Let mixture cool 10 minutes. Slowly add beaten egg yolks, beating them in vigorously. Fold in beaten egg whites gently but thoroughly. Pour into prepared 1-pint soufflé dish. Bake in 325° F. (slow) oven for 25 to 35 minutes.

YIELD: 2 servings.

PUMPKIN PUFFS

3 tablespoons flour
2 tablespoons cold milk
2 egg yolks, well beaten
½ cup hot mashed, cooked or canned pumpkin
1 teaspoon butter or margarine
½ teaspoon salt
⅛ teaspoon pumpkin pie spice
2 egg whites, beaten stiff but not dry

HAVE READY: Two 8-ounce or 10-ounce soufflé dishes or baking dishes, lightly buttered.

Measure flour into bowl; slowly add milk and blend to smooth mixture. Briskly stir in beaten egg yolks, then thoroughly blend in pumpkin, butter, salt, and spice. Fold in beaten egg whites gently but thoroughly. Divide evenly into two prepared 8-ounce or 10-ounce soufflé or baking dishes. Bake in 375° F. (moderate) oven for 20 to 25 minutes.

YIELD: 2 servings.

SAVORY RICE SOUFFLÉ

2 tablespoons butter or margarine
2 tablespoons flour
½ teaspoon salt
⅛ teaspoon pepper
1 cup hot milk
¼ cup dairy sour cream
¼ cup creamed cottage cheese
2 egg yolks, well beaten
¾ cup cooked drained, herbed or curried rice
3 egg whites, beaten stiff but not dry

HAVE READY: 1-quart soufflé dish, buttered.

Melt butter or margarine in saucepan over low heat. Blend in flour and seasonings, and cook for 1 minute. Remove from heat. Gradually add hot milk, stirring to smooth mixture. Cook and stir over medium heat until sauce boils and thickens. Remove from heat. Blend in sour cream and cottage cheese and let cool 10 minutes. Slowly add beaten egg yolks, stirring briskly. Mix in cooked herbed or curried rice thoroughly. Fold in beaten egg whites gently but thoroughly. Pour into prepared 1-quart soufflé dish. Bake in 375° F. (moderate) oven for 30 to 35 minutes. YIELD: 3 servings.

NOTE: If desired, substitute ½ cup cooked, drained fine noodles for herbed or curried rice.

SALMON OR TUNA SOUFFLÉ

2 tablespoons butter or margarine
1 tablespoon minced celery
2 teaspoons minced onion
2 tablespoons flour
½ cup hot milk
½ teaspoon grated lemon peel
1 teaspoon lemon juice
2 drops hot pepper sauce
2 egg yolks, well beaten
1 small can (6½ ounces) salmon or tuna, drained and flaked
2 teaspoons minced parsley
3 egg whites, beaten stiff but not dry

HAVE READY: 1-quart soufflé dish, lightly buttered.

Melt butter or margarine in saucepan over low heat. Add

minced celery and onion, and sauté 1 minute. Blend in flour, and cook for 2 minutes. Remove from heat. Gradually add hot milk, stirring to smooth mixture. Cook and stir over medium heat until sauce thickens. Remove from heat and cool 5 to 10 minutes. Stir in lemon peel and juice and hot pepper sauce. Slowly add beaten egg yolks, stirring briskly. Blend in flaked salmon or tuna and minced parsley. Fold in beaten egg whites gently but thoroughly. Pour into prepared 1-quart soufflé dish set in shallow pan containing 1 inch hot water. Bake in 350° F. (moderate) oven for 40 to 50 minutes.

YIELD: 3 servings.

SEAFOOD SOUFFLÉ

1½ tablespoons butter or margarine
1 tablespoon cornstarch
¼ teaspoon salt
⅛ teaspoon pepper
½ cup cold milk
2⅔ cups finely chopped cooked shrimp, crab meat, or lobster
2 egg yolks, well beaten
3 egg whites, beaten stiff but not dry

HAVE READY: 1-quart soufflé dish, buttered.

Melt butter or margarine in saucepan over low heat. Remove from heat. Blend in cornstarch and seasonings until smooth. Slowly add cold milk, stirring to smooth mixture. Cook and stir over medium heat until sauce boils and thickens, about 3 or 4 minutes. Add chopped cooked seafood of choice. Remove from heat and cool 3 or 4 minutes. Slowly add beaten egg yolks, stirring briskly. Cool sauce 5 minutes more. Fold in beaten egg whites gently but thoroughly. Pour into prepared 1-quart soufflé dish set in shallow pan containing 1 inch hot water. Bake in 350° F. (moderate) oven for 50 to 60 minutes.

YIELD: 3 servings.

NOTE: To repuff this soufflé, leave in soufflé dish. Set dish in shallow pan containing 1 inch hot water. Reheat in 350° F. (moderate) oven until puffed, about 25 minutes.

SQUASH PUFFS

2 tablespoons flour
2 tablespoons cold milk
2 egg yolks, well beaten
½ cup hot mashed cooked or canned squash
1 teaspoon butter or margarine
½ teaspoon onion salt
few grains cayenne pepper
2 egg whites, beaten stiff but not dry

HAVE READY: Two 8-ounce or 10-ounce soufflé dishes or baking dishes, lightly buttered.

Measure flour into bowl; slowly add milk and blend to smooth mixture. Briskly stir in beaten egg yolks, then thoroughly blend in squash, butter or margarine, and seasonings. Fold in beaten egg whites gently but thoroughly. Divide evenly into two prepared 8-ounce or 10-ounce soufflé or baking dishes. Bake in 375° F. (moderate) oven for 20 to 25 minutes.

YIELD: 2 servings.

VANILLA CREAM SOUFFLÉ

¼ cup flour
¼ cup sugar
¾ cup cold light cream
1 teaspoon vanilla extract
3 egg yolks, well beaten
3 egg whites, beaten stiff but not dry

HAVE READY: 1½-pint or 1-quart soufflé dish, buttered, and dusted with sugar or finely ground nuts.

Blend together flour and sugar in top of double boiler, mixing well. Gradually stir in cold light cream to make a smooth mixture. Cook over boiling water, stirring frequently, until sauce thickens. Remove from heat, add vanilla extract, and let cool about 20 minutes, covered to keep skin from forming. Add beaten egg yolks, stirring briskly. Fold in beaten egg whites gently but thoroughly. Pour into prepared 1½-pint or 1-quart soufflé dish. Bake in 325° F. (slow) oven for 25 to 35 minutes.

YIELD: 2 to 3 servings.

VANILLA CUSTARD SOUFFLÉ

2 tablespoons butter or margarine
2 tablespoons flour
¾ cup hot milk
⅛ teaspoon salt
3 egg yolks, well beaten
¼ cup sugar
1 teaspoon vanilla extract
3 egg whites, beaten stiff but not dry

HAVE READY: 1½-pint or 1-quart soufflé dish, buttered and dusted with sugar or fine dry macaroon crumbs.

Cream butter or margarine and flour together in saucepan. Slowly add hot milk and salt, stirring constantly to make smooth mixture. Cook and stir over low heat until sauce comes just to a boil and thickens slightly. Remove from heat and cool 5 minutes. Combine beaten egg yolks, sugar, and vanilla extract. Slowly add egg-yolk mixture to sauce, stirring briskly. Fold in beaten egg whites gently but thoroughly. Pour into prepared 1½-pint or 1-quart soufflé dish set in shallow pan containing 1 inch hot water. Bake in 350° F. (moderate) oven for 35 to 45 minutes.

YIELD: 3 servings.

VANILLA DOUBLE BOILER SOUFFLÉ I

1 tablespoon butter or margarine
2 teaspoons flour
few grains salt
¼ cup hot milk
½ teaspoon vanilla extract
1 egg yolk, well beaten
1 egg white
3 tablespoons sugar

HAVE READY: 3-cup (1½ pints) double boiler, ungreased, but with inside of cover buttered.

Melt butter or margarine in small saucepan over low heat. Blend in flour and salt, and cook ½ minute. Remove from heat. Gradually add hot milk, stirring until smooth. Cook and stir until sauce thickens. Remove from heat. Add vanilla extract and let cool 4 to 5 minutes. Briskly stir in beaten egg yolk. Beat egg white until thick foam, gradually add sugar, and continue beating to firm shiny peaks. Fold into sauce mixture gently but thoroughly. Pour into top of 3-cup double boiler. Cover and cook over hot water 30 to 35 minutes.

YIELD: 2 servings.

NOTE: For flavor variation, substitute apricot, peach, or pear nectar for the milk in this recipe.

VANILLA DOUBLE BOILER SOUFFLÉ II

1 tablespoon butter or margarine
1 tablespoon flour
few grains salt
⅓ cup hot milk
1 teaspoon vanilla extract
4 drops almond extract
2 egg yolks, well beaten
2 egg whites
¼ cup sugar

HAVE READY: 1-quart double boiler, buttered including inside of cover.

Melt butter or margarine in saucepan over low heat. Blend in flour and salt, and cook for 1 minute. Remove from heat and gradually stir in hot milk to make smooth mixture. Cook and stir over medium heat until sauce thickens. Remove from heat, cool 2 or 3 minutes, and add vanilla and almond extracts. Gradually add beaten egg yolks, stirring briskly. Beat egg whites to soft peaks. Gradually add sugar, beating continuously until stiff glossy peaks form. Fold into sauce gently but thoroughly. Pour into prepared 1-quart double boiler top. Cover. Cook over simmering (not boiling) water for 30 minutes. If not served at once, turn off heat and leave over hot water for 10 to 15 minutes more. Do not remove cover until ready to serve, then turn out on plate or platter.

YIELD: 3 servings.

VEGETABLE SOUFFLÉ

1½ tablespoons butter or margarine
1 tablespoon cornstarch
¼ teaspoon salt
⅛ teaspoon pepper
½ cup cold milk
½ cup finely chopped cooked vegetable
2 egg yolks, well beaten
3 egg whites, beaten stiff but not dry

HAVE READY: 1½-pint or 1-quart soufflé dish, buttered.

Melt butter or margarine in saucepan over low heat. Remove from heat. Blend in cornstarch and seasonings until smooth. Slowly add cold milk, stirring to smooth mixture. Cook and stir over medium heat until sauce boils and thickens, about 3 or 4 minutes. Remove from heat. Add chopped cooked vegetable, mixing well. Slowly add beaten egg yolks, stirring briskly. Cool sauce 5 minutes. Fold in beaten egg whites gently but thoroughly. Pour into prepared 1½-pint or 1-quart soufflé dish set in shallow pan containing 1 inch hot water. Bake in 350° F. (moderate) oven for 50 to 60 minutes.

YIELD: 2 to 3 servings.

NOTE: To repuff this soufflé, leave in soufflé dish. Set dish in shallow pan with 1 inch hot water. Reheat in 350° F. (moderate) oven until puffed, about 25 minutes.

YAM OR SWEET POTATO SOUFFLÉ PUFF

1 cup hot mashed cooked or canned yams or sweet potatoes
⅓ cup hot milk
2 tablespoons butter or margarine
¼ teaspoon salt
few grains pepper
1 teaspoon grated orange peel
few grains ground cinnamon
2 egg yolks, well beaten
2 egg whites, beaten stiff but not dry

HAVE READY: 1½-pint or 1-quart soufflé dish, buttered, and dusted with very finely ground nuts, if desired.

Blend together hot mashed yams or sweet potatoes and hot milk. Beat in butter or margarine, salt, pepper, grated orange peel, and cinnamon. Let cool 10 minutes. Slowly add beaten egg yolks, stirring briskly. Fold in beaten egg whites gently but thoroughly. Pour into prepared 1½-pint or 1-quart soufflé dish. Bake in 375° F. (moderate) oven for 30 to 40 minutes.

YIELD: 2 to 3 servings.

7

PSEUDO-SOUFFLÉS

These soufflélike puffs, puddings, and omelets include many old favorites for use in a variety of meals. Though not truly soufflés, they are similar to soufflés in taste and texture and full of eating pleasure.

CARROT PUFF

3 cups hot mashed cooked carrots
1 teaspoon salt
¼ teaspoon pepper
½ teaspoon monosodium glutamate
¼ cup butter or margarine, melted
4 egg yolks, well beaten
5 egg whites, beaten stiff but not dry

HAVE READY: 1½-quart soufflé dish or deep casserole, lightly buttered.

Combine first 5 ingredients and beat together with wire whisk or spoon until well blended. Let cool 5 to 10 minutes. Gradually add beaten egg yolks, stirring briskly. Fold in beaten egg whites gently but thoroughly. Pour into prepared 1½-quart soufflé dish or casserole. Bake in 375° F. (moderate) oven for 35 to 45 minutes.

YIELD: 4 to 5 servings.

COTTAGE CHEESE PUFF

1 cup creamed cottage cheese
1 cup light cream
½ teaspoon salt
¼ teaspoon white pepper
4 egg yolks, beaten thick and light
1 tablespoon minced parsley or chives (optional)
5 egg whites, beaten stiff but not dry

HAVE READY: 1½-quart soufflé dish or deep casserole, buttered.

Combine cottage cheese, light cream, and seasonings in bowl, and beat until smooth. Gradually beat in beaten egg yolks. Stir in minced parsley or chives, if desired. Fold in beaten egg whites gently but thoroughly. Pour into prepared 1½-quart soufflé dish. Bake in 350° F. (moderate) oven for 40 to 50 minutes.

YIELD: 4 to 5 servings.

CREAMY COTTAGE CHEESE PUFF

¾ cup dairy sour cream
½ cup flour
1 teaspoon salt
½ teaspoon pepper
few grains cayenne pepper
¾ cup creamed cottage cheese
5 egg yolks, well beaten
5 egg whites, beaten stiff but not dry

HAVE READY: 1½-quart soufflé dish, buttered.

Combine sour cream, flour, salt, and peppers in bowl and beat until mixture is very smooth. Gradually beat in creamed cottage cheese. Add beaten egg yolks slowly, beating continuously. Fold in beaten egg whites gently but thoroughly. Pour into prepared 1½-quart soufflé dish set in shallow pan containing 1 inch of hot water. Bake in 350° F. (moderate) oven for 40 to 50 minutes.

YIELD: 4 to 5 servings.

CREAMY CHEESE DESSERT PUFF

⅔ cup (6 ounces) cream cheese
¾ cup dairy sour cream
¼ cup confectioners' sugar
⅛ teaspoon salt
½ teaspoon vanilla extract
3 egg yolks, well beaten
4 egg whites, beaten stiff but not dry

HAVE READY: 1-quart soufflé dish, buttered, and dusted with confectioners' sugar.

Beat cream cheese in a bowl with fork or wire whisk until soft and fluffy. Add sour cream and beat until smoothly blended. Stir in confectioners' sugar, salt, and vanilla extract, then add beaten egg yolks and stir vigorously. Fold in beaten egg whites gently but thoroughly. Pour into prepared 1-quart soufflé dish. Bake in 350° F. (moderate) oven for 35 to 40 minutes. Serve with fresh berries or sliced peaches.

YIELD: 4 servings.

QUICK CREAMY CHEESE PUFF

1 cup instant-blending flour
½ teaspoon salt
¾ teaspoon white pepper
1½ cups dairy sour cream
¼ cup grated Parmesan cheese
5 egg yolks
5 egg whites, beaten to soft peaks

HAVE READY: 1½-quart soufflé dish, well buttered, and sprinkled with grated Parmesan cheese.

Combine instant-blending flour, salt, and pepper in bowl. Blend in sour cream and ¼ cup grated cheese; beat with wire whisk or spoon until thick and creamy. Add egg yolks and beat vigorously until mixture is ivory-colored. Gently fold beaten whites into sour cream mixture. Pour into prepared 1½-quart soufflé dish. Set in shallow pan containing 1 inch hot water.

Bake in 350° F. (moderate) oven for 40 to 50 minutes, until puffed and golden brown. If serving is delayed, reduce oven heat to 250° F. (very slow) and leave soufflé in pan of water to hold until needed. YIELD: 4 to 6 servings.

QUICK AND EASY CHEESE PUFF

½ cup evaporated milk, undiluted
1 cup shredded sharp cheese
¼ teaspoon salt
4 drops hot pepper sauce
5 egg yolks, well beaten
5 egg whites, beaten stiff but not dry

HAVE READY: 1½-quart soufflé dish or deep casserole, ungreased.

Scald evaporated milk in saucepan over low heat. Add cheese and seasonings, and stir until cheese melts and blends in well. Remove from heat and cool 5 to 10 minutes. Gradually add beaten egg yolks, stirring briskly. Fold in beaten egg whites gently but thoroughly. Pour into 1½-quart soufflé dish or deep casserole. Bake in 350° F. (moderate) oven for 35 to 40 minutes. YIELD: 4 to 5 servings.

DOUBLE CHERRY PUFF

1½ cups drained, pitted canned Bing cherries
¼ cup sugar
2 teaspoons lemon juice
¼ teaspoon almond extract
¼ cup Edelkirsch liqueur
4 egg yolks, well beaten
5 egg whites, beaten stiff but not dry

HAVE READY: 1½-quart soufflé dish, buttered, and dusted with sugar.

Press cherries through sieve or whirl in blender until a smooth pulp. Combine cherry pulp, sugar, and lemon juice in saucepan. Bring to a boil over low heat, stirring constantly. Remove from heat and stir in almond extract and Edelkirsch liqueur. Let cool 5 to 10 minutes. Slowly add beaten egg yolks, stirring briskly. Fold in beaten egg whites gently but thoroughly. Pour into prepared 1½-quart soufflé dish set in shallow pan containing 1 to 2 inches of hot water. Bake in 375° F. (moderate) oven for 30 to 40 minutes. YIELD: 4 to 5 servings.

BLENDER CHOCOLATE PUFF

½ cup light cream or milk
2 tablespoons butter or margarine
1 cup (6-ounce package) semi-sweet chocolate pieces
4 egg yolks
½ teaspoon vanilla extract
5 egg whites
2 tablespoons sugar

HAVE READY: 1½-quart soufflé dish, ungreased.

Heat cream or milk and butter or margarine in saucepan over low heat until butter or margarine melts. Empty chocolate pieces into blender container, add hot milk mixture, and cover. Blend at high or blend speed for about 20 seconds. Turn off motor and remove cover; add egg yolks and vanilla extract. Cover and blend for 20 more seconds. Beat egg whites with electric or rotary beater to soft peaks. Gradually add sugar, beating continuously until stiff peaks form. Fold chocolate mixture into beaten egg whites gently but thoroughly. Pour into 1½-quart soufflé dish. Bake in 375° F. (moderate) oven for 30 to 35 minutes. YIELD: 4 to 5 servings.

BLENDER CHOCO-CHEESE PUFF

1 cup hot light cream or evaporated milk
1 cup (6-ounce package) semi-sweet chocolate pieces
2 packages (3 ounces each) cream cheese, cut up
½ teaspoon salt
1 teaspoon vanilla extract
5 egg yolks
6 egg whites
¼ cup sugar

HAVE READY: 2-quart soufflé dish or deep casserole, ungreased.

Pour hot cream or evaporated milk into blender container, add chocolate pieces, cover, and whirl at high or blend speed until mixture is smooth. Immediately remove cover and drop in cream cheese pieces one at a time. Turn off motor. Add salt, vanilla extract, and egg yolks. Cover and whirl at high or blend speed until mixture is smooth, about 20 to 25 seconds. Beat egg whites to soft peaks with electric or rotary beater. Gradually add sugar, beating continuously until stiff glossy peaks form. Fold chocolate mixture into beaten egg whites gently but thoroughly. Pour into 2-quart soufflé dish or deep casserole. Bake in 325° F. (slow) oven for 40 to 50 minutes.

YIELD: 6 to 8 servings.

CORN PUFF

3 egg yolks, well beaten
1 cup evaporated milk (undiluted)
3 tablespoons melted butter or margarine
3 cups canned or cooked whole kernel corn
1 teaspoon salt
4 drops hot pepper sauce
¼ teaspoon nutmeg
4 egg whites, beaten stiff but not dry
paprika

HAVE READY: 2-quart soufflé dish or deep casserole, buttered.

Blend beaten egg yolks, evaporated milk, and melted butter or margarine together in large bowl. Stir in corn and seasonings. Gently but thoroughly fold in beaten egg whites. Pour into prepared 2-quart soufflé dish or casserole. Sprinkle paprika on top. Bake in 350° F. (moderate) oven for 40 to 50 minutes.

YIELD: 6 servings.

EASY FISH PUFF

1 cup hot milk
3 cups soft bread crumbs
½ teaspoon salt
¼ teaspoon pepper
1 cup cooked sole, haddock, or salmon
1 tablespoon minced parsley
3 egg yolks, well beaten
4 egg whites, beaten stiff but not dry

HAVE READY: 1½-quart soufflé dish or deep casserole, buttered.

Combine hot milk and soft bread crumbs in saucepan. Cook and stir over medium heat for 5 to 8 minutes until mixture is well heated and smooth. Add seasonings and remove from heat. Flake cooked fish, then mash thoroughly or push through coarse sieve. Add fish and parsley to bread mixture and mix well. Slowly add beaten egg yolks stirring briskly. Fold in beaten egg whites gently but thoroughly. Pour into prepared 1½-quart soufflé dish or deep casserole. Bake in 350° F. (moderate) oven 45 to 55 minutes.

YIELD: 4 to 5 servings.

HAM PUFF

1 cup finely diced cooked ham
2 cups hot milk
2 tablespoons melted butter or margarine
2 cups soft fresh bread crumbs
1 teaspoon salt
¼ teaspoon pepper
6 egg yolks, well beaten
6 egg whites, beaten stiff but not dry

HAVE READY: 2-quart soufflé dish, lightly buttered.

Combine first 6 ingredients in bowl and mix well. Add beaten egg yolks and stir to blend. Fold in beaten egg whites gently but thoroughly. Pour into prepared 2-quart soufflé dish. Bake in 325° F. (slow) oven for 40 to 50 minutes.

YIELD: 6 servings.

HOMINY PUFF

¾ cup cold milk
½ cup water
⅓ cup hominy grits
¼ cup cold water (additional)
½ teaspoon salt
2 tablespoons butter or margarine
⅛ teaspoon white pepper
3 egg yolks, well beaten
2 strips crisp cooked bacon, crumbled (optional)
4 egg whites, beaten stiff but not dry

HAVE READY: 1½-quart soufflé dish or deep casserole, buttered.

Combine milk and ½ cup water in top of double boiler and bring to a boil over direct heat. Moisten hominy grits thoroughly with ¼ cup cold water, add salt, and stir into boiling liquid. Place over boiling water, and cook, stirring occasionally, until liquid is absorbed by hominy, about 30 minutes. Remove from heat, stir in butter or margarine and pepper, and let cool 15 to 20 minutes. Gradually add beaten egg yolks, stirring briskly. If desired, lightly blend in crumbled bacon. Fold in beaten egg whites gently but thoroughly. Pour into prepared 1½-quart soufflé dish or deep casserole. Bake in 350° F. (moderate) oven for 35 to 45 minutes.

YIELD: 4 to 5 servings.

HONEY NUT PUFF

4 egg yolks
1 tablespoon brandy
½ cup confectioners' sugar
½ cup granulated sugar
1 tablespoon flour
¼ teaspoon salt
⅛ teaspoon ground nutmeg
¼ cup butter or margarine
½ cup strained honey
2 tablespoons finely chopped pecans, filberts, or California walnuts
5 egg whites, beaten stiff but not dry

HAVE READY: 1½-quart soufflé dish, buttered, and dusted with sugar or finely ground nuts.

Beat egg yolks until light, add brandy, and continue beating until thick. Sift together sugars and flour. Add gradually to egg-yolk mixture, beating continuously until very light and thick. Beat in salt and ground nutmeg. Cream butter or margarine well. Gradually add strained honey, creaming and beating until mixture is fluffy. Beat into egg-yolk mixture a little at a time. Stir in finely chopped nuts of choice. Fold in beaten egg whites gently but thoroughly. Pour into prepared 1½-quart soufflé dish. Bake in 375° F. (moderate) oven for 35 to 45 minutes.

YIELD: 4 to 5 servings.

PIQUANT LEMON PUFF

4 egg yolks
⅓ cup confectioners' sugar
2 tablespoons lemon juice
1 tablespoon grated lemon peel
4 egg whites
few grains salt

HAVE READY: 1½-quart soufflé dish or deep casserole, buttered and dusted with sugar.

Beat egg yolks until thick and light. Gradually beat in confectioners' sugar, lemon juice, and lemon peel. Beat egg whites and salt to stiff glossy peaks. Fold lemon mixture into beaten egg whites gently but thoroughly. Pour into prepared 1½-quart soufflé dish or deep casserole set in shallow pan containing 1 or 2 inches of hot water. Bake in 350° F. (moderate) oven for 45 to 50 minutes.

YIELD: 4 to 6 servings.

SAUCY LEMON PUFF

5 egg whites
¼ teaspoon salt
5 egg yolks
⅓ cup sugar
2 teaspoons grated lemon peel
3 tablespoons lemon juice

HAVE READY: 1½-quart soufflé dish, buttered, and dusted with sugar.

Beat egg whites until foamy, add salt, and continue beating until stiff glossy peaks form. Beat egg yolks until thick and light, gradually add sugar, and continue beating until sugar dissolves. Stir in grated lemon peel and lemon juice. Fold lemon mixture into beaten egg whites gently but thoroughly. Pour into prepared 1½-quart soufflé dish set in shallow pan containing 1 inch hot water. Bake in 350° F. (moderate) oven for 35 to 45 minutes, until center is firm to touch. Loosen edges of soufflé, invert on warm large serving plate, and shake gently to unmold. Sauce formed in bottom of dish will flow over warm soufflé.

YIELD: 6 servings.

FLUFFY LEMON PUFF

4 egg yolks
½ cup sugar
2 tablespoons lemon juice
1 tablespoon grated lemon peel
4 egg whites
⅛ teaspoon salt
½ cup sugar (additional)
½ teaspoon vanilla extract

HAVE READY: 1½-quart soufflé dish or deep casserole, buttered, and dusted with sugar.

Combine egg yolks with ½ cup sugar and beat until thick and light. Blend in lemon juice and grated lemon peel. Beat egg whites and salt to very soft peaks, then gradually add ½ cup sugar beating constantly until stiff glossy peaks form. Add vanilla extract to egg-yolk mixture. Fold in beaten egg whites gently but thoroughly. Pour into prepared 1½-quart soufflé dish or deep casserole set in shallow pan containing 1 inch hot water. Bake in 325° F. (slow) oven for 35 to 40 minutes.

YIELD: 5 to 6 servings.

RUM NUT PUFF

6 egg yolks
1¼ cups confectioners' sugar
2 to 3 teaspoons light or dark rum
¾ cup ground California walnuts, pecans, or filberts
7 egg whites
¼ teaspoon salt

HAVE READY: 2-quart soufflé dish, lightly buttered, and dusted with sugar or finely ground nuts.

Beat egg yolks until light and thick. Slowly add confectioners' sugar, beating until mixture is creamy. Fold in rum and ground nuts of choice. Beat egg whites and salt until stiff glossy peaks form. Fold into nut mixture gently but thoroughly. Pour into prepared 2-quart soufflé dish. Bake in 350° F. (moderate) oven for 45 to 55 minutes.

YIELD: 8 servings.

BRANDIED PEACH PUFF

¾ cup coarse macaroon or ladyfinger crumbs
2 to 3 tablespoons peach brandy
½ cup butter or margarine
½ cup sugar
4 egg yolks, lightly beaten
1½ cups puréed fresh, frozen, or canned peaches
5 egg whites, beaten stiff but not dry

HAVE READY: 1½-quart soufflé dish or deep casserole, buttered, and dusted with sugar.

Moisten macaroon or ladyfinger crumbs with peach brandy and set aside. Cream butter or margarine, gradually add sugar, and continue creaming until mixture is light and fluffy. Add egg yolks slowly, beating vigorously. Stir in reserved moist crumbs and puréed peaches until well blended. Fold in beaten egg whites gently but thoroughly. Pour into prepared 1½-quart soufflé dish or casserole. Bake in 350° F. (moderate) oven for 40 to 50 minutes.

YIELD: 6 servings.

POLENTA PUFF

½ cup cold milk
⅓ cup corn meal
1½ cups hot milk
1 tablespoon butter or margarine
3 tablespoons grated Parmesan or Romano cheese
½ teaspoon salt
¼ teaspoon pepper
3 egg yolks, well beaten
¼ cup crisp bacon bits or chopped cooked ham
4 egg whites, beaten stiff but not dry

HAVE READY: 1½-quart soufflé dish, buttered.

Stir cold milk into corn meal until every grain is moistened. Add slowly to hot milk, stirring briskly to avoid lumps, then add butter or margarine. Cook and stir over low heat until thick and smooth. Add grated cheese and seasonings, and cook, stirring frequently, for 4 to 5 minutes. Remove from heat and cool 5 to 10 minutes. Slowly add beaten egg yolks, stirring vigorously. Stir in bacon bits or chopped ham. Gently but thoroughly fold in beaten egg whites. Pour into prepared 1½-quart soufflé dish. Bake in 350° F. (moderate) oven for 35 to 45 minutes.

YIELD: 4 to 5 servings.

POTATO PUFF I

¼ cup butter or margarine
3 cups hot mashed potatoes
1 cup hot milk
1 teaspoon salt
¼ teaspoon white pepper
few grains ground nutmeg
1 tablespoon minced parsley
5 egg yolks, well beaten
6 egg whites, beaten stiff but not dry

HAVE READY: 2-quart soufflé dish, buttered.

Beat butter or margarine into hot mashed potatoes, using wire whisk or fork. Gradually add hot milk, then salt, pepper, nutmeg, and parsley, beating well. Let mixture cool for 10 minutes. Slowly add beaten egg yolks, beating them in vigorously. Fold in beaten egg whites gently but thoroughly. Pour into prepared 2-quart soufflé dish. Bake in 325° F. (slow) oven for 45 to 55 minutes.

YIELD: 6 servings.

POTATO PUFF II

1 envelope (4 servings) instant mashed potato
1 tablespoon minced onion
½ teaspoon salt
1 teaspoon monosodium glutamate
3 egg yolks, slightly beaten
3 egg whites, beaten stiff but not dry

HAVE READY: 1½-quart soufflé dish or deep casserole, ungreased.

Prepare instant mashed potato according to package directions. Blend in minced onion, salt, and monosodium glutamate. Add egg yolks quickly, stirring briskly. Fold in beaten egg whites. Pour into 1½-quart soufflé dish or casserole. Bake in 375° F. (moderate) oven for 35 to 40 minutes.

YIELD: 6 servings.

CHEESY POTATO PUFF

2 cups thick mashed potatoes, freshly made
½ cup light cream or evaporated milk
½ teaspoon salt
¼ teaspoon pepper
few grains ground nutmeg
3 tablespoons grated Parmesan or Romano cheese
3 egg yolks, well beaten
4 egg whites, beaten stiff but not dry

HAVE READY: 1½-quart soufflé dish, ungreased.

Blend together first 5 ingredients. Cook and stir over very low heat until mixture is thoroughly heated. Avoid scorching. Remove from heat. Stir in grated cheese to blend well. Slowly add beaten egg yolks, stirring vigorously. Cool for 10 to 15 minutes. Gently but thoroughly fold in beaten egg whites. Pour into 1½-quart soufflé dish. Bake in 375° F. (moderate) oven for 30 to 35 minutes, until puffed and lightly browned.

YIELD: 4 to 5 servings.

POTATO SPINACH PUFF

1½ cups hot mashed potato
1 cup chopped raw or thawed frozen spinach, drained
1 teaspoon salt
¼ teaspoon pepper
1 teaspoon monosodium glutamate
¼ cup butter or margarine, melted
4 egg yolks, well beaten
5 egg whites, beaten stiff but not dry

HAVE READY: 1½-quart soufflé dish or deep casserole, lightly buttered.

Combine first 6 ingredients and beat together with wire whisk or spoon until well blended. Let cool 5 minutes. Gradually add beaten egg yolks, stirring briskly. Fold in beaten egg whites gently but thoroughly. Pour into prepared 1½-quart soufflé dish or casserole. Bake in 375° F. (moderate) oven for 35 to 45 minutes.

YIELD: 5 to 6 servings.

SPICY PUMPKIN PUFF

3 cups hot mashed cooked or canned pumpkin
1 teaspoon salt
¼ teaspoon pepper
½ teaspoon monosodium glutamate
½ to 1 teaspoon pumpkin pie spice, to taste
¼ cup butter or margarine, melted
4 egg yolks, well beaten
5 egg whites, beaten stiff but not dry

HAVE READY: 1½-quart soufflé dish or deep casserole, lightly buttered.

Combine first 6 ingredients and beat together with wire whisk or spoon until well blended. Let cool 10 minutes. Gradually add beaten egg yolks, stirring briskly. Fold in beaten egg whites gently but thoroughly. Pour into prepared 1½-quart soufflé dish or casserole. Bake in 375° F. (moderate) oven for 35 to 45 minutes. YIELD: 5 to 6 servings.

RICE AND CHEESE PUFF

1½ cups hot milk
1½ cups shredded process American cheese
3 tablespoons butter or margarine
3 drops hot pepper sauce
3 egg yolks, well beaten
1 cup cooked rice
1 cup soft bread crumbs
¼ cup minced sweet red pepper or pimiento
1 tablespoon minced parsley
1 tablespoon minced chives or green onions
3 egg whites, beaten stiff but not dry

HAVE READY: 1½-quart soufflé dish or casserole, ungreased.

Combine hot milk, shredded cheese, and butter or margarine in saucepan, stirring over low heat until cheese melts and is blended in. Remove from heat, add hot pepper sauce, and cool for 5 to 10 minutes. Gradually blend into beaten egg yolks, stirring briskly. Mix in next 5 ingredients. Gently but thoroughly fold in beaten egg whites. Pour into ungreased 1½-quart soufflé dish or casserole. Bake in 325° F. (slow) oven for 50 to 60 minutes. YIELD: 5 to 6 servings.

RAISIN ANGEL PUFF

1 cup seedless raisins
¼ teaspoon grated orange peel
1 tablespoon lemon juice
¼ cup sherry
4 egg whites
¼ teaspoon salt
½ cup sugar
3 to 4 cups small torn pieces of angel food cake

HAVE READY: 1½-quart soufflé dish or deep casserole, lightly buttered.

Combine first 4 ingredients in bowl, stirring well. Cover and let stand several hours or overnight. Beat egg whites and salt to soft peaks. Gradually add sugar, beating continuously until stiff glossy peaks form. Fold angel food cake pieces gently into beaten egg whites, then fold in raisin mixture carefully but thoroughly. Pour into prepared 1½-quart soufflé dish or deep casserole. Bake in 350° F. (moderate) oven for 25 to 35 minutes.

YIELD: 6 to 8 servings.

SEAFOOD PUFF

1 cup finely shredded cooked crab meat, shrimp, or lobster
1 tablespoon sherry (optional)
1 tablespoon grated onion
2 tablespoons minced parsley
1½ tablespoons fine dry bread or cracker crumbs
1 teaspoon salt
¼ teaspoon pepper
few grains cayenne pepper
4 egg yolks, beaten thick and light
4 egg whites, beaten stiff but not dry

HAVE READY: 1½-quart soufflé dish or deep casserole, ungreased.

Sprinkle seafood of choice with sherry, if desired. Combine seafood with next 6 ingredients, mixing thoroughly. Add beaten egg yolks, blending well with seafood mixture. Fold in beaten egg whites gently but thoroughly. Pour into 1½-quart soufflé dish or deep casserole set in shallow pan containing 1 or 2 inches hot water. Bake in 350° F. (moderate) oven for 30 to 35 minutes.

YIELD: 4 to 5 servings.

DEVILED SEAFOOD PUFF

1/3 cup butter or margarine
1/2 cup shredded blue cheese
2 to 3 teaspoons Worcestershire sauce
1/2 teaspoon salt
1/2 teaspoon coarsely ground pepper
3 drops hot pepper sauce
1 teaspoon minced fresh basil leaves (1/4 teaspoon, dried)
2 cups soft fresh bread crumbs
1/4 cup dry white wine or water
1 1/2 cups finely flaked cooked king crab meat, shrimp or lobster
4 egg whites, beaten stiff but not dry

HAVE READY: 1 1/2-quart soufflé dish, buttered, and dusted with fine dry bread crumbs.

Melt butter or margarine in saucepan over low heat. Add next 6 ingredients. Cook and stir over low heat until cheese melts and ingredients are smoothly blended, about 4 minutes. Remove from heat. Moisten soft bread crumbs with wine or water. Mix into sauce, then stir in flaked crab meat, shrimp, or lobster. Let cool 5 to 10 minutes. Fold in beaten egg whites gently but thoroughly. Pour into prepared 1 1/2-quart soufflé dish. Bake in 375° F. (moderate) oven for 40 to 50 minutes.

YIELD: 6 servings.

SQUASH PUFF

1 1/2 cups hot mashed cooked squash
1 teaspoon salt
1/4 teaspoon pepper
few grains nutmeg
1/4 cup butter or margarine
5 egg yolks, well beaten
6 egg whites, beaten stiff but not dry

HAVE READY: 1 1/2-quart soufflé dish or deep casserole, lightly buttered.

Combine first 5 ingredients and beat together with wire whisk or spoon until well blended. Cool 5 minutes. Gradually add beaten egg yolks, stirring briskly. Fold in beaten egg whites gently but thoroughly. Pour into prepared 1½-quart soufflé dish or deep casserole. Bake in 350° F. (moderate) oven for 40 to 45 minutes. YIELD: 5 to 6 servings.

SWEET POTATO PUFF

2 cups hot sieved cooked sweet potatoes (about 6)
¾ cup hot milk
¼ cup melted butter or margarine
½ teaspoon salt
⅛ teaspoon pepper
1 to 1½ teaspoons grated orange peel
⅛ teaspoon ground cinnamon
2 egg yolks, well beaten
4 egg whites, beaten stiff but not dry

HAVE READY: 1½-quart soufflé dish, buttered, and dusted with fine dry bread crumbs or very finely ground nuts.

Combine hot sieved sweet potatoes with hot milk. Beat in melted butter or margarine, salt, pepper, grated orange peel, and ground cinnamon. Let cool 10 minutes. Slowly add beaten egg yolks, stirring briskly. Fold in beaten egg whites gently but thoroughly. Pour into prepared 1½-quart soufflé dish. Bake in 375° F. (moderate) oven for 40 to 50 minutes.
YIELD: 4 to 5 servings.

FRESH TOMATO PUFF

1½ cups chopped peeled and seeded tomatoes
¾ cup cooked rice
1 teaspoon salt
¼ teaspoon pepper
few grains cayenne pepper
1 tablespoon minced green pepper
1 tablespoon minced chives
4 egg yolks, well beaten
4 egg whites, beaten stiff but not dry

HAVE READY: 1½-quart soufflé dish, buttered, and dusted with fine dry bread crumbs.

Simmer chopped tomatoes in saucepan over low heat until just soft enough to mash with a fork. Remove from heat. Add next 6 ingredients, mixing well. Cool 5 minutes. Slowly add beaten egg yolks, stirring briskly. Cook and stir over low heat until sauce is thickened, about 8 to 10 minutes. Remove from heat and cool 15 minutes. Fold in beaten egg whites gently but thoroughly. Pour into prepared 1½-quart soufflé dish. Bake in 325° F. (slow) oven for 40 to 50 minutes.

YIELD: 4 to 5 servings.

YAM OR SWEET POTATO PUFF

3 cups hot cooked and mashed yams or sweet potatoes
½ teaspoon salt
⅛ teaspoon pepper
1 teaspoon grated orange peel
¼ teaspoon ground cinnamon
¼ cup butter or margarine, melted
4 egg yolks, well beaten
5 egg whites, beaten stiff but not dry
¼ cup flaked or grated coconut (optional)

HAVE READY: 1½-quart soufflé dish or deep casserole, lightly buttered.

Combine first 6 ingredients and beat together with wire whisk or spoon until well blended. Let cool 10 minutes. Gradually add beaten egg yolks, stirring briskly. Fold in beaten egg whites gently but thoroughly. Pour into prepared 1½-quart soufflé dish or casserole. Sprinkle flaked or grated coconut on top, if desired. Bake in 375° F. (moderate) oven for 35 to 45 minutes.

YIELD: 5 to 6 servings.

YAM AND COCONUT PUFF

2 cups hot mashed cooked or canned yams
2 tablespoons melted butter or margarine
½ teaspoon salt
⅛ teaspoon pepper
1 teaspoon grated orange or lemon peel
1 tablespoon orange or lemon juice
1 tablespoon sugar
¾ cup flaked or grated coconut
3 egg yolks, well beaten
4 egg whites, beaten stiff but not dry

HAVE READY: 1½-quart soufflé dish, buttered, and dusted with cinnamon sugar.

Combine hot mashed yams with next 6 ingredients and beat well together. Stir in flaked or grated coconut. Cool 5 minutes. Slowly add beaten egg yolks, stirring briskly. Fold in beaten egg whites gently but thoroughly. Pour into prepared 1½-quart soufflé dish. Bake in 375° F. (moderate) oven for 35 to 45 minutes. YIELD: 4 to 5 servings.

YAM AND PECAN SOUFFLÉ PUFF

2 cups hot mashed cooked or canned yams
2 tablespoons melted butter or margarine
½ teaspoon salt
⅛ teaspoon pepper
⅛ teaspoon ground cinnamon
1½ teaspoons grated orange peel
2 tablespoons orange juice
½ cup finely chopped pecans
3 egg yolks, well beaten
4 egg whites, beaten stiff but not dry

HAVE READY: 1½-quart soufflé dish, buttered, and dusted with finely ground pecans.

Combine hot mashed yams with next 6 ingredients and beat well together. Stir in chopped pecans. Cool 5 minutes. Slowly add beaten egg yolks, stirring briskly. Fold in beaten egg whites gently but thoroughly. Pour into prepared 1½-quart soufflé dish. Bake in 375° F. (moderate) oven for 35 to 45 minutes. YIELD: 4 to 5 servings.

GOLDEN YAM PUFF

2 cups mashed cooked or canned yams
½ to 1 teaspoon salt
1 tablespoon brown sugar
½ teaspoon ground cinnamon
⅛ teaspoon ground nutmeg
2 teaspoons grated orange peel
¼ cup orange juice
¾ cup hot milk
2 tablespoons melted butter or margarine
5 egg yolks, well beaten
6 egg whites, beaten stiff but not dry
1 tablespoon chopped California walnuts

HAVE READY: 2-quart soufflé dish, buttered, and dusted with fine dry bread crumbs or very finely ground nuts.

Place smoothly mashed yams in large bowl. Using wire whisk or wooden spoon, beat in next 6 ingredients, one at a time. Stir in hot milk, then melted butter or margarine until smoothly and thoroughly blended. Add beaten egg yolks, and stir vigorously. Fold in beaten egg whites. Pour into prepared 2-quart soufflé dish. Sprinkle chopped walnuts on top. Bake in 375° F. (moderate) oven for 45 to 50 minutes. YIELD: 6 servings.

ALMOND PUDDING SOUFFLÉ

¼ cup butter or margarine
½ cup flour
2 tablespoons confectioners' sugar
1 cup hot light cream
4 egg yolks
⅛ teaspoon salt
¼ cup sugar
1 teaspoon vanilla extract
2 teaspoons Orgeat syrup or ¼ teaspoon almond extract
4 egg whites, beaten stiff but not dry
1 tablespoon ground toasted almonds

HAVE READY: 1- or 1½-quart soufflé dish or casserole, buttered, and dusted with sugar and finely ground toasted almonds.

Cream butter or margarine in saucepan until soft. Add flour and confectioners' sugar, and continue creaming until well blended and light. Slowly add hot cream, stirring to smooth mixture. Cook, stirring vigorously, over low heat until mixture no longer clings to sides of pan. Remove from heat. Beat egg yolks and salt until light, then gradually beat in sugar, vanilla extract, and Orgeat syrup or almond extract. Slowly add egg-yolk mixture to cooked mixture, blending by beating vigorously and constantly with wire whisk or spoon. Let cool 8 to 10 minutes. Fold beaten egg whites into cooled mixture gently but thoroughly. Pour into prepared 1- or 1½-quart soufflé dish or casserole set in shallow pan containing 2 inches hot water. Sprinkle 1 tablespoon ground toasted almonds on top. Bake in 350° F. (moderate) oven for 60 to 70 minutes. Serve from baking dish or unmolded. To unmold, let cool 2 or 3 minutes after removing from oven. Loosen edge with tip of knife, and turn soufflé out onto warmed plate or platter.

YIELD: 5 to 6 servings.

CHOCOLATE CEREAL PUDDING SOUFFLÉ

¾ cup hot milk
¾ cup crushed shredded wheat biscuits
4 egg yolks, well beaten
½ cup sugar
1 teaspoon baking powder
1 teaspoon salt
2 squares (2 ounces) unsweetened chocolate, melted
4 egg whites, beaten stiff but not dry

HAVE READY: 1-quart soufflé dish or deep casserole, buttered.

Pour hot milk over crushed shredded wheat in a bowl and beat with wire whisk or spoon until mixture is smooth. Slowly add beaten egg yolks, stirring briskly. Blend together sugar, baking powder, and salt. Stir into egg-yolk mixture. Add melted chocolate. Fold in beaten egg whites gently but thoroughly. Pour into prepared 1-quart soufflé dish or deep casserole. Bake in 325° F. (slow) oven for 40 to 45 minutes.

YIELD: 4 to 5 servings.

CHOCOLATE PUDDING SOUFFLÉ

1 cup hot milk
2 squares (2 ounces) unsweetened chocolate, broken up
⅓ cup sugar
1 tablespoon butter or margarine
1 cup coarse fresh bread crumbs
¼ teaspoon salt
1 teaspoon vanilla extract
3 egg yolks, well beaten
3 egg whites, beaten stiff but not dry

HAVE READY: 1-quart soufflé dish or deep casserole, lightly buttered.

Combine hot milk, chocolate, sugar, and butter or margarine in saucepan over low heat. Cook and stir until chocolate melts and mixture is smoothly blended. Remove from heat, and add fresh bread crumbs, salt, and vanilla extract. Let cool 10 minutes. Slowly add beaten egg yolks, stirring briskly. Fold in beaten egg whites gently but thoroughly. Pour into prepared 1-quart soufflé dish or deep casserole, set in shallow pan containing 1 inch hot water. Bake in 350° F. (moderate) oven for 50 to 60 minutes.

YIELD: 4 to 5 servings.

GINGER PUDDING SOUFFLÉ

1 cup evaporated milk, undiluted
¼ cup butter or margarine
½ cup fresh bread crumbs
½ cup minced preserved ginger
½ cup syrup from preserved ginger
1 tablespoon ginger brandy (optional)
5 egg yolks, well beaten
5 egg whites, beaten stiff but not dry

HAVE READY: 2-quart soufflé dish, lightly buttered, and dusted with sugar.

Heat evaporated milk and butter or margarine together in saucepan over low heat until butter melts. Remove from heat. Measure fresh bread crumbs into bowl. Add hot milk mixture and beat vigorously with wire whisk until smooth. Beat in ginger, ginger syrup, and ginger brandy, if desired. Cool 5 minutes. Gradually add beaten egg yolks, stirring briskly. Fold mixture into beaten egg whites gently but thoroughly. Pour into prepared 2-quart soufflé dish. Bake in 375° F. (moderate) oven for 35 to 40 minutes.

YIELD: 6 servings.

LEMON PUDDING SOUFFLÉ

¾ cup sugar
3 tablespoons cornstarch
⅛ teaspoon salt
2 egg yolks
1 cup milk
1 teaspoon grated lemon peel
3 tablespoons lemon juice
2 tablespoons butter or margarine, melted
2 or 3 egg whites
¼ cup sugar (additional)

HAVE READY: 1½-quart soufflé dish or deep casserole, buttered.

Sift ¾ cup sugar, cornstarch, and salt together into large bowl. Beat egg yolks until foamy, add milk, and gradually stir into dry ingredients to make a smooth mixture. Blend in grated lemon peel, lemon juice, and melted butter or margarine. Beat egg whites to soft peaks. Gradually add ¼ cup sugar, beating continuously until stiff glossy peaks form. Fold beaten egg whites into lemon mixture. Pour into prepared 1½-quart soufflé dish or deep casserole set in shallow pan containing 1½ inches hot water. Bake in 350° F. (moderate) oven 50 to 55 minutes until puffed and browned. YIELD: 6 servings.

LEMON MACAROON PUDDING SOUFFLÉ

3 tablespoons butter or margarine
6 tablespoons flour
2 tablespoons confectioners' sugar
¾ cup hot milk
4 egg yolks
⅛ teaspoon salt
2 tablespoons sugar
2 tablespoons lemon juice
1 teaspoon grated lemon peel
½ cup finely crumbled almond macaroons
4 egg whites, beaten stiff but not dry

HAVE READY: 1- or 1½-quart soufflé dish or deep casserole, buttered, and dusted with sugar.

Cream butter or margarine in saucepan until soft. Add flour and confectioners' sugar and continue creaming until well blended and light. Slowly add hot milk, stirring to smooth mixture. Cook, stirring vigorously, over low heat until mixture no longer clings to the sides of the pan. Remove from heat. Beat egg yolks, salt, and sugar until thick and light, then gradually beat in lemon juice and grated lemon peel. Slowly add egg-yolk mixture to cooked mixture, blending by beating vigorously and constantly with wire whisk or spoon. Let cool 8 to 10 minutes, then stir in crumbled almond macaroons. Fold beaten egg whites into macaroon mixture gently but thoroughly. Pour into prepared 1- or 1½-quart soufflé dish or deep casserole, set in shallow pan containing 1 to 2 inches hot water. Bake in 350° F. (moderate) oven for 55 to 65 minutes. Remove from oven and let cool 2 or 3 minutes. Loosen edge with tip of knife, and turn soufflé out onto warmed plate or platter to serve.

YIELD: 5 to 6 servings.

LIQUEUR PUDDING SOUFFLÉ

¼ cup confectioners' sugar
½ cup granulated sugar
¾ cup flour
½ cup butter or margarine
1½ cups hot milk or light cream
5 egg yolks, beaten until thick and light
½ cup any fruit-flavored liqueur
5 egg whites, beaten stiff but not dry

HAVE READY: 1½-quart soufflé dish or deep casserole, well buttered.

Combine sugars and flour, mixing well together. Melt butter or margarine in saucepan over low heat. Blend in sugar and flour mixture, stirring to prevent lumps. When well blended remove from heat. Gradually add hot milk or cream, stirring to a smooth mixture. Cook and stir over low heat until the sauce is very thick and smooth. Remove from heat and let cool 10 minutes. Beat together thick egg yolks and liqueur of choice. Slowly add to cooled sauce, stirring briskly. Fold in beaten egg whites gently but thoroughly. Pour into prepared 1½-quart soufflé dish or deep casserole set in shallow pan containing 1 to 2 inches hot water. Bake in 350° F. (moderate) oven for 40 to 50 minutes. This soufflé may be unmolded onto a warm plate for serving, if desired.

YIELD: 5 to 6 servings.

SOUTHERN LEMON PUDDING PUFF

1 cup sugar
4 egg yolks, well beaten
2 tablespoons lemon juice
1 tablespoon grated lemon peel
4 egg whites, beaten stiff but not dry

HAVE READY: 1- or 1½-quart soufflé dish or deep casserole, lightly buttered.

Combine sugar gradually with beaten egg yolks, beating mixture until thick and light. Beat in lemon juice and grated lemon peel. Fold in beaten egg whites gently but thoroughly. Pour into prepared 1- or 1½-quart soufflé dish or deep casserole. Bake in 350° F. (moderate) oven for 35 to 40 minutes.

YIELD: 5 to 6 servings.

ORANGE PUDDING SOUFFLÉ

3 egg yolks
2 tablespoons sugar
3 tablespoons flour
2 tablespoons butter or margarine, melted
½ cup diluted evaporated milk
1 tablespoon grated orange peel
1 cup orange juice
3 egg whites
¼ teaspoon salt
⅓ cup sugar (additional)

HAVE READY: 1½-quart soufflé dish or 6 custard cups, buttered.

Beat egg yolks with 2 tablespoons sugar until thick and light. Gradually stir in flour and melted butter or margarine. Blend in evaporated milk, grated orange peel, and orange juice, stirring to smooth mixture. Beat egg whites and salt to soft peaks. Gradually add ⅓ cup sugar, beating continuously until stiff glossy peaks form. Fold egg-yolk mixture into beaten egg whites gently but thoroughly. Pour into prepared 1½-quart soufflé dish or divide evenly into 6 prepared custard cups. Set in shallow pan containing 2 inches hot water. Bake in 350° F. (moderate) oven for 60 to 70 minutes (soufflé dish) or 40 to 50 minutes (custard cups). Cool before serving, and turn out on dessert plates, if desired. YIELD: 6 servings.

RICE PUDDING SOUFFLÉ

1 cup rice
2 cups boiling water
½ teaspoon salt
2 cups hot milk
1 cup hot light cream
2 tablespoons butter or margarine
¼ cup sugar
3 egg yolks, beaten
1 teaspoon grated lemon peel
2 to 3 tablespoons dark or light seedless raisins
4 egg whites, beaten stiff but not dry
¼ teaspoon ground cinnamon

HAVE READY: 2-quart soufflé dish or deep casserole, buttered.

Cook rice in boiling salted water for 10 minutes. Drain. Add hot milk and light cream to drained rice. Cook, stirring occasionally, over low heat until rice is tender and liquid nearly absorbed, about 20 minutes. Remove from heat and let cool 20 minutes. Cream butter or margarine with sugar until light and fluffy. Add egg yolks and cream well together. Stir in grated lemon peel. Combine raisins with rice, add egg-yolk mixture, and mix well. Fold in beaten egg whites gently but thoroughly. Pour into prepared 2-quart soufflé dish or deep casserole. Sprinkle ground cinnamon on top. Bake in 400° F. (hot) oven for 35 to 45 minutes. YIELD: 6 servings.

SOUR CREAM PUDDING SOUFFLÉ

4 egg yolks, well beaten
½ cup sugar
⅓ cup flour
1 tablespoon grated lemon peel
1 teaspoon vanilla extract
2 cups dairy sour cream
5 egg whites, beaten stiff but not dry

HAVE READY: 1½-quart soufflé dish, buttered, and dusted with sugar.

Combine beaten egg yolks and sugar and beat until light and thick. Gradually sprinkle on flour and beat it in well, then beat in grated lemon peel and vanilla extract. Fold in sour cream until well blended. Fold in beaten egg whites gently but thoroughly. Pour into prepared 1½-quart soufflé dish. Bake in 350° F. (moderate) oven for 45 to 55 minutes.

YIELD: 5 to 6 servings.

VANILLA PUDDING SOUFFLÉ PIE

3 tablespoons cornstarch
¾ cup hot milk
3 tablespoons butter or margarine
1 teaspoon vanilla extract
4 egg yolks
3 tablespoons sugar
4 egg whites
⅛ teaspoon salt

HAVE READY: one unbaked 9-inch pie shell.

Measure cornstarch into saucepan. Very slowly add hot milk, stirring vigorously to keep mixture smooth. Cook and stir over medium heat until thick and smooth. If any lumps should form during cooking, beat them out with a spoon. Remove from heat and add butter or margarine and vanilla extract. Beat egg yolks with 3 tablespoons sugar until thick and light. Slowly add to cornstarch mixture, stirring briskly. Place saucepan over low heat, and cook and stir sauce for 1 minute. Remove from heat and cool 5 minutes. Beat egg whites and salt to stiff but not dry peaks. Fold cooled sauce into beaten egg whites gently but thoroughly. Pour into unbaked 9-inch pie shell. Bake on low rack in 350° F. (moderate) oven for 50 to 55 minutes, until puffed and browned. If pie is not to be served at once, reheat in 350° F. (moderate) oven for 20 minutes to repuff filling. YIELD: 6 to 8 servings.

VANILLA BREAD PUDDING SOUFFLÉ

1 cup hot milk
⅓ cup sugar
1 tablespoon butter or margarine
1 cup coarse fresh bread crumbs
¼ teaspoon salt
1 teaspoon vanilla extract
3 egg yolks, well beaten
3 egg whites, beaten stiff but not dry

HAVE READY: 1-quart soufflé dish or deep casserole, lightly buttered.

Combine hot milk, sugar, and butter or margarine in saucepan, stirring over low heat until sugar dissolves and fat melts. Remove from heat. Blend in fresh bread crumbs and salt. Add vanilla extract. Let cool 5 minutes. Slowly add beaten egg yolks, stirring briskly. Fold in beaten egg whites. Pour into prepared 1-quart soufflé dish or deep casserole set in shallow pan containing 1 inch hot water. Bake in 350° F. (moderate) oven for 50 to 60 minutes. YIELD: 4 to 5 servings.

COLD WALNUT SOUFFLÉ PUDDING

1 envelope unflavored gelatine
¼ cup cold water
1 cup heavy cream
¾ cup cold milk
½ cup sugar
½ cup drained canned crushed pineapple
½ cup sliced fresh or frozen (drained) strawberries
1 cup chopped California walnuts
1 egg white, beaten stiff but not dry

HAVE READY: 1½-pint soufflé dish with collar rising 2 inches above rim, or 6 uncollared dessert dishes.

Sprinkle gelatine on cold water and set aside to soften. Combine cream, cold milk, and sugar in saucepan over medium heat. Cook and stir until mixture just reaches boiling point. Remove from heat and stir in softened gelatine until dissolved. Refrigerate and chill, stirring occasionally, until mixture mounds up. Blend in crushed pineapple, sliced strawberries, and chopped walnuts. Fold in beaten egg white gently but thoroughly. Pour into collared 1½-pint soufflé dish or divide evenly into 6 uncollared dessert dishes. Refrigerate until chilled, about 1 to 2 hours. Carefully peel off collar of soufflé dish before serving.

YIELD: 6 servings.

CHOCOLATE SOUFFLÉ OMELET

4 egg yolks
2 tablespoons confectioners' sugar
2 squares (2 ounces) unsweetened chocolate, melted
6 egg whites
few grains salt
1 tablespoon fine granulated or superfine sugar

HAVE READY: Large ovenproof platter, skillet, or shallow baking dish, buttered.

Beat egg yolks until light. Gradually add confectioners' sugar, beating until thick and very light. Slowly beat in melted chocolate. Beat egg whites and salt to soft peaks. Gradually add 1 tablespoon sugar, beating continuously until stiff glossy peaks form. Fold about ⅓ beaten egg whites gently but thoroughly into chocolate mixture, then lightly fold in remaining beaten egg whites. Pile onto prepared ovenproof platter, skillet, or shallow baking dish. Bake in 450° F. (very hot) oven for 15 to 18 minutes.

YIELD: 4 to 5 servings.

BRANDY SOUFFLÉ OMELET

6 egg yolks
¼ cup confectioners' sugar
¼ cup cognac or brandy
6 egg whites, beaten stiff but not dry
1 tablespoon confectioners' sugar (additional)

HAVE READY: large ovenproof platter, skillet, or shallow baking dish, buttered, and dusted with sugar.

Beat egg yolks until light. Gradually add confectioners' sugar, beating until thick and light. Beat in cognac or brandy. Fold beaten egg whites into egg-yolk mixture gently but thoroughly. Pile lightly on prepared ovenproof platter, skillet, or shallow dish. Sprinkle with 1 tablespoon confectioners' sugar. Bake in 350° F. (moderate) oven for 15 to 18 minutes.

YIELD: 6 servings.

CELESTIAL LEMON SOUFFLÉ OMELET

8 egg whites
½ teaspoon salt
3 tablespoons superfine sugar
5 egg yolks, well beaten
1 tablespoon flour
½ teaspoon grated lemon peel

HAVE READY: 1½-quart shallow soufflé or baking dish, well buttered, and dusted with superfine sugar.

In large bowl, beat egg whites until foamy, using electric or rotary beater or wire whisk. Add salt and continue beating until soft peaks form. Add superfine sugar, 1 tablespoonful at a time, and continue beating until meringue is very stiff and glossy. Add beaten egg yolks, sprinkle on flour and grated lemon peel, and stir gently until blended into meringue. With large spoon, pile lightly on prepared 1½-quart shallow soufflé or baking dish. Bake in 350° F. (moderate) oven for 10 to 12 minutes. Inside of baked omelet should be moist and creamy.

YIELD: 6 to 8 servings.

LIQUEUR SOUFFLÉ OMELET

3 egg yolks
2 teaspoons flour
1 teaspoon grated orange or lemon peel
1 tablespoon any fruit-flavored liqueur
8 egg whites
⅛ teaspoon salt
¼ cup fine granulated or superfine sugar
1 tablespoon confectioners' sugar

HAVE READY: Large ovenproof platter, skillet, or shallow baking dish, buttered, and dusted with sugar.

Beat egg yolks until light. Gradually add flour, then grated orange or lemon peel, beating until thick and light. Add liqueur of choice. Beat egg whites and salt to soft peaks. Gradually add ¼ cup sugar, beating continuously until stiff glossy peaks form. Fold egg-yolk mixture into beaten egg whites gently but thoroughly. Pile onto prepared large platter, skillet, or shallow baking dish. Sprinkle top with 1 tablespoon confectioners' sugar. Bake in 450° F. (very hot) oven for 10 to 12 minutes.

YIELD: 6 to 8 servings.

SWEET SKILLET SOUFFLÉ OMELET

6 egg yolks
½ cup fine granulated or superfine sugar
1 teaspoon vanilla extract
6 egg whites
⅛ teaspoon salt
2 tablespoons confectioners' sugar

HAVE READY: Deep 10-inch or 12-inch covered ovenproof skillet, buttered.

Beat egg yolks until light. Gradually add ½ cup sugar, beating until thick and very light. Beat in vanilla extract. Beat egg whites and salt to stiff glossy peaks. Fold into egg-yolk mixture gently but thoroughly. Pour into prepared skillet and set cover in place. Cook over low heat until puffed, about 18 to 20 minutes. Remove cover. Quickly sprinkle top with 2 tablespoons confectioners' sugar. Bake in 375° F. (moderate) oven until browned and glazed, about 8 to 10 minutes.

YIELD: 4 to 5 servings.

VANILLA SOUFFLÉ OMELET I

- *5 egg whites*
- *3 tablespoons fine granulated or superfine sugar*
- *4 egg yolks*
- *2 tablespoons fine granulated or superfine sugar (additional)*
- *1 teaspoon vanilla extract*

HAVE READY: Large ovenproof platter or skillet, buttered, and dusted with sugar.

Beat egg whites to soft peaks. Gradually add 3 tablespoons sugar, beating continuously until stiff glossy peaks form and sugar is dissolved. Beat egg yolks until light. Gradually add 2 tablespoons sugar, beating constantly until thick and very light, with sugar dissolved. Beat in vanilla extract. Fold egg-yolk mixture into beaten egg whites gently but thoroughly. Pile onto prepared large ovenproof platter or skillet. Bake in 400° F. (hot) oven for 18 to 20 minutes until puffed and well browned.

YIELD: 4 to 5 servings.

VANILLA SOUFFLÉ OMELET II

- *6 egg whites*
- *⅔ cup fine granulated or superfine sugar*
- *5 egg yolks*
- *1 teaspoon vanilla extract*
- *2 tablespoons flour*

HAVE READY: 1½- or 2-quart shallow soufflé or baking dish, buttered, and heated in 400° F. (hot) oven.

Beat egg whites to soft peaks. Gradually add sugar, beating continuously until stiff glossy peaks form. Beat egg yolks and vanilla extract until light. Gradually beat in flour until well blended. Fold egg-yolk mixture into beaten egg whites gently but thoroughly. Spoon into prepared and heated 1½- or 2-quart shallow soufflé dish or baking dish and place in oven. Immediately reduce oven heat to 300° F. (slow) and bake for 15 to 18 minutes.

YIELD: 5 to 6 servings.

8

TIMESAVER SOUFFLÉS

Quick and Easy Soufflés make it possible to be a gourmet cook at short notice. Emergency shelf canned soups and packaged puddings as well as freezer-stored juices and soup concentrates help short cut preparation time.

QUICK COLD BERRY SOUFFLÉ

1 package (10 ounces) frozen sweetened raspberries or sliced strawberries, thawed
cold water
1 package strawberry whipped dessert mix
1 egg white
2 tablespoons sugar

HAVE READY: 1½-pint soufflé dish, with collar rising 2 or 3 inches above rim.

Drain thawed raspberries or strawberries, and reserve syrup. Add enough cold water to reserved syrup to make 1 cup. Blend strawberry whipped dessert mix according to package directions, using cold syrup mixture as required liquid. Beat egg white to soft peaks. Gradually add sugar, beating continuously until stiff glossy peaks form. Fold beaten egg white into prepared dessert mix. Chill until mixture mounds up when spooned. Fold in drained raspberries or strawberries. Pile into collared 1½-pint soufflé dish. Chill until delicately firm, about 2 to 2½ hours. Carefully remove collar before serving.

YIELD: 4 to 5 servings.

EASY FROZEN CARAMEL NUT SOUFFLÉ

2 cups cold milk
2 packages instant caramel nut pudding
2 cups heavy cream, whipped
6 egg whites, beaten stiff but not dry

HAVE READY: 1-quart soufflé dish, ungreased, with collar rising 2 to 3 inches above rim.

Measure cold milk into bowl. Add instant caramel nut pudding and beat with a rotary beater until well blended, about 1 minute. Fold pudding and whipped cream into beaten egg whites gently but thoroughly. Pour into collared 1-quart soufflé dish. Freeze until firm. Remove from freezer about 15 minutes before serving, and carefully remove collar.

YIELD: 8 servings.

NOTE: For 4 servings, use half as much of each ingredient. Pour into 1½-pint soufflé dish, ungreased, with collar rising 2 inches above rim. Freeze and serve as directed above.

EASY CHEESE SOUFFLÉ

1 can (10¾ ounces) condensed Cheddar cheese soup
6 egg yolks
6 egg whites

HAVE READY: 1½-quart soufflé dish or deep casserole, ungreased.

Cook and stir undiluted condensed Cheddar cheese soup in saucepan over medium heat until thoroughly heated. Remove from heat. Beat egg yolks until thick and very light. Slowly add to hot soup, stirring briskly. Beat egg whites to stiff glossy peaks. Fold soup mixture into egg whites gently but thoroughly. Pour into 1½-quart soufflé dish or deep casserole. Bake in 300° F. (slow) oven for 1 to 1¼ hours.

YIELD: 5 to 6 servings.

QUICK CELERY CHEESE SOUFFLÉ

1 can (10½ ounces) condensed cream of celery soup
1½ cups shredded American cheese
4 egg yolks, beaten thick and light
¼ cup minced dried chipped beef
¼ teaspoon pepper
½ teaspoon Worcestershire sauce
4 egg whites, beaten stiff but not dry

HAVE READY: 1½-quart soufflé dish or deep casserole, ungreased.

Heat undiluted soup over low heat, stirring frequently. Add shredded cheese and stir until melted. Remove from heat. Slowly add to beaten egg yolks, stirring briskly. Return mixture to saucepan. Cook and stir over low heat until sauce thickens, about 5 minutes. Remove from heat. Add minced dried beef, pepper, and Worcestershire sauce. Let cool 15 minutes. Fold into beaten egg whites gently but thoroughly. Pour into 1½-quart soufflé dish or deep casserole set in shallow pan containing 1 inch hot water. Bake in 325° F. (slow) oven 55 to 60 minutes.

YIELD: 6 servings.

QUICK PIQUANT CHEESE SOUFFLÉ

1 can (10¾ ounces) condensed Cheddar cheese soup
½ teaspoon dry mustard
½ teaspoon Worcestershire sauce
few grains cayenne pepper
3 egg yolks, slightly beaten
3 egg whites
⅛ teaspoon salt

HAVE READY: 1½-quart soufflé dish or deep casserole, ungreased.

Cook and stir undiluted condensed Cheddar cheese soup over low heat until warm and smooth. Add dry mustard, Worcestershire sauce, cayenne pepper, and beaten egg yolks, stirring briskly. Continue to cook and stir over low heat until thickened and smooth, but do not allow to boil. Remove from heat and let cool 10 minutes. Beat egg whites and salt to stiff glossy peaks. Fold beaten egg whites into cooled soup mixture gently but thoroughly. Pour into 1½-quart soufflé dish or deep casserole. Bake in 375° F. (moderate) oven for 45 to 55 minutes.

YIELD: 5 to 6 servings.

QUICK COLD CHOCOLATE SOUFFLÉ

1 package chocolate whipped dessert mix
½ cup cold milk
½ cup cold water
1 package (3 ounces) cream cheese, softened
1 teaspoon vanilla extract
1 egg white
2 tablespoons sugar

HAVE READY: 1½-pint soufflé dish, with collar rising 2 or 3 inches above rim.

Blend chocolate whipped dessert mix with cold milk and cold water according to package directions. Add softened cream cheese, a little at a time, beating to smooth mixture after each addition, then beat in vanilla extract. Chill until mixture mounds up when spooned. Beat egg white to soft peaks. Gradually add sugar, beating continuously until stiff glossy peaks form. Fold beaten egg white into chilled prepared dessert mix gently but thoroughly. Pile into collared 1½-pint soufflé dish. Chill until delicately firm, about 2 to 2½ hours. Carefully remove collar before serving.

YIELD: 4 to 5 servings.

EASY FROZEN CHOCOLATE SOUFFLÉ

2 packages (4 ounces each) chocolate pudding
2 cups cold milk
1 teaspoon vanilla extract
6 eggs
2 cups heavy cream, whipped
¼ cup heavy cream (additional)
¼ cup currant jelly, melted

HAVE READY: 1½-quart soufflé dish with collar extending 2 inches above rim.

Empty pudding into saucepan. Gradually add milk, stirring to smooth mixture. Cook and stir over medium heat until pudding thickens and begins to bubble. Remove from heat and add vanilla extract. Beat eggs rapidly until they are light and fluffy. Gradually add hot pudding, beating constantly. Continue beating until mixture is cool, about 8 to 10 minutes. Fold in whipped cream gently but thoroughly. Pour into collared 1½-quart soufflé dish. Freeze until firm, about 4 hours.

Before serving, carefully remove collar. Whip ¼ cup heavy cream and spread on top of soufflé. Drizzle melted jelly in thin rows an inch apart on top of cream. Mark rows with tip of knife in alternating directions to give wavy appearance.

YIELD: 8 servings.

QUICK CHOCOLATE PUDDING SOUFFLÉ

1 package dark and sweet chocolate pudding mix
1 cup milk
1 tablespoon butter or margarine
3 egg yolks
½ teaspoon vanilla extract
3 egg whites, beaten stiff but not dry

HAVE READY: 1½-quart soufflé dish or deep casserole, ungreased.

Empty chocolate pudding mix into saucepan; gradually stir in milk to make smooth mixture. Add butter or margarine. Cook and stir over medium heat until pudding begins to boil. Remove from heat. Beat egg yolks in large bowl until thick and light. Slowly beat in cooked pudding. Continue beating until cool, about 5 minutes with electric beater, about 8 to 10 minutes with rotary beater. Add vanilla extract. Fold in beaten egg whites gently but thoroughly. Pour into 1½-quart soufflé dish or deep casserole set in shallow pan containing 1 to 2 inches hot water. Bake in 350° F. (moderate) oven 60 to 75 minutes, until knife plunged in center comes out clean.

YIELD: 8 servings.

QUICK CHICKEN LIVER SOUFFLÉ

1 can condensed cream of chicken or mushroom soup
1 cup minced cooked chicken livers
½ teaspoon salt
¼ teaspoon pepper
1 small can (3 ounces) chopped mushrooms (optional)
3 egg yolks, well beaten
4 egg whites, beaten stiff but not dry

HAVE READY: 1½-quart soufflé dish or deep casserole, ungreased.

Heat undiluted soup in saucepan over low heat, stirring occasionally. Add minced chicken livers, seasonings, and chopped mushrooms, if desired. Cook and stir over medium heat for 1 to 2 minutes. Remove from heat and let cool 10 minutes. Slowly add beaten egg yolks, stirring briskly. Fold in beaten egg whites gently but thoroughly. Pour into 1½-quart soufflé dish or deep casserole. Bake in 350° F. (moderate) oven for 35 to 40 minutes.

YIELD: 4 servings.

QUICK DINNER SOUFFLÉ

1 can (1 pound) roast beef or corned beef hash
1 can (10¾ ounces) condensed Cheddar cheese, cream of mushroom or tomato soup
2 tablespoons minced onion
⅛ teaspoon hot pepper sauce
2 egg yolks, beaten thick and light
3 egg whites, beaten stiff but not dry

HAVE READY: 1½-quart soufflé dish or deep casserole, buttered.

Break up hash with fork in large bowl. Add undiluted condensed cream soup of choice, minced onion, and hot pepper sauce. Blend thoroughly, then stir in beaten egg yolks. Fold beaten egg whites into meat mixture gently but thoroughly. Pour into prepared 1½-quart soufflé dish or deep casserole. Bake in 350° F. (moderate) oven for 55 to 65 minutes.

YIELD: 5 to 6 servings.

QUICK LEMONADE SOUFFLÉ I

4 egg yolks, beaten thick and light
⅓ cup thawed frozen lemonade concentrate
5 egg whites
⅛ teaspoon salt
⅓ cup sugar

HAVE READY: 1-quart soufflé dish or deep casserole, ungreased.

Blend together well beaten egg yolks and thawed lemonade concentrate. Beat egg whites and salt to soft peaks. Gradually add sugar, beating continuously until stiff glossy peaks form. Fold into lemonade mixture gently but thoroughly. Pour into 1-quart soufflé dish set in shallow pan containing 1 inch hot water. Bake in 350° F. (moderate) oven for 45 to 50 minutes.

YIELD: 4 to 5 servings.

NOTE: For Quick Limeade Soufflé substitute ⅓ cup thawed frozen limeade concentrate for lemonade.

QUICK LEMONADE SOUFFLÉ II

5 egg yolks
½ cup sugar
¼ cup thawed frozen lemonade concentrate
1 teaspoon grated lemon peel
5 egg whites, beaten stiff but not dry

HAVE READY: 1½-quart soufflé dish or deep casserole, ungreased.

Using electric or rotary beater, beat egg yolks slightly in large bowl. Gradually add sugar, beating until thick and light. Add lemonade concentrate and grated lemon peel and beat for 2 minutes. Fold in beaten egg whites gently but thoroughly. Pour into 1½-quart soufflé dish or deep casserole set in pan containing 2 inches hot water. Bake in 325° F. (slow) oven for 50 minutes if served hot or for 60 minutes if served cold. To serve cold, cool soufflé for 15 minutes, then refrigerate and chill for 2 hours before serving.

YIELD: 6 servings.

QUICK ORANGE SOUFFLÉ

4 egg yolks, beaten thick and light
⅓ cup thawed frozen orange juice concentrate
1 to 2 teaspoons grated orange peel
5 egg whites
⅛ teaspoon salt
⅓ cup sugar

HAVE READY: 1-quart soufflé dish or deep casserole, ungreased.

Blend together beaten egg yolks, thawed frozen orange juice concentrate, and grated orange peel. Beat egg whites and salt to soft peaks. Gradually add sugar, beating continuously until stiff glossy peaks form. Fold beaten egg whites into orange mixture gently but thoroughly. Pour into 1-quart soufflé dish or deep casserole set in shallow pan containing 1 inch hot water. Bake in 350° F. (moderate) oven for 45 to 50 minutes.

YIELD: 4 to 5 servings.

QUICK COLD ORANGE SOUFFLÉ

1 package lemon whipped dessert mix
½ cup cold water
½ cup chilled orange juice
2 teaspoons grated orange peel
1 egg white
2 tablespoons sugar

HAVE READY: 1-quart soufflé dish, ungreased.

Blend dessert mix and the 2 cold liquids in a deep narrow bowl according to package label directions. Fold in grated orange peel. Beat egg white until very soft peaks form. Add sugar gradually, beating constantly until meringue will stand in stiff glossy peaks. Fold gently but thoroughly into orange mixture. Pour or pile gently into 1-quart soufflé dish. Refrigerate for 3 to 4 hours.

YIELD: 4 to 5 servings.

EASY COLD ORANGE CREAM SOUFFLÉ

2 packages (3 ounces each) orange-flavored gelatin
2 cups boiling water
1 large package (8 ounces) cream cheese
¼ cup sugar
1 cup orange juice
1 teaspoon grated orange peel
1 cup heavy cream, whipped

HAVE READY: 1-quart soufflé dish with collar rising 1½ to 2 inches above rim.

Stir gelatin into boiling water until dissolved, then set aside. Soften cream cheese by beating with a fork, then beat in sugar thoroughly. Gradually add gelatin mixture, orange juice, and grated orange peel, stirring until smooth. Refrigerate and cool, stirring occasionally, until mixture mounds up slightly. Fold in whipped cream gently but thoroughly. Pour into collared 1-quart soufflé dish. Chill 3 to 4 hours until firm. Carefully peel off collar before serving. YIELD: 6 servings.

EASY COLD MOCHA SOUFFLÉ

2 envelopes unflavored gelatine
¼ cup cold water
1 package (3 ounces) chocolate pudding and pie filling mix
2 cups cold milk
2 egg yolks, well beaten
1 pound creamed cottage cheese
2 tablespoons sugar
1 to 2 tablespoons coffee-flavored liqueur
⅓ cup finely chopped California walnuts
3 egg whites, beaten stiff but not dry
1 cup heavy cream, whipped

HAVE READY: 1-quart soufflé dish with collar rising 2 inches above rim, or 1½-quart soufflé dish with collar rising 1 inch above rim.

Sprinkle gelatine on cold water and set aside to soften. Cook chocolate pudding and pie filling mix with milk according to package directions. Remove from heat, add softened gelatine, and stir vigorously until gelatine dissolves. Slowly add hot pudding to beaten egg yolks, stirring briskly. Let cool about 15 minutes. Add cottage cheese, sugar, liqueur, and nuts all at once and fold into pudding mixture until well blended. Fold in beaten egg whites gently but thoroughly, then fold in whipped cream. Pour into collared 1- or 1½-quart soufflé dish. Chill 3 to 4 hours until firm. Carefully remove collar before serving. YIELD: 6 to 8 servings.

QUICK MUSHROOM SOUFFLÉ

1 can (10½ ounces) condensed cream of mushroom soup
1 can (4 ounces) chopped mushrooms, drained
3 egg yolks, beaten thick and light
¼ teaspoon salt
few grains cayenne pepper
4 egg whites, beaten stiff but not dry

HAVE READY: 1-quart soufflé dish or deep casserole, ungreased.

Heat undiluted soup over low heat, stirring frequently. Add drained chopped mushrooms. Remove from heat. Slowly stir into beaten egg yolks. Return mixture to saucepan. Cook and stir over low heat until thickened, about 4 or 5 minutes. Remove from heat, add seasonings, and let cool 15 minutes. Fold into beaten egg whites gently but thoroughly. Pour into 1-quart soufflé dish or deep casserole. Bake in 350° F. (moderate) oven for 45 to 55 minutes.

YIELD: 4 servings.

QUICK SEAFOOD SOUFFLÉ

1 can (10 ounces) frozen cream of shrimp soup
1 tablespoon sherry
½ cup chopped cooked or canned shrimp, crab meat, or lobster
6 egg yolks
6 egg whites

HAVE READY: 1½-quart soufflé dish or deep casserole, ungreased.

Cook and stir undiluted frozen cream of shrimp soup over low heat until thawed and thoroughly hot. Remove from heat.

Stir in sherry and chopped seafood of choice. Beat egg yolks until thick and very light. Slowly add to hot soup mixture, stirring briskly. Beat egg whites to stiff glossy peaks. Fold soup mixture into beaten egg whites gently but thoroughly. Pour into 1½-quart soufflé dish or deep casserole. Bake in 325° F. (slow) oven for 60 to 70 minutes.

YIELD: 5 to 6 servings.

QUICK HERBED SOUP SOUFFLÉ

1 can (10½ ounces) condensed cream of mushroom soup
1 cup shredded sharp Cheddar cheese
¼ teaspoon dried chervil
½ cup minced cooked ham or tongue
2 tablespoons chopped parsley
6 egg yolks, beaten thick and light
6 egg whites
⅛ teaspoon salt

HAVE READY: 2-quart soufflé dish or deep casserole, ungreased.

Combine undiluted condensed cream of mushroom soup, shredded cheese, and chervil in saucepan. Cook and stir over low heat until cheese melts and mixture is smoothly blended. Remove from heat and stir in minced cooked ham or tongue and parsley. Slowly add beaten egg yolks, stirring briskly. Beat egg whites and salt to stiff glossy peaks. Fold soup mixture into beaten egg whites gently but thoroughly. Pour into 2-quart soufflé dish or deep casserole. Bake in 300° F. (slow) oven for 1 to 1¼ hours.

YIELD: 5 to 6 servings.

9

SOME SAUCES AND GARNISHES TO SERVE WITH SOUFFLÉS

Though well-made soufflés are a perfect balance of taste and texture, many lend themselves to the extra enhancement of a complementary sauce. Here then, are recipes for savory or sweet sauces from which to choose. Use your own judgment as to which sauce best suits your taste and the soufflé you've made.

Savory Sauces for Main Dish or Accompaniment Soufflés

CAPER BUTTER SAUCE

2 tablespoons butter or margarine
2 tablespoons flour
¼ teaspoon salt
⅛ teaspoon pepper
1 cup water
2 tablespoons butter (additional)
1 tablespoon vinegar from bottled capers
3 tablespoons drained capers

Melt 2 tablespoons butter or margarine in saucepan over low heat. Blend in flour and seasonings. Slowly stir in water, keeping mixture smooth. Cook and stir until sauce thickens and comes to a boil. Add 2 tablespoons additional butter in 4 portions, alternating with vinegar, stirring briskly and constantly. Stir in drained capers. Keep warm, and stir vigorously for a few seconds before serving.

YIELD: about 1⅓ cups.

PEPPY CHEESE SAUCE

3 tablespoons butter or margarine
3 tablespoons flour
2 cups hot milk
½ pound sharp cheese, shredded
½ teaspoon salt
⅛ teaspoon pepper
⅛ teaspoon hot pepper sauce
½ teaspoon dry mustard
½ teaspoon Worcestershire sauce

Melt butter or margarine in saucepan over low heat. Blend in flour, and cook for 2 minutes. Remove from heat. Slowly add hot milk, stirring to smooth mixture. Cook and stir over medium heat until sauce thickens and comes to a boil. Reduce heat. Add shredded cheese and seasonings, and stir until cheese melts. Serve warm.

YIELD: about 2½ cups.

QUICK CURRY SAUCE

1 can (10¾ ounces) condensed cream of chicken soup
¼ cup milk or water
½ to 1 teaspoon curry powder, to taste
1 teaspoon butter or margarine

Combine soup and milk or water in saucepan. Cook and stir over low heat until heated through but not quite boiling. Blend together curry powder and butter or margarine. Stir into heated soup. Reduce heat and keep warm to serve.

YIELD: about 1½ cups.

HERB BUTTER SAUCE

½ cup butter or margarine
2 teaspoons lemon juice
2 tablespoons minced parsley, chives, chervil, tarragon, or shallots

Melt butter or margarine in saucepan over low heat. Blend in lemon juice and herb of choice. Keep warm to serve.

YIELD: ½ cup.

NUT BUTTER SAUCE

½ cup butter or margarine
⅓ cup toasted almonds, filberts, pecans, or California walnuts
2 drops hot pepper sauce
salt to taste

Melt butter or margarine in saucepan. Chop choice of nuts finely, or whirl in blender for 1 or 2 seconds. Add, with hot pepper sauce, to melted butter or margarine. Correct seasoning with salt, if necessary.

YIELD: about ¾ cup.

LEMON BUTTER SAUCE

½ cup butter or margarine
2 tablespoons lemon juice
1 teaspoon grated lemon peel (optional)
½ teaspoon salt
¼ teaspoon pepper
3 drops hot pepper sauce
1 tablespoon chopped parsley

Melt butter or margarine in saucepan over low heat. Blend in remaining ingredients. Keep warm to serve.

YIELD: ½ cup.

MADEIRA SAUCE

1 cup cold beef broth or consommé
2 tablespoons meat drippings or 1 teaspoon beef stock base or 1 teaspoon meat extract
2 tablespoons instant-blending flour
1 to 1½ tablespoons Madeira wine

Combine cold beef broth or consommé with meat drippings or beef stock base or meat extract. Sprinkle on instant-blending flour. Cook and stir over medium heat until thickened and boiling. Lower heat, stir in wine, and keep warm for serving.
YIELD: 1 cup.

MUSHROOM SAUCE

3 tablespoons butter or margarine
½ pound mushrooms, cleaned, trimmed, and sliced
2 tablespoons flour
½ teaspoon salt
⅛ teaspoon pepper
few grains cayenne pepper
1 cup hot chicken broth
½ cup hot medium cream

Melt butter or margarine in saucepan over low heat. Add mushrooms, and sauté, stirring frequently, for 4 or 5 minutes, but do not brown. Blend in flour and seasonings and cook 1 more minute. Remove from heat. Slowly add hot chicken broth, then hot cream, stirring to smooth mixture. Cook and stir over medium heat until sauce thickens and comes to a boil. Reduce heat and keep warm to serve.
YIELD: about 2½ cups.

NOTE: For sherried mushroom sauce, add 1 to 1½ tablespoons sherry when sauce reaches boiling point.

QUICK MUSHROOM CHEESE SAUCE

1 can (10¾ ounces) condensed cream of mushroom soup
¼ cup milk
½ cup shredded Cheddar cheese
½ teaspoon Worcestershire sauce
few grains cayenne pepper

Cook and stir mushroom soup and milk over low heat until blended and well heated. Add cheese and stir until melted. Blend in Worcestershire sauce and cayenne pepper. Serve hot.

YIELD: about 1½ cups.

QUICK MUSHROOM NUT SAUCE

1 can (10¾ ounces) condensed cream of mushroom soup
½ cup milk or light cream
⅓ cup chopped California walnuts

Combine soup and milk or cream in saucepan. Cook and stir over low heat until heated through but not quite boiling. Stir in walnuts. Reduce heat and keep warm to serve.

YIELD: about 1⅔ cups.

FISH SOUFFLÉ SAUCE

2 egg yolks
2 tablespoons heavy cream
⅔ cup fish stock in which fish was poached
2 tablespoons butter, cut in pieces

Beat egg yolks until light colored, then beat in heavy cream. Heat fish stock just to a boil, then remove from heat. Gradually stir egg and cream mixture into hot stock. Briskly stir in butter pieces, one at a time, until well blended. Serve at once over Fish Soufflé (see Index).

YIELD: about 1 cup.

ONION SAUCE

3 tablespoons butter or margarine
1 cup thinly sliced onions
2 tablespoons flour
1 teaspoon salt
¼ teaspoon pepper
few grains cayenne pepper
¼ teaspoon paprika
1½ cups hot milk

Melt butter or margarine in saucepan over low heat. Add sliced onions, and sauté until golden, but do not brown. Remove cooked onions with slotted spoon and set aside. To fat in pan add next 5 ingredients, blending well. Let cook for 1 minute. Remove from heat. Slowly stir in hot milk to smooth mixture. Cook and stir over medium heat until sauce thickens and boils. Reduce heat, add reserved cooked onions, and keep warm to serve.

YIELD: about 2¼ cups.

PARMESAN BUTTER SAUCE

½ cup butter or margarine
¼ cup grated Parmesan cheese
2 drops hot pepper sauce

Melt butter or margarine in saucepan over low heat. Stir in grated cheese and hot pepper sauce. Keep warm to serve.

YIELD: about ¾ cup.

MUSTARDY LEMON SAUCE

¼ cup butter or margarine
½ cup flour
2 cups hot water
1 teaspoon salt
1 to 2 teaspoons prepared mustard, to taste
2 tablespoons lemon juice

Melt butter or margarine in saucepan over low heat. Blend in flour and cook, stirring occasionally, for 2 or 3 minutes. Remove from heat. Slowly stir in hot water to smooth mixture, then add salt. Cook and stir over medium heat until sauce thickens. Reduce heat, add mustard and lemon juice and simmer for 3 minutes. Do not allow to boil.

YIELD: about 2½ cups.

SEAFOOD SAUCE

1 tablespoon butter or margarine
1 tablespoon flour
1 cup hot chicken broth or milk
½ cup medium cream
½ teaspoon salt
⅛ teaspoon pepper
few grains nutmeg
3 drops hot pepper sauce
½ to ¾ cup diced cooked lobster or shrimp or coarsely shredded crab meat
2 tablespoons sherry

Melt butter or margarine in saucepan. Blend in flour, and cook about 1 minute. Remove from heat. Slowly stir in hot chicken broth or milk to smooth mixture. Cook and stir over medium heat until sauce boils and thickens. Reduce heat, add cream and seasonings, and simmer 5 minutes, stirring occasionally. Add seafood of choice and sherry and heat for 2 or 3 more minutes. Keep warm to serve.

YIELD: about 2 cups.

QUICK SHRIMP SAUCE

1 can (10 ounces) frozen cream of shrimp soup
⅓ cup milk or light cream
1 to 2 tablespoons sherry

Combine frozen shrimp soup and milk or cream in saucepan. Heat very slowly, stirring occasionally, until heated through but not quite boiling. Remove from heat, and add sherry. Serve warm.

YIELD: about 1½ cups.

SHERRIED SHRIMP SAUCE

2 tablespoons butter or margarine
2 tablespoons flour
¼ teaspoon salt
¼ teaspoon hot pepper sauce
¾ cup hot milk
¼ cup sherry
½ pound cooked, deveined shrimp (cut in two, if large)

Melt butter or margarine in saucepan over low heat. Blend in flour, salt, and hot pepper sauce, and cook for 1 minute. Remove from heat. Slowly add hot milk, stirring to smooth mixture. Cook and stir over medium heat until sauce thickens. Add sherry and cooked shrimp. Continue cooking until shrimp are heated through, but do not allow sauce to boil. Serve warm.

YIELD: about 2 cups.

SOUR CREAM SAUCE

3 egg yolks, well beaten
1 cup dairy sour cream
½ teaspoon salt
few grains cayenne pepper
1½ tablespoons lemon juice
2 tablespoons minced parsley

Blend together beaten egg yolks and sour cream in top of double boiler. Add salt, cayenne pepper, and lemon juice. Cook and stir over hot water until sauce is thick and smooth. Add minced parsley. Turn off heat under double boiler and leave over hot water to keep warm for serving.

YIELD: about 1½ cups.

TOMATO SAUCE

2 tablespoons butter or margarine
2 tablespoons flour
½ teaspoon salt
⅛ teaspoon pepper
1½ cups hot tomato juice
1 tablespoon minced parsley or chives

Melt butter or margarine in saucepan over low heat. Blend in flour and seasonings, and cook for 1 minute. Remove from heat. Slowly add hot tomato juice, stirring until smooth. Cook and stir over medium heat until thickened and boiling. Add minced parsley or chives. Reduce heat and keep warm to serve.

YIELD: about 1½ cups.

PIQUANT TOMATO SAUCE

3 tablespoons salad oil
2 tablespoons chopped onion
1 tablespoon chopped parsley
¼ teaspoon dried basil (1 teaspoon if fresh)
¼ teaspoon hot pepper sauce
1 can (20 ounces) solid pack tomatoes
1 can (8 ounces) tomato or tomato mushroom sauce

Heat salad oil in saucepan, add chopped onion, and sauté until tender but not browned. Add next 3 ingredients and remove from heat. Blend in canned tomatoes and tomato or tomato mushroom sauce. Simmer over low heat, stirring occasionally, for about 30 minutes.

YIELD: about 1½ cups.

FRESH VEGETABLE SAUCE

3 tablespoons butter or margarine
½ cup thinly sliced celery
⅓ cup slivered carrots
3 tablespoons thinly sliced scallions
3 tablespoons flour
1 teaspoon salt
⅛ teaspoon pepper
2 cups hot milk

Melt butter or margarine in saucepan. Add vegetables and sauté until golden but not browned. Sprinkle on flour, salt, and pepper and blend well. Remove from heat. Slowly add hot milk, stirring constantly to prevent lumping. Cook and stir over medium heat until sauce is thickened and smooth.

YIELD: about 2¼ cups.

Sweet Sauces for Dessert Soufflés

APRICOT, PEAR, OR PEACH SAUCE

2 tablespoons cornstarch
1½ tablespoons sugar
⅛ teaspoon salt
1 can (12 ounces) apricot, pear, or peach nectar
½ cup light corn syrup
2 teaspoons butter or margarine

Blend first 3 ingredients together in saucepan. Slowly stir in apricot, pear, or peach nectar and light corn syrup. Cook over medium heat, stirring constantly until sauce thickens and boils for 3 minutes. Remove from heat. Stir in butter or margarine until well blended. Serve warm.

YIELD: about 2 cups.

BERRY SAUCE

2 tablespoons cornstarch
¼ cup sugar
1 cup cold water
1 cup raspberries or sliced strawberries, fresh or frozen
¼ cup sherry or Madeira wine or 1 tablespoon lemon juice

Blend cornstarch and sugar together in saucepan. Slowly stir in cold water to make smooth mixture. Cook and stir over medium heat until sauce is thick and clear. Remove from heat and add raspberries or sliced strawberries. Let cool, then add wine or lemon juice. Serve chilled.

YIELD: about 2 cups.

BRANDY SAUCE

1½ cups sugar
¾ cup boiling water
1 teaspoon grated lemon or orange peel
¼ cup brandy

Stir sugar and boiling water together in saucepan until sugar dissolves. Bring to a boil and let cook, without stirring, for 10 to 12 minutes. Remove from heat and stir in grated lemon or orange peel and brandy. Serve warm.

YIELD: about 1½ cups.

SPICY COFFEE SAUCE

1 cup sugar
1 cup strong coffee
few grains salt
2 whole cloves
⅛ teaspoon ground cinnamon
⅛ teaspoon ground nutmeg
¼ cup coffee-flavored liqueur

Combine first 6 ingredients in saucepan. Cook, stirring occasionally, until sugar dissolves and mixture boils 5 minutes. Remove from heat and stir in coffee-flavored liqueur. Remove whole cloves. Serve warm. YIELD: about 2 cups.

RICH CHOCOLATE SAUCE

3 squares (3 ounces) unsweetened chocolate
1 cup (6-ounce package) semi-sweet chocolate pieces
2 tablespoons butter or margarine
2 tablespoons light corn syrup
⅓ cup sugar
1 cup light cream
1 teaspoon vanilla extract

Combine first 3 ingredients in top of double boiler. Cook over hot water, stirring frequently, until chocolate melts and mixture is blended. Add corn syrup, sugar, and cream, mixing well. Continue to cook and stir until sauce is smooth and thickened. Add vanilla extract. Serve warm. YIELD: about 2 cups.

TIPSY CREAM SAUCE

1 cup heavy cream
2 tablespoons confectioners' sugar
1½ tablespoons sherry, brandy, or liqueur

Combine cream and sugar in cold bowl. Beat with rotary beater until stiff shiny peaks form when beater is withdrawn. Fold in sherry, brandy, or liqueur. YIELD: 2 cups.

CUSTARD SAUCE

2 eggs, slightly beaten
¼ cup sugar
⅛ teaspoon salt
1¼ cups hot milk
1 teaspoon vanilla extract

Blend together first 3 ingredients in top of double boiler. Slowly add hot milk, stirring constantly to keep mixture smooth. Cook and stir over hot (not boiling) water until mixture coats a metal spoon. Remove from heat and set over cold water. Stir in vanilla extract. Pour into bowl, cover, and refrigerate. Serve chilled. YIELD: about 1¾ cups.

LEMON SAUCE

1 tablespoon cornstarch
⅓ to ½ cup sugar, to taste
⅛ teaspoon salt
1 cup boiling water or any syrup from canned fruit
1 tablespoon grated lemon peel
¼ cup lemon juice
1 tablespoon butter or margarine

Blend together first 3 ingredients in saucepan. Gradually stir in boiling water or syrup from canned fruit. Cook and stir over medium heat until clear and thickened. Remove from heat, add grated lemon peel and lemon juice. Stir in butter or margarine until melted. Serve warm.

YIELD: 1 cup.

ORANGE SAUCE

1 tablespoon cornstarch
½ cup sugar
¼ teaspoon salt
1 cup orange juice
2 teaspoons grated orange peel
1 tablespoon butter or margarine
1 orange peeled and sectioned

Blend together first 3 ingredients in saucepan. Slowly stir in orange juice to smooth mixture, then add grated orange peel. Cook and stir over medium heat until sauce boils and is thick and clear. Add butter or margarine and peeled orange sections. Keep warm to serve.

YIELD: about 1¼ cups.

QUICK FRUIT SAUCE

1 package (10 ounces) frozen raspberries or sliced strawberries, thawed
¼ cup sugar
2 tablespoons fruit-flavored liqueur

Stir together thawed raspberries or strawberries and sugar until sugar is dissolved. Add liqueur. Serve chilled.

YIELD: about 1⅓ cups.

BRANDIED JAM SAUCE

1½ cups apricot, strawberry, or raspberry jam
½ cup water
3 tablespoons brandy or kirsch

Blend together jam and water in saucepan. Cook and stir over medium heat until mixture boils. Reduce heat and simmer for 8 or 10 minutes, stirring frequently. Add brandy or kirsch. Serve warm or chilled.

YIELD: about 1¾ cups.

GINGERED PEAR SAUCE

1 tablespoon cornstarch
⅓ to ½ cup sugar, to taste
⅛ teaspoon salt
1 cup hot syrup from canned pears or pear nectar
1 teaspoon grated lemon peel
1 tablespoon lemon juice
1 tablespoon chopped crystallized ginger
1 tablespoon butter or margarine

Blend first 3 ingredients together in saucepan. Slowly stir in hot pear syrup or nectar to make smooth mixture. Cook and stir over medium heat until sauce is thickened and clear. Remove from heat and add remaining ingredients. Serve warm.

YIELD: about 1 cup.

BUTTERSCOTCH CUSTARD CREAM

¼ cup butter or margarine
¾ cup light brown sugar, firmly packed
1 tablespoon hot coffee
2 egg yolks, slightly beaten
1 teaspoon vanilla extract
1 cup heavy cream, whipped

Combine first 4 ingredients in top of double boiler, blending well together. Cook and stir over hot water until sugar is melted and sauce thickens slightly. Remove from heat, add vanilla extract, and let cool. Fold in whipped cream. Serve slightly warm or well chilled.

YIELD: about 2 cups.

CREAMY LIQUEUR SAUCE

4 egg yolks, well beaten
½ cup sugar
few grains salt
¼ cup any fruit-flavored liqueur
1 tablespoon lemon juice
½ cup heavy cream, whipped

Combine beaten egg yolks, sugar, and salt, and continue beating until sugar is dissolved and mixture is very thick and light. Cook and stir over hot water for about 8 minutes. Remove from heat. Gradually beat in liqueur and lemon juice. Chill, stirring occasionally. Fold in whipped cream. Serve chilled. YIELD: about 2½ cups.

CARAMEL NUT SAUCE

1 cup granulated sugar
½ cup boiling water
½ cup medium cream
½ cup chopped toasted almonds
1 teaspoon vanilla extract

Spread sugar in thin layer in a large heavy frying pan. Let stand over low heat until sugar melts and forms golden brown liquid. Slowly and cautiously stir in boiling water. Cook and stir for 5 minutes. Remove from heat. Blend cream into hot syrup, then add chopped nuts and vanilla extract. Serve warm. YIELD: 2 cups.

HONEY NUT SAUCE

1½ cups honey
¼ cup butter or margarine
few grains salt
½ cup chopped California walnuts, almonds, pecans or filberts
¼ cup light rum or 1 teaspoon vanilla extract

Combine honey, butter or margarine, and salt in saucepan. Cook and stir over low heat for 5 minutes. Add chopped nuts of choice and cook for 3 more minutes. Remove from heat and add rum or vanilla extract. Serve warm.

YIELD: about 2¼ cups.

MOCHA SAUCE

4 squares (4 ounces) unsweetened chocolate
1 cup sugar
2 teaspoons instant coffee
1 cup boiling water
⅛ teaspoon salt
1 teaspoon vanilla extract

Combine first 5 ingredients in double boiler. Cook and stir over boiling water until chocolate melts. Cover and cook for ½ hour, stirring occasionally, until sauce is thickened and smooth. Remove from heat and add vanilla extract. Serve warm or cold.

YIELD: about 1½ cups.

COLD SABAYON SAUCE

⅓ cup sugar
⅔ cup sherry or marsala wine
4 egg yolks

Stir sugar and wine together in top of double boiler. Add egg yolks. Place over hot (not boiling) water, making sure water does not touch top pan. Beat with rotary or electric beater until mixture thickens and mounds up slightly. Remove top of double boiler and continue beating until mixture is almost cold. Pour into bowl and chill.

YIELD: about 1½ cups.

HOT SABAYON SAUCE

4 egg yolks
½ cup sugar
¾ cup sherry or marsala wine
2 teaspoons brandy

Beat egg yolks and sugar together in bowl until sugar dissolves and mixture is thick and very light. Transfer to top of double boiler and add wine. Cook and stir over hot (not boiling) water until sauce is thick. Make sure hot water does not touch top pan. Add brandy. Remove from heat, pour into bowl, and serve warm. YIELD: about 1⅔ cups.

VELVET WINE SAUCE

½ cup heavy cream, whipped
2 tablespoons sugar
3 egg yolks
2 egg whites
few grains salt
2 or 3 tablespoons sherry or Madeira wine

Combine whipped cream and sugar in top of double boiler. Beat egg yolks and whites and salt together in a bowl until light and thick, then add to cream mixture. Cook over hot, not boiling water, stirring constantly with wire whisk or spoon until sauce is thick and smoothly blended. Remove from heat and add wine of choice. Serve warm. YIELD: about 2 cups.

WHIPPED CREAM

1 cup heavy cream
2 tablespoons confectioners' sugar
1 teaspoon vanilla extract

Combine cream and sugar in cold bowl. Beat with rotary beater until soft shiny peaks are formed when beater is lifted. Fold in vanilla extract. YIELD: 2 cups.

FRUITED WHIPPED CREAM

1 cup heavy cream
2 tablespoons confectioners' sugar
½ cup crushed peaches, raspberries, or strawberries
1 tablespoon fruit-flavored liqueur or kirsch

Combine cream and sugar in cold bowl. Beat with rotary beater until stiff shiny peaks form when beater is lifted. Fold in crushed fruit and liqueur or kirsch.

YIELD: about 2½ cups.

Some Garnish Accompaniments to Serve with Soufflés

These garnishes may be used in several ways: On top of a cold soufflé; around and on top of an unmolded soufflé; in the center of a soufflé omelet; on the serving plate or platter, surrounding a hot soufflé in its dish. The color and flavor of the garnish should, of course, complement the soufflé that is being decorated.

SAVORY

Sautéed mushroom caps
Lemon or orange slices
Parsley or chervil sprigs or bouquets
Unpeeled cucumber and radish slices
Tomato slices and green pepper rings
Pimiento-topped egg slices

SWEET

Whole berries dusted with sugar
Sugar-frosted grapes

Pear or peach halves sprinkled with liqueur
Brandied fruits
Dollops of whipped or sour cream
Mandarin orange sections

For additional sauces to serve with soufflés see *The Art of Making Sauces and Gravies* by Frederica L. Beinert, published by Doubleday and Company, September 1966.

GLOSSARY OF TERMS FREQUENTLY USED IN MAKING SOUFFLÉS

BEAT To make a mixture light and smooth by using a lifting motion with a spoon, or by using a wire whisk, rotary hand beater, or electric beater.

BLEND Combining two or more ingredients thoroughly by mixing or stirring with a spoon or fork until no clumps or streaks of any of the ingredients are visible.

BOIL To heat liquids so that bubbles constantly rise and break on the surface, at the same time agitating the entire amount.

BOILING POINT The moment when bubbles in a heated liquid rise to the surface and break and the whole amount begins to move.

BREAD CRUMBS Fresh crumbs made by crumbling sliced fresh bread with the fingers or by tearing an unsliced loaf (without crust) with a fork. Dry crumbs made by rolling, grinding, or blending (electric blender) broken slices of very dry bread.

CHILL To refrigerate a food until it is cold throughout.

CHOP To cut into small pieces with a knife or special sharp chopping tool.

COLLAR Folded waxed paper, foil, or brown paper tied or pinned around soufflé dish so that several inches extend above rim of dish. A device used to increase height of dish and keep shape of finished soufflé uniform.

COOL Let stand at room temperature until hot mixture is barely warm to the touch.

DISSOLVE To mix a dry substance, such as gelatine, with hot liquid until it melts. To mix a crystalline substance, such as sugar, with a moist substance until it melts and no crystals remain.

DUST To sprinkle greased surface of a soufflé dish with a dry substance such as sugar, flour, fine crumbs or ground nuts. Particles which do not cling should be shaken out of the dish.

FOAMY Egg white beaten until it takes on a sudsy appearance with a mixture of large and small bubbles.

FOLD To combine sauce and beaten egg whites or whipped cream by a gentle cutting and lifting motion so as not to lose air bubbles. Spatula or spoon is passed through the mixture, drawn across bottom of bowl and to the top. Bowl should be given a quarter turn with each folding motion.

MASH To crush to a pulpy mass.

MINCE To chop or cut with knife or scissors into very small pieces.

MIX To distribute ingredients and blend them together by stirring with spoon, fork, or whisk.

MOUNDS UP A small portion of a mixture dropped onto the rest from a spoon heaps up slightly and doesn't sink in. A spoonful dropped onto a flat surface keeps its heaped-up shape.

PURÉE To press food through a sieve or food mill or to whirl it in an electric blender until it is nearly liquefied.

SAUTÉ To cook lightly in a small amount of fat.

SCALLIONS Green-topped young spring onions.

SHALLOT One of the onion family, with clustered bulbs like garlic but with flavor more like onion.

SIEVE To purée by pushing food through a fine-meshed sieve.

SIMMER To heat food just below the boiling point so that small bubbles form slowly and collapse below the surface.

SLIGHTLY BEATEN Applied to egg yolks means beaten just enough to blend yolks together.

SOFT PEAKS Droopy moist peaks formed by beaten egg whites when beater is withdrawn.

SOFTEN GELATINE Appearance of gelatine granules changes from opaque to clear when sprinkled on cold water and allowed to stand until water is absorbed.

SPRINKLE To scatter drops of liquid or dry food particles evenly over the surface of a food.

STIFF BUT NOT DRY Used to describe peaks in beaten egg whites that hold shape when beater is withdrawn but are glossy. Peaks may droop slightly at top when beater leaves them.

TOP HAT Finishing touch for a baked soufflé. To make soufflé rise higher in center a circle 1 inch deep and 1 inch from edge of dish is traced with spoon or spatula before soufflé is placed in oven.

WELL BEATEN Applied to egg yolks means beaten until thick and light in color.

WHISK A cluster of evenly-spaced wires fastened to a sturdy handle, used for beating, stirring, and mixing. Available in a number of graduated sizes.

GLOSSARY

[illegible] used to describe peaks in bottom [illegible] when [illegible] the [illegible] water [illegible] the glossy [illegible] may [illegible] and [illegible] top [illegible]

[illegible] plumbing [illegible] finger [illegible]. To move [illegible] the [illegible] and 1 inch [illegible] edge. [illegible] with [illegible] or [illegible] used [illegible] [illegible] until [illegible]

[illegible] A [illegible] spaced [illegible] used [illegible] handles, [illegible] used for [illegible] stirring, and [illegible] [illegible] of [illegible] [illegible]

INDEX

1/2
1/3